The New Age Ethic and the Spirit of Postmodernity

CRITICAL BODIES
Joseph Pilotta, series editor

Knowledge and the Production of Nonknowledge:
An Exploration of Alien Mythology in Postwar America
Mark Featherstone

The New Age Ethic and the Spirit of Postmodernity
Carmen L. Kuhling

Plato's Cave: Revised Edition
Television and its Discontents
John O'Neill

Why I [Still] Want My MTV
Kevin Williams

forthcoming

The Body in Human Inquiry:
Interdisciplinary Explorations of Embodiment
Vicente Berdayes, Luigi Esposito and John M. Murphy (eds.)

Visceral Manifestation and the East Asian Communicative Body
Jay Goulding

Phenomenolgy, Body Politics, and the Future of Communication Theory
Hwa Yol Jung

Hispanic Tele-visions in the United States
Television Discourse and the Cultural Construction of Ethnicity
Elizabeth Lozano

Abjection and its correction in Ethnic Studies
Jill McCaughan

The Seductive Aesthetics of Post-Colonialism
Rekha Menon

Body Works: Essays on Modernity and Morality
John O'Neill

The New Age Ethic and the Spirit of Postmodernity

Carmen Kuhling
University of Limerick

HAMPTON PRESS INC.
CRESSKILL, NEW JERSEY

Printed in the United States of America

Library of Congress Cataloging-in-Publication Data

Kuhling, Carmen.
The new age ethic and the spirit of postmodernity / Carmen Kuhling
p. cm. -- (The Hampton Press communication series)
Includes bibliographic references and index.
ISBN 1-57273-520-1 (cl) -- ISBN 1-57273-521-X (ppb)
1. Ethics. 2. Postmodernism. I. Title. II. Series

BJ1012K74 2004
306'.1--dc22

2003067582

Hampton Press, Inc.
23 Broadway
Cresskill, NJ 07626

Contents

Preface

What is the New Age? The New Age is not a unified social movement or a cultural phenomenon. Rather, it can be characterised as the materialisation of various desires: for integration, for a spiritual life, for connectedness with others, for a union with nature, for health. I do not want to argue in this book that there is something *essentially* New Age, something that defines this movement. Neither is it in my agenda to identify clearly defined boundaries between what specifically differentiates the New Age movement from consumerism and the extension of commodification of leisure time pursuits on the one hand, and from green politics, feminism, Marxism, or other social movements on the other. Rather, the New Age is best understood as encapsulated within a number of circles, some of which overlap significantly with the concerns of left politics, and others which are perfectly consistent with a Yuppie work ethic. Nor is the New Age new; some activities central to the New Age such as astrology, an interest in African art, and vegetarianism, predate the New Age by centuries. What *is* New however, is the enthusiasm, the passion, the desperation with which people are turning to holistic health, astrology, self-help therapy, paranormal phenomena, and the like, as an alternative to conventional scientific, medical, and psychiatric authorities.

What is most significant about the New Age is that it can be seen as a response to what people perceive as the spiritual vacuum at the heart of late capitalism. New Age spirituality, an eclectic mix of Eastern mysticism, self-help therapy, paganism, and other philosophies, is not a religious movement per se; it is a response to the secularisation of modern social life or the increasing disenchantment with the world. In

The *Protestant Ethic and the Spirit of Capitalism*, Weber claimed that is the early stages of modern capitalism, Christian asceticism or the pursuit of wealth was simply the means to the end of religious salvation. Rationalised acquisition or the pursuit of wealth became "stripped of its religious and ethical meaning" (Weber, 1976, p. 182) and dislocated from its original association with higher spiritual or religious ideals. Materialism, understood in this context as "care for external goods", has now become an end in itself, or the "iron cage" (p. 181). He does not see any alternative to this cage, or see it as reversible, but rather says "the great question is . . . what can we oppose to this machinery in order to keep a portion of mankind free from this parceling out of the soul, from this supreme mastery of the bureaucratic way of life (Weber, in Coser & Rosenberg, 1965, p. 473). To Weber, there are several possible ways of offsetting this cage. In his words:

> No one knows who will live in this cage in the future, or whether at the end of this tremendous development entirely new prophets will arise, or there will be a great rebirth of old ideas and ideals, or if neither, mechanised petrification, embellished with a sort of convulsive self-importance. For the last stage of this cultural development, it might well be truly said: "Specialists without spirit, sensualists without heart; this nullity imagines that it has attained a level of civilisation never before achieved". (Weber, 1976, p. 182)

Contrary to its more common association the "iron cage" does not simply refer to the mechanisms of instrumental rationality which render us objects of rational accounting and administration, as this notion is commonly understood, but also the process by which rationalised acquisitiveness deprives us of our spiritual relationship to "our calling."

Seemingly, embracing new prophets, or old religious beliefs are ways of escaping this state of "mechanised petrification," this state of becoming the "specialists without spirit." What I argue here is that as an attempt to create new gurus and leaders and revive old forms of spirituality and magic, the New Age illustrates precisely the first two of the three outcomes that Weber predicts. This is not to say that New Age spirituality, in both its old and new guises, enables us to break out to the cage, for Weber's point is not that we can escape, for as he sees it, those very forces that shackle us within the iron cage (namely, rationalisation and capitalism) are those same forces that bring about, paradoxically, the freedom, creativity, and spontaneity that accompany material abundance, characteristics that keep us from even testing the cage door. Rather than escape, he prophesied that we would try to bring other spirits and demons to live in this cage with us, for embracing new prophets and old religious beliefs to Weber is one way of making modern life bearable. The New Age to Weber would not be a satisfactory solution to the "disenchantment of the world," but rather as an inward escape, a flight from "the fate of the times." Instead, he prefers that one possess "the trained relentlessness in viewing the realities of life, and the ability to face such realities and to measure up to them inwardly" (Weber, 1958, pp. 126-127), or his ideal characteristics of a social scientists.

My work here is based primarily on two case studies: observations of the role of the New Age plays in an urban, metropolitan setting conducted in downtown Toronto, Canada, and observations of a deliberately self-marginalised New Age community who chose to settle in West Cork, Ireland. The former provided an opportunity to observe the role the New Age plays in the lives of predominantly urban, middle-class, professional, and predominantly white Canadian constituency, where New Age practices are inextricably bound up withe consumption. Within this context, I rely on Weber's thesis that seeking refuge in established religion or in new forms of mysticism are no more than an escape from the demands of the modern social order (Giddens, 1971, p. 241). This part of my analysis illustrates the New Age as a symptom of the disenchantment with the world, and as a symptom of the spiritual crisis at the heart of secular society, where the idea of the good life has been reduced to materialism and to rationalised acquisitiveness. However, it is not my intention to simplistically denounce the New Age as an extension of the ethic of hedonistic consumerism, but rather to illustrate how in this community, affiliation with the New Age is in fact a quest for higher values, for spiritual regeneration, for some transcendent principles, even if it does take place within a very limited, compartmentalised, and easily consumable form. Here, spiritual quests are limited to a form consistent with the compartmentalisation of the working day, and where regeneration taking place during clearly defined leisure time is subject to the same standards of productivity as the work that precedes them. In this context, the New Age shows us that Yuppies are not simply hedonists, but are also alternately, hedonists and ascetisists and alternately productive and consumptive.

Although my analysis of the case study of the New Age in Toronto focuses largely on ways in which the New Age adheres to the ideology of consumer society, my other case study of New Age Travellers living in very sparse conditions in rural Ireland enables an analysis of the New Age as explicitly a form of resistance to such aspects of modern life. These mostly British New Age Travellers have a complex and somewhat paradoxical relationship to consumer society. On the one hand, they perceive themselves aw being "refugees from modernity"; form consumerism, as well as from urban development and decay, and from the violence and crime that accompanies city life. They deliberately place themselves on the margins of society. On the other hand, they have attempted to develop a principled relationship to consumption, and to make an intervention by living off the excess of consumer society. By living in abandoned vehicles, self-made shacks, and tipis made of plastic bags, by clothing themselves in second-hand clothes, and by feeding themselves on self-grown food or leftover supermarket refuse, these Travellers are practising New Age environmentalism in a way that is much more integrated into every aspect of their daily lives than simply a leisure time activity.

Although my analysis generally focuses on how the New Age in Toronto expresses various ideologies consistent with consumer society, and how the New Age in Ireland is an example of a "subculture of resistance," it is not sufficient to claim that Toronto New Agers are "cultural dupes" whereas those living in the est of Ireland are not. Rather, I try to show here that both movements' relationship to dominant cultural authorities is complex and diverse. For instance, despite the fact that some aspects of the New Age apparent in my Toronto case study render it simply a commodified leisure activity, holistic health and self-help therapy are a strong attempt toward the democratisation of scientific, medical, and psychiatric authority. Furthermore, the New Age Traveller lifestyle of living off the waste of modernity is not always simply an expression of an environmentalist ethic,or self-consciously and deliberately a political strategy. However, I have described these two cases studies in a manner consistent with Weber's strategy of identifying "ideal types"; some tendencies are maximised, and others are minimised because they both illustrate in exaggerated form the two opposing tendencies characteristic of this movement.

What I really wish to show is that both case studies can be seen in the context of what Alisdair MacIntyre (1981) described as representative of two positions on the spectrum of options facing the modern subject who is attempting to live "the good life." In *After Virtue*, MacIntyre argues that modern society is in moral disarray or crisis because the moral paradigms that inform contemporary moral theory have become disarticulated from the contexts within which they were originally located. Specifically, he argues that the Aristotelian notion of virtue as a end in itself, which linked morality with practical activity, has been replaced by the modern exigencies of instrumental rationality. This fragmentation of morality, has been accompanied by a fragmentation of the modern subject because modern life "partitions each human life into a variety of segments, each with its own norms and modes of behaviour" whereby "work is divided into leisure, private life from public, the corporate from the personal" (MacIntyre. 1981, p. 190). In the context of the disarray of morality and the disunity of modern subject, competing moral claims are at a stalemate, and we no longer have a notion of "the good life" or a moral code that transcends the particular instance. In MacIntyre's words this modern standpoint he is criticising is "that which envisages moral debate in terms of a confrontation between incompatible and incommensurable moral premises and moral commitment as the expression of a criterionless choice between such premises, a type of choice for which no rational justification can be given" (MacIntyre, 1981, p. 38).

MacIntyre's concern with "the good life" can be seen as a response to the fragmenting effect of modern life on a unitary notion of the subject and a universalisable notion of "the good life." Both my Toronto and Ireland case studies illustrate how the New Age is animated by a similar concern. As I demonstrate in the following pages, New Age Travellers attempt to live an ethical life through integrating New Age environmentalism into all aspects of everyday life. Furthermore, what I show here is that although the Toronto New Age is in some ways ideologically consistent with consumer society, and its compartmentalisation into commodified leisure activity is consistent with MacIntyre's critique of the fragmentation of the modern moral subject, even this aspect of the New Age expresses a desire for the good life which transcends its immediate expression—for unity, wholeness, transcendence, and the cosmic universal that can raise us above the fragmented experience of modern life.

For all its negative aspects, New Agers are on a quest for a better life, a quest for transcendence. Although much more naive in form, the New Age, like theorists such as MacIntyre, is concerned with whether we can conceive of a notion of a unitary subject or of a more universal morality that transcends the fragmented, particular notion of the common good we are left with in a (post)modern era. In this fashion, the New Age movement is integrally related to debates around modernity/postmodernity. If we agree that the contemporary ear (whether we choose to periodise it as modern or postmodern) is characterised as Hebdige claims by a move against totalization, teleology, and utopias (Hebdige, 1988, pp. 186-202), then the new age movement is perhaps the return of the repressed of modernism, for it refuses to renounce such absolutes, universals, or foundations. In fact, "good life" for the New Age is perhaps that very quest, the search for growth, the search for answers. If, as MacIntyre concludes, "the good life for man is the life spent in seeking the good life for man" (1981, p. 204), the New Agers are in a sense already living such a life.

I

The Commodification of the New Age

One

The New Age Ethic and the Spirit of Postmodernity

The New Age movement has become increasingly influential in shaping various political religious, and popular discourses in the last decade. In North America, the growing popularity of this movement can be seen in the proliferation of business seminars and television talk shows that espouse the New Age rhetoric of "potential," "growth," and "personal space," Reagan's reputed consultation with various astrologists, the use of psychics by police in missing persons cases, and the emergence of the "Natural Law Party" in Canada. In Europe, there has been a recent proliferation of New Age Travellers living in communes, squats, and travelling encampments in Spain, Holland, England, Germany, Denmark, and Ireland as a form of resistance either to what they perceive as suburban values, to a culture of overregulation, or as a proactive response to a crisis in unemployment or homelessness that characterises their country of origin. In both America and Europe, there has been a rapid expansion of health food stores, alternative health practices such as homeopathic and naturopathic medicine, and midwifery. Although the New Age movement may be seen by some to be restricted to a marginal group of "flaky" practitioners and consumers, New Age practices and rhetoric have achieved a sufficient visibility or cultural currency in the public sphere in both America and Europe to make them a legitimate object of inquiry to social and cultural theorists.

The New Age movement is also integrally related to the claim of several recent cultural commentators (Jameson, 1992; Kingwell, 1996) that we live in an era dominated by millenarianism. This millennium anxiety, as Kingwell calls it, is apparent in the post-apocalyptic aesthetic of urban dance clubs, in the popularity of tattoos and body piercing as a symptom of the collapse of political possibilities to (literally) the politics of the local, in the public fascination with millenarianist themes in television shows such as *The X-Files* and *Millennium* (Kingwell, 1996), and the popularity of the aesthetic of nostalgia and pastiche apparent in disco fashion and films such as *Pulp Fiction*. In the social sciences, such millenarianism is apparent in the barrage of references (since about 1968) to the end of philosophy, the end of history, the end of ideology, the death of the subject, the end of artistic innovation, the collapse of communism as a viable alternative to capitalism, and the loss of universally applicable ethical standards in the context of postmodern critiques of modern metanarratives. If millenarianism is the depressive, anxious unconscious of a schizophrenic modernity, then the New Age movement is its inversion: Where millenarianism emphasizes exhaustion, death, the end, and the apocalypse, the New Age focuses on recharging, rebirthing, reinvigorating, and renewal.

However, to use the term *New Age movement* in the singular is somewhat misleading, as it is neither a unified movement nor necessarily new, but rather a disparate pastiche of practices, ideas, and philosophies some of which have their roots in 17th-century romanticism, herbalism, and other long-standing beliefs and practices. Although New Agers perceive themselves in some ways as reinvigorating and preserving traditional beliefs and practices, they tend to be thoroughly modern subjects who have lived in cities in highly modernized countries in Europe and North America and whose adoption of the New Age is a reflection of their own ambivalence to what Berman (1985) calls the experience of modernity (p. 15). Thus, the New Age, like the category of the "traditional" itself, is a modern invention. Unlike the Hutterites or Amish in Canada, or residual peasant communities in the west of Ireland, they are not uniformly and resolutely premodern, but rather are interested in combining what is perceived as the old with the new, the traditional with the modern, as well as what they see as the Eastern with the Western.

The diversity of this movement is captured in Andrew Ross' (1991) description of the American New Age as an "eclectic and colourful mix of healers, psychics, holistic foodsters, folk metaphysicians, psychotechnologists, UFO contactees, crystal therapists, dolphin advocates, channellers, and a roster of New Age stars such as Timothy Leary" (p. 15). My most basic approach to defining the New Age is phenomenological, and is based on who defines his or herself as New Age, for I am presuming, in accordance with the interpretive tradition in the social sciences, that the New Age, like culture, is not some coherent, reified entity but rather that it is constituted in meaning. This understanding is consistent with what Rabinow and Sullivan (1987) call the "interpretive turn" in the social sciences, a turn that has been influenced by Foucault's claim, that "we are both subjects and objects of the discourse of modernity" (Hekman, 1986), Wittgenstein's (1994) acknowledgment of the intersubjective character of language and hence meaning (the "linguistic turn"), and Gadamer's recognition that all knowledge, even the "hard sciences" is limited by the horizon of meaning within which it is understood (Hekman, 1986), known as the "hermeneutic turn."

In my observations of this movement in America and Europe, most strains of New Ageism can be subsumed under the separate, but by no means mutually exclusive headings of alternative health, environmentalism, paranormal phenomena, self-help therapy, futurology, or alternative religion. Within these categories, the various practices, ideas, philosophies, and beliefs range from powerful and legitimate critiques of various aspects of modernity to what has been called by Andrew Ross the "flaky fringe." For example, the alternative health movement ranges from the holistic health critique of the medicalization of the body propagated by mainstream biomedicine, and the naturopathic condemnation of the use of pesticides, antibiotics, veal pens, and genetic manipulation of livestock or crops, to the arbitrary and sometimes dangerous advocacy of cleansing rituals and fad diets such as the Scarsdale diet and macrobiotics. The environmentalist fringe ranges from imperatives to heighten both personal and industrial responsibility in the global economy of waste, by reducing air emissions and garbage by, for instance, cycling and recycling, to the extreme but provocative contention of proponents of "Deep Ecology" that killing deadly bacteria is species-centric.

The people who make up this community are also diverse. For instance, those who believe in paranormal phenomena such as psychic abilities or the existence of extraterrestrials range from positivist scientists themselves to those who completely reject the scientific worldview. Members of the self-help therapy movement range from those who merely seek empowerment and autonomy from psychiatric and medical experts in their quest for self-knowledge to those who fetishize the self in the search for the "inner child," the "past life," the "Iron John"/"Wild Woman," and espouse essentialist, reductionist, and dualistic concepts of the self and of gender. Those who participate in tarot card readings, palmistry, and astrology range from those who read their horoscope ironically or as an interpretive device that provides an opportunity for self-reflection, to those who develop such elaborate pseudoscientific schemata to guide their everyday life that they refuse to date partners with the wrong astrological sign. Finally, New Age spirituality ranges from those who have a belief in various Eastern and Oriental religions such as Buddhism, Taoism, Hinduism as a reaction to the spiritual vacuum at the heart of what they perceive as an increasingly secularized, materialistic, consumption-oriented culture, to those such as the Heaven's Gate and Japanese doomsday cult members who fill this vacuum with obedience to an arbitrary, and in these cases, megelomaniacal authority.

Furthermore, the New Age is inhabited by both the high and the low end of the commodity spectrum. Although some of my research conducted in crystal shops, New Age book stores, music stores, and in an upscale end of Toronto illustrates clearly how the New Age has been commodified, New Age Travellers in West Cork, and their Canadian counterparts in British Columbia illustrate how aspects of the New Age movement are an explicit critique of consumer society. For example, New Age Travellers living on "Cool Mountain" in West Cork, a mostly British community of self-proclaimed "refugees from modernity" settled in self-made shacks, abandoned vehicles, and makeshift tipis in order to practice holistic health, alternative spirituality, and other "alternative rationalities," unhindered by what they perceive as the materialistic values of city life. Through their environmentalist ethic of constructing an entire lifestyle based on living off the waste, the garbage, the excess of modernity, New Age Travellers express a movement of New Age environmentalism that is not simply a commodified leisure activity or a sporadic practice such as recycling, but rather a total way of life.

Although aspects of the New Age are strongly integrated into consumer culture, much of the New Age impulse adopts a critical stance regarding contemporary social life. As Ross (1991) noted, this movement can be seen on one hand as the repository for radical impulses of the 1960s counterculture, as well as for a disenchanted and devitalized left politics, yet at another level, as ideologically confused. At this level of analysis, the New Age movements, like most contemporary social movements, can be seen as a configuration of many diverse, sometimes marginalized, and contradictory discourses. It is simultaneously what Foucault (1980) would call a "reverse discourse" (p. 101) or what Laclau and Mouffe (1985) would call a "counterhegemonic movement," and ideological or in Marcuse's terms (1964) "affirmative." New Ageism's critiques of Western rationality, of positivist science, of Christian dogma, and of the medicalization of the body are potentially emancipatory. Yet, the New Age selective appropriation and (mis)representation of various aspects of third world culture and religion, the valorization of the "natural"/"primitive"/"goddess" are in fact a replication of dualistic and colonialist tendencies of Enlightenment rationality that New Ageism is critiquing in the first place. Furthermore, its emphasis on personal transformation, on "energy," and its holistic picture of the self-regulating body–mind–spirit, reflects and expresses, respectively, the ideology of possessive individualism, of industrial efficiency, and of the free market economy (Ross, 1991).

However, an approach that takes account of the recent critiques of the Marxist versions of a unified subject and a coherent social totality inherent in both ideology critique and in theories of resistance (see, e.g., Laclau & Mouffe, 1985) is the approach that examines the New Age movement as a "symptom" of various crises of modernity. The New Age movement, like contemporary social theory, is animated by an anxiety about the limits of modern narratives of progress. Twentieth-century critiques of modernity documented the inability of science, positivism, democracy, liberalism, humanism, and other modern narratives of progress to deliver their promise of unlimited social and technological growth through the pursuit of reason. These critiques have revealed how the modernist scientific project's promise to liberate humanity from toil, on one hand, and the modernist political project's promise of the gradual extension of human rights and freedoms (enshrined in concepts of democracy and liberalism) on the other, have failed to fulfill their utopian aspirations. The proliferation of debates about the "crisis" of reason, technology, science, and positivism on one hand, and of reason, the political, community, and identity on the other are a testament to the limits of these narratives of technological and social growth. It is these debates around the crises and limits of modernity that have both reflected and facilitated what some theorists are calling the loss of utopia in contemporary society (Hebdige, 1988).

Holistic health and self-help therapy dimensions of the New Age represent a critique of "expert knowledge," a critique of medical and psychiatric authority, or an expression of what some social scientists would call the *crisis of science*. Furthermore, the New Age Traveller creation of a subcultural community is a response to the contemporary crises of community and identity. As such, the New Age movement can be very clearly located within debates on the various crises of modernity/postmodernity (i.e., the crises of science, reason, identity, community, and legitimation). In many ways, the New Age movement can be seen as a symptom of these various crises of modernity, specifically debates around the crisis of Reason, or the failure of enlightenment Reason to deliver its emancipatory promise. Holistic health and self-help therapy can be seen in the context of this crisis, or more specifically the related "crisis of science" indicated by the proliferation of critiques of positivism, technology, the scientific method, and objectivity advanced by environmentalists, feminists, social scientists, philosophers, and even positivist scientists themselves. As well, New Age literature frequently appeals to the fantasy of an undifferentiated, unified community characterized by face-to-face interaction and a unified notion of the "common good" that is a reaction to the heterogeneity and social differentiation that theorists such as Simmel, Durkheim, and Tonnies claim sets apart modern from premodern societies. Thus, New Age science and the New Age version of community are both strongly related to what various contemporary theorists are calling the crisis of cultural authority (Ross, 1988), or crisis of legitimation (Lyotard, 1994) characterizing contemporary society.

THEORETICAL PERSPECTIVES

There are a wide range of theoretical perspectives that are relevant to a sociology of the New Age movement, ranging from contemporary critiques of gender, orthodox Freudian psychoanalysis, existentialist feminism, and Marxist ideology critique, to contemporary critiques of the body in social theory. For example, the phenomenon of "Iron John," and the "Wild Woman" can be seen in the context of feminism and gender studies. The search for the Iron John and the Wild Woman can be seen as an essentialized and reactionary response to the reorganization of gender scripts in contemporary society induced by such demographic and attitudinal changes in the 20th century such as the increased labor force participation of women, decreased levels of fertility, increased levels of marital breakdown, and the rise of feminism. As some feminists such as Margaret Eichler (1988) have argued, the destabilization of traditional versions of masculine and feminine identities that these social changes both reflect and encourage have facilitated both the rise of feminism and a conservative anti-feminist backlash.

As well, spirit channelling, past-life regression and other New Age practices, lend themselves readily to an orthodox Freudian psychoanalytic interpretation. Within such a model, spirit channelling and past-life regression could be seen as an example of the "return of the repressed"—an expression of the eruption of desires normally repressed in everyday life. Many undergoing past-life regression "discover" that they were exotic warriors, princesses, and leaders rather than servants, slaves, or peasants, because they are, like Walter Mitty, metaphorically the latter in real life. Within a Freudian framework, the more severe the superegoic or societal injunction on enjoyment for the individual, the more flamboyant the self-romanticizing fantasy. One of the people with whom I spoke was a very warm and creative Canadian woman who succumbed to the moral regulation accompanying her station as a single, middle-aged primary schoolteacher by being extremely nondescript, conservative-looking, gentle, and polite, but claimed that in a past life she was a warrior princess with a bloodcurdling battlecry who killed all aggressors against the meek. Within this perspective, these previous lives and spirit voices not only expressed her fantasy that she had an exotic inner life, but also gave a voice to her own desire for agency and passion and her own anger suppressed under the veneer of the "good woman." A more explicit example of the New Age as expressing repressed desire is illustrated in those who claim to have had erotic encounters with aliens, a central theme of the 1992 independent U.S. film *Road Scholar* directed by Romanian filmmaker Andrei Codresceu. Many cases of so-called "possession" have been explained in a similar fashion. Although the content of these fantasies may involve contemporary themes such as aliens, the form of course is consistent with Freud's case studies of "hysterical" and "neurotic" individuals in early 20th century Vienna: Rather than psychopathologizing or labeling these individuals, it is my intention to illustrate how the desires they express are shared by members of the broader society.

A more Lacanian application of psychoanalysis to the New Age might see the self-help movement rhetoric of finding the inner child and allowing it to speak as a literalization of the Lacanian dictum regarding the impossibility of reconciling the divided parts of the self. Lacan's psychoanalytic critique of the rational subject holds that we are all split subjects, with chaotic and contradictory desires. In this way, the New Age self-help search for the inner child can be seen as an expression of the desire for reconciliation with the divided parts of the self. This tendency to compartmentalize spheres of life is discussed not only in clinical psychiatric terms as an individual pathology, namely schizophrenia, but also as a collective pathos, as the contemporary, albeit distorted, form of subjectivity in various contemporary discussions of the schizophrenic subject of modernity (see, e.g., Jameson, 1991).

As well, the resurgence of interest in Wicca and witch cults, which is another aspect of the New Age movement, can be seen in the context of psychoanalytic or existentialist feminist constructions of woman as Other. Feminists such as Judith Butler (1993) illustrate how the relegation of women to the category of matter, the body, and man to the mind, and the cosmos is a long-standing tradition in Western philosophy. This tradition is generally associated with male ambivalence regarding female power, or more generally in the dialectic of fear and desire between men and women. From this point of view, the New Age cults of the goddess and the witch can be seen as actively embracing the positive rather than the negative connotations of the ambivalent identity imposed on them, a sort of a semiotic affirmative action.

New Age spiritualism and the phenomena of Harmonic Convergence can be seen in the context of Marx's critique of religion as illusory, and as the "opiate of people" (Giddens, 1971, p. 220). The New Age doctrine of Harmonic Convergence, based of Ferguson's (1980) book *The Aquarian Conspiracy*, lends itself well to Marx's critique that "in religion, men participate in an unreal, fantasy world of harmony, beauty, and contentment, while living in a practical everyday world of pain and misery" (Giddens, 1971, p. 5). Ferguson's book, seen by some as the canonical New Age text, claims that New Agers are the creative minority who will be catalysts to a global transformation to a "higher consciousness" where we, in the words of one of my research subjects, will "explode in an ecstasy of light and sound." New Age spiritualism, like religious illusion, can be seen as deflecting concern with the material conditions of life and all the social hierarchies these conditions involve, onto the afterlife. Ferguson's emphasizes that this revolution is a revolution in consciousness evades the question as to how embodiment, concrete material relations, and social inequality might be experienced after the revolution, an oversight shared by other revolutionary and religious perspectives as well.

Harmonic Convergence, as well as the New Age self-help ethic of individual responsibility and self-empowerment are now becoming a part of corporate thinking in Canada (as is indicated by the wide-scale use of motivational speakers, "the power of positive thinking" encounter groups, and Dale Carnegie seminars in business training programs) and can also be comprehended in the context of Marx's critique of idealism. He argues idealism falsely privileges the world of the mind, awareness, consciousness, over the material, matter, the body. Marx (1965) claims that to the young Hegelians "the relationships of men, all their doings, their chains, and their limitations are products of their consciousness" (p. 41). To Marx, this focus on the mind, on consciousness, of Being, detracts us from material conditions, inequalities, and hierarchies, and thus advocates a model of philosophical reflection that is, in contemporary terms, politically conservative. As implied earlier, this ethic of individual responsibility can be seen on the one hand as a form of resistance to the medicalization and stigmatization of mental health. However, from the perspective of Marx's ideology critique, this self-help ethic, in certain guises, is inseparable from the laissez-faire ideology of the New Right who use this same ethic of individual responsibility to justify cutbacks to the welfare state. Thus, both spiritualist impulses of the New Age movement such as Harmonic Convergence, and idealist impulses, such as aspects of self-help therapy can be seen in the context of ideology critique as ways of thinking that distort, legitimate, or deflect attention from the existing material, productive relations.

From this perspective, the New Age is ideological. But I also examine the New Age as a form of resistance to what New Agers perceive as the alienating and dehumanizing processes of modernity such as the rationalization, bureaucratization, and urbanization. For instance, the New Age perspective on the body, specifically holistic health, can be seen as a form of resistance to the failure of the biomedical model of contemporary medicine to acknowledge the relationship between mind and body, a dualism that is a part of a more general legacy of a mind-matter split inherent in Western science and philosophy. The attempt by the holistic health movement to integrate the disparate elements of mind/body/spirit, is a reaction to the failure of biomedical model of mainstream medicine to acknowledge this connection between mind and body, or psychological/emotional and physiological health. From a Foucauldian perspective, the holistic health movement and self-help therapy represents an attempt at democratizing expert psychiatric knowledge in opposition to the dividing practices of social and spatial exclusion, and to the processes of scientific categorization practiced on the insane, the marginalized, and the ill in psychiatric and medical institutions. However, the holistic health and self-help therapy could in fact be the latest form of subjectivization, or the internalization of the normalizing, collective gaze (Foucault, 1991). From this point of view, the New Age imperative to "be healthy" and to liberate ourselves and our bodies from the expert control of science and medicine simply renders us complicit in the very mechanisms of surveillance and normalization from which we are trying to escape.

As well as ascribing to New Age critique of scientific rationality in their rejection of modern medicine, many New Age Travellers I studied in Ireland lead a lifestyle that is an explicit rejection of the organization of space and time underpinning the modern household. First, the New Age Traveller advocacy of (geographical and spiritual) nomadicism is a rejection of the notion of the permanent habitat and stable identity that has played a crucial role in processes of modernization. Because the mobility of New Age Traveller life and the practice of living in single room shacks, tipis, vehicles, and so on precludes the possibility of modern conveniences such as a separate "bathroom," this lifestyle explicitly rejects the modern obsession with sanitation and the ideology that "civilized" individuals engage in the daily ritual of cleaning, scrubbing, and soaking the surface, hair and orifices of the unclean body. Furthermore, their innovative, multifunctional living spaces are an implicit challenge to the spatial imposition of the division of labor onto the modern house wherein houses are fragmented into specialized rooms; into bathrooms, bedrooms, and kitchens in which individual bodies are fed, cleaned, and regenerated to the tempo of the working day. More generally, the multifunctional spaces that comprise New Age Traveller homes run contrary to the spatial and temporal ordering central to work and home life that is a part of the civilizing and moralizing processes of modernity.

Although these theoretical paradigms derived from contemporary critiques of gender, orthodox Freudian psychoanalysis, existentialist feminism, and so on, do inform my discussion of the New Age, I look at them more generally in terms of their possible application to cultural analysis of the New Age in terms of the categories of ideology and resistance. Specifically, I use these perspectives in terms of how they inform an analysis of the New Age as both the commodification of counterrationalities and thus as "ideological," and as a form of resistance to the dividing, labeling, and rationalizing processes of modernity. At a more general level, I have tried to locate my discussion of the New Age in the context of debates on the various crises of modernity, debates that problematize both the concept of ideology's assumption of the "extra-ideological position," as well as the totalizing view of the social implied by the notion of "resistance."

I generally look at the New Age movement as three levels of abstraction. At the most microsociological level of analysis, I look at various New Age phenomena such as the phenomenon of Iron John, Goddess cults, spirit channelling, past-life regression, self-help therapy, Wicca, holistic health, and Harmonic Convergence in the context of various theoretical paradigms ranging from feminism, psychoanalysis, Marxism, existentialism, a Foucauldian analysis of the biopolitics of power, and so on. At a higher level of abstraction, I will look at these phenomena in terms of how these theoretical analyses reveal them to be either ideological or forms of resistance. My analysis at this level takes into consideration that labeling aspects of the New Age as either ideological or emancipatory can only be done provisionally, because critical theory is only now coming to terms with its own desire to occupy the extra-ideological position or the fantasy of the coherent social totality from which one can resist or be liberated. At an even higher level of abstraction, and at a level that takes account of the problems of the totalizing and essentializing assumptions underpinning notions of ideology and resistance, I look at these phenomena in terms of how they are symptoms of the limits of various modern narratives of progress. This section, therefore, looks at New Age phenomena in terms of how they are symptoms of various crises of (post)modernity.

Thus, my analysis moves from a specific theme to greater level of abstraction and back down again, moves among different paradigms, and moves from the personal to the political to the philosophical, with regards to this phenomenon. In moving among these various levels of abstraction, I demonstrate a "sociological imagination," which to Mills (1959) is:

> the capacity to shift from one perspective to another—from the political to the psychological; from examination of a single family to comparative assessment of the national budgets of the world; from the theological school to the military establishment; from considerations of an oil industry to studies of contemporary poetry. (p. 7)

In Mills' analysis, theorizing requires a dexterity, a certain agility to move from biography to history, from private to public, from self to society, and so on. In his words, the sociological imagination is also "the capacity to range from the most impersonal and remote transformations to the most intimate features of the self-and to see the relations between the two" (Mills, 1959, p. 8). Following Mills' description, if we can see for a moment each paradigm or theoretical perspective as a colored thread in a tapestry, any final account or piece of sociological work will resemble a tapestry, and will have woven within it several different hues. This creation, this tapestry of theoretical perspectives will probably be more one shade than another, but still multicolored. In accordance with my understanding of the interpretive tradition, I have tried to let the particular New Age phenomena guide the type of theoretical perspectives I used.

METHODOLOGY

My own relationship to the New Age began when I moved to Toronto. As a small-town Saskatchewanian moving to the big city for the first time, I moved in with another "prairie girl" like myself, who had joined "est," Warner Erhart's self-help and personal empowerment seminar series, a program mockingly referred to in Woody Allen films as capturing the self-seeking Zeitgeist of the 1970s, but which is still a lucrative industry. The actual philosophy of self-empowerment est ascribes to is innocuous and common-sensical enough to defy criticism albeit rooted in a competitive individualist paradigm of self-actualization: principles such as "don't give up on the dream of establishing the career or business you want," "the power of goal setting and positive thinking," and so on. However, the problem was rather the extent to which est began to dominate my roommate's whole life whereby this program slowly became for her a total way of life and an all-encompassing worldview: She dropped out of graduate school, began working for them voluntarily fulltime, continued to donate large sums of money to their "cause." Although she was smart, tough, and sassy, est became the latest in a long line of paradigms or "isms" with which she had become fascinated: First Catholicism, then Marxism and feminism, although never with the dogmatism she expressed with regards to est. Although all these perspectives sometimes lend themselves to the self-justificatory creation of their own hermetically sealed communities, self-explanatory metanarratives, and charismatic leaders, est was more explicitly "cult-like" in that individuals are "hooked" by the allure of its manifest function, self-empowerment, which ensures that it fulfills its latent function, to collect large donations. What was most frightening about est was that its ethos of self-empowerment so clearly taps into a collective unconscious or longing in a context where both faith in formal politics and large-scale political movements of the left are in decline, and a "politics of the local" is seemingly all that remains. Although this woman's exploration of various paradigms and her subsequent devotion to est is symptomatic of aspects of the modern search for meaning more generally, I was unable to remain roommates with her and thus eventually moved into a very cheap, six bedroom house in downtown Toronto with a houseful of people that was and still is my template for the cosmopolitan experience.

My new household was a fascinating array of 20 (and 30) something countercultural bohemianism in the 1990s: a strange, beautiful, and inarticulate artist who wore only secondhand, torn clothes and made films with no dialogue; a White, uppermiddle-class African studies major with a loving but racist family and a boyfriend from Zimbabwe; a Danish Earth-mother lesbian; a vegetarian, pro-animal rights, ex-Deadhead manager of a health food store who read Heidegger in German; a guitar-playing young playwright (who actually really wrote); an English lit graduate who was waitressing just long enough to finance her eighth trip to India; a demure, "small-town girl" who loved sushi, sake, and all things Japanese; an ex-con who sold drugs in order to tour with the Grateful Dead; and a brilliant but guilt-riddled political science major with a penchant for Black feminist literature major who had spent years in eastern Europe and who is still my best friend. Together we burned incense and candles, cooked communal vegetarian feasts, stopped shaving and perfuming, became "Green," recycled and composted, discussed ethnocentrism and politics, toyed with monogamy, sexual orientation, and the meaning of life, and ran a surprisingly successful collective household for more than 3 years. Although only two of these roommates would explicitly identity with the label "New Age," the fascination with Africa, Japan, the move toward becoming green, and the quest for self-knowledge signified by the interest in therapy and self-knowledge were all characteristic of some aspects of the New Age.

One of the most short-lived roommates, the "Deadhead" and his girlfriend were perhaps the most clearly identifiable New Agers. In a sense, their relationship to the New Age was even more problematic than that of my previous roommate, not because of an over zealousness, but because their beliefs were so fraught with contradictions: They criticized those of us who were not strictly vegetarian, yet they wore leather. They sporadically practiced homeopathic medicine, lectured the rest of us on the evils of alcohol, yet chain-smoked cigarettes, smoked marijuana by the bagful, and regularly consumed "acid" and mushrooms. They spoke of "getting in touch with their inner child," or "self-actualization," yet masked their own drug dependence behind a liberal/ hippie rhetoric of freedom of action. They talked about the "mind/body connection" yet were practically anorexic and got no exercise. They listened to raggae and World music, wore clothes from Indonesia and Thailand, decorated the house with African carvings and Aboriginal "dream catchers," burned incense from India, yet had no real knowledge or interest in the politics or histories of these cultures beyond proclaiming them "authentic." They frequently spoke of sharing, of communal ethics, yet fled the house when it was their turn to cook, and "forgot" when they borrowed money. They claimed to be anti-materialistic, but moved in to an expensive condominium on the lakefront belonging to one of their parents when out of work. They were anti-technologists and rural-philes, but unable to move out of the city. In our 20-something search for identity in the city, all of us were a mass of contradictions (I myself was a case in point as I tried to refashion myself from "prairie girl" to "urban cool") but these two individuals are perhaps my most contradictory example to date of one of the defining features of New Age: the tendency to take bits and pieces of the grab-bag of New Age practices and to fashion or sew them together as it suits them.

From these experiences, I derived a general sense that the New Age is concerned with consciousness, and individual empowerment, with the limitations of Western art, music, and culture, with the ramifications of modern industry on human and non-human life, and with the limitations of modern science to explain paranormal phenomena or effectively cure health problems. I became increasingly convinced that there was something about this movement worth researching to begin examining these phenomena in earnest. I then tried to get a more broad sense of the themes, symbols, rhetoric, and desires of this movement by immersing myself in the New Age in my neighborhood: I got massages from holistic masseuses, had tarot card readings, had my astrological chart and my palm read. I read New Age books, magazines, and pamphlets, went to psychic fairs, Emin meetings, New Age book shops, I ate in vegetarian restaurants, hung around coffee shops frequented by New Age members. I approached some of the more visible and perhaps unusual New Age members: White North American Sikhs, Hindus, and Buddhists. Out of these general observations, I noticed recurring themes in the New Age, themes such as "rebirthing," "recharging," "regenerating," "healing," "wholeness," "tradition," and "primitive."

In sociological language, this stage of data collection involved the use of classical sociological research methods or techniques such as observation and participant observation at various New Age shops, events, meetings, and lectures organized around these themes, as well as interviews with people in the fields of alternative health, environmentalism, paranormal phenomena, self-help therapy, futurology, and alternative religion. It also involved various techniques in the anthropological tradition such as establishing a rapport, selecting informants, transcribing texts, keeping fieldnotes, and other techniques associated with doing ethnography. However, as Geertz (1973) points out, elaborating the types of methods used tells us nothing about what ethnographers really do. He says "it is not these things, techniques, and received procedures that define the enterprise" of doing ethnography (p. 5). Furthermore, the scientific resonance of these "methods," and their apparent characterization of the sociologist as "observer" is in a way misleading insofar as they characterise the sociologist as somehow immune, apart, or distanced from "culture," from "the field" that comprises the site of her or his investigation.

Much of my data, however, was accumulated in a much less coordinated or scientific fashion, and involved interpreting or theorizing about dominant New Age symbols as they appeared to me in my neighborhood. Contrary to the image of the "field" of the ethnographer as radically distinct from his or her everyday life, my topic of investigation or my field was culturally and geographically close to me; I was, at times, embedded within it. Living in downtown Toronto, crystals and health foods, green products and self-help books, Thai clothes, and Latin American wall hangings were all around me in the coffee shops, bookstores, and sidewalk vendors. As a result, my preliminary data was largely based on observations and interpretations that emerged when I encountered phenomena associated with the New Age. I learned to take a fieldnote diary with me when I went to the shop, the bookstore, the pub, or just for a walk, because at any moment, I could "step into the field." Nor did I have to go "undercover," for many acquaintances and several friends involved in this movement went to great lengths to help me when they heard the topic of my research. In this sense, I was not distanced from the "field" at all, this phenomenon was in my neighborhood, at times in my house, and more recently (and interestingly, from my point of view), in my family, insofar as my own mother, who was previously not spiritually inclined has become a recent convert to the notion of "past-life regression."

I would thus define a large part of my research process as ethnographic. As Clifford (1998) documents, *ethnography* has been variously defined as "sometimes requiring extensive reading, sometimes fieldwork, sometimes a totalizing theoretical framework, sometimes a dialogic inclusion of differing views, including the views of the people being studied, sometimes a combination of these possibilities" (p. 5). In this research, I encountered some of the moral/ethical issues that are currently occupying debates on ethnography, issues such as "going native," primitivism, intellectual imperialism, the subject-object relation in ethnography, the importance of intuition in ethnography, and the problem of maintaining a critical distance versus merging with research subjects. I have also in the sociological tradition, conducted in-depth interviews with New Age practitioners, but with the recognition that the epistemological assumptions underlying this discipline's approach to the phenomenon ascribes to the structuralist fantasy of the coherent and connected social totality, of a logic within the structure, a legacy of rationalist epistemology. Such attempts to reconstruct each research subject's version of the lifeworld rely on the assumption that these accounts allow the researcher to construct the entire symbolic order of the New Age.

Insofar as distance from one's research subjects is frequently posited as an ideal in the social sciences by proponents of "objectivity," my acknowledgment of embeddedness, of proximity to the phenomena I am examining may from some points of view be seen as problematic. This notion of the necessity of "distance" between the researcher and the research enshrined in more positivistic versions of "objectivity" in the social sciences is often apparent in what Bordo (1990) calls methodologism. To Bordo, methodologism, is the belief that rigorous adherence to the "right" methods and sufficient distance between researcher and researched will themselves guarantee the validity of the research results.

Methodologism also entails the assumption that the rigorous adherence to certain established precepts within its own tradition ensures that whatever method is employed is self-cleansing, and that the "proper" employment of method can eliminate bias. This perspective, particularly characteristic of positivism is similar to the linguistic structuralism inherent in the contemporary assumption that the use of the "proper" politically correct anti-racist and anti-sexist language can eradicate racist and sexist thought. As many 20th-century philosophers have pointed out, this fetishization of method characteristic of positivism extends far beyond the perimeters of positivist philosophy and methodology itself, but rather is a symptom of our society's obsession with technical procedures and the formalistic organization of knowledge (Rabinow & Sullivan, 1987). This concern about methodologism in the social sciences is apparent in critiques of instrumental rationality originating from Weber's concern over the danger of substituting technical expertise and procedures for political debate (Rabinow & Sullivan, 1987), to the Frankfurt school's critique of identity thinking on up to Habermas' notion of the "colonisation of the lifeworld" (Habermas, 1987, p. 332).

Furthermore, as Bordo pointed out, this version of objectivity presumes a disembedded, autonomous, knowing subject immune from the effects of history, culture, or social location that "speaks from nowhere" (Bordo, 1990). This is linked to the Enlightenment fantasy that one uses the right method man will be "freed from his passions, his history, and his traditions" (Rabinow & Sullivan, 1987, p. 2). Despite these problems, the social scientific insistence that we define our method in our research often ascribes to such methodologism. However, in Rabinow and Sullivan's words, "we must challenge the very ideal that inquiry into the social world and the value of the understanding that results is to be determined by methodology" (p. 20).

However, this model of the knowing subject that emerges from Enlightenment epistemology has been critiqued insofar as it represses materiality (Butler, 1993), and represses the body (Bordo, 1990), which fixes the knower in space and time. In denying itself a body that would situate it, this modern epistemic subject, in Bordo's words, "claims to descend from the heavens of pure rationality or reflect the inevitable and progressive logic of intellectual or scientific discovery" (p. 137). In light of the fact that all knowledge claims have a point of origin, are located in history, in culture, and are in minute ways influenced by the race, class, or gender of the knower, Haraway (1991) argued that we should replace the notion of "objectivity" with the recognition that all knowledges are "situated knowledges" (p. 183), that all knowledges are perspectival, for one's range of vision is always dependent on from where one "sees."

Despite the more or less explicit repudiation of positivism in the social sciences, the unwillingness to give up the doctrine of "objectivity" has had the effect of reproducing a dichotomy between objectivity and subjectivity, between subject and object (Hekman, 1990). However, recent shifts in the philosophy of the social sciences that focus on discourse, language, and interpretation have challenged the classic rationalist dichotomy between subject and object. These shifts involve, for example, the recognition that both the subject and object in the classical epistemological sense are enmeshed in the complex world of signification, and that neither the actions of the spectator subject nor the object of study can be understood in abstraction from the languages used to describe them. These debates claim that knowledge does not involve a radically separate knower and known, but rather a world in which "both the object of investigation—the web of language, symbol, and institutions that constitutes signification-and the tools by which investigation is carried out share inescapably the same pervasive context that is the human world" (Rabinow & Sullivan, 1987, p. 7). As Geertz (1973) phrased it, following Weber, "man is an animal suspended in webs of signification he himself has spun" (p. 5).

In this way of thinking, the "object" of investigation becomes meaning itself. Moreover, the classic division between knower and known is called into question, because both are dependent on the prior existence of the shared world of meaning within which the subjects of human discourse constitute themselves. As Rabinow and Sullivan (1987) put it "there is no outside, detached viewpoint from which we can gather and present brute data" (p. 7). In other words, as social scientists, we are irrevocably enmeshed in the very culture we are trying to describe, and are in a paradoxical situation whereby, in Hekman's (1986) words:

> the "man" of the human sciences is on one hand the object of those sciences, the entity that is studied in these disciplines just as the natural scientists study the physical world. But "man"; is also the subject that constitutes knowledge, the being that makes knowledge, even knowledge of himself, possible. (p. 69)

From this point of view, my embeddedness in New Age culture, my proximity to the phenomenon was not a "problem," as the positivists would have it, but rather a fundamental aspect of the study of culture. Furthermore, my geographical and cultural proximity gave me a valuable opportunity to examine this phenomenon in intricate detail. As Gadamer acknowledged, prejudice (in the sense of one's embeddedness in history and culture) is not an impediment to knowledge, but rather a precondition for it (Hekman, 1986). In Gadamer's understanding, the world is only made present to us from within our own horizon of meaning, from within the "range of vision that includes everything that can be seen from a particular vantage point" (Hekman, 1986, p. 104). Within this framework, achieving an understanding of another does not mean the abandoning of one's own horizon (which to Gadamer entails self-alienation, or is impossible), but rather involves self-reflexively acknowledging how one's own horizons will color the interpretations of another. Thus, to Gadamer, self-understanding is a precondition to understanding. Efforts to claim a stance outside history and culture, are, to Gadamer, irresponsible, and misrecognize the fundamental character of knowing.

In this sense, my overall epistemological position that influences my methodology is based on what Rabinow and Sullivan call the interpretive turn in the social sciences. This turn has been influenced by the discursive/linguistic/hermeneutic turn elaborated earlier. Based on this interpretive turn, my approach to the New Age presumes that there is no coherent reified entity called the New Age, but rather that it is constituted in meaning. This perspective acknowledges that there is no essential meaning of "the New Age," but rather that it is inseparable from the beliefs, definitions, and self-perceptions of those who practice it.

On acknowledging that there is no Archimedean, neutral, or external point of view that can tell us what the New Age actually is, I began a phenomenological investigation into what self-proclaimed New Age devotees themselves actually thought constituted New Age practices. This involved a collection of the various signifiers that emerged alongside the terms "New Age" in magazines, journals, books, crystal shops, and coffee shops. There is by no means common agreement about what is and is not the New Age: The New Age movement has no paradigmatic unity regarding what constitutes New Age practices, no clearly defined boundaries or easily locatable discursive space. However, out of the amalgamation of signifiers associated with the New Age, out of the diversity of meanings and associations, and the contradictory and disparate understanding, there was a sufficient overlap or consensus, a generalised agreement, for me to organize New Age practices into six general categories: environmentalism, holistic health, self-help, futurologist, paranormal, and alternative religion. Thus, despite the diversity, complexity, and the contradictory character of the various accounts I received about the New Age, I was able to impose some unifying categories on this phenomenon.

However, an analysis of any cultural phenomenon entails much more than merely a description and classification of the practices it involves, just as an account of any methodological approach to research involves much more than an account of the methods used to produce "data." For instance, to Geertz (1973):

> The concept of culture I espouse . . . is essentially a semiotic one. Believing, with Marx Weber, that man is an animal suspended in webs of significance he himself has spun, I take culture to be those webs, and the analysis of it to be therefore not an experimental science in search of law but an interpretive one in search of meaning. (p. 5)

Geertz thus defines the interpretive process that defines ethnography as "thick description"; as uncovering "a stratified hierarchy of meaningful structures" or "piled up structures of inference and implication" (Geertz, 1973, p. 7). Moreover, the real work of the ethnographer, in Geertz's view, is not the description, but rather the interpretation, the "sorting out of the structures of signification" or codes. To Geertz, we have to look at what symbolic action signifies, what is getting said.

Out of the reservoir of information that these ethnographies produced, I tried to pick out areas where these accounts that coalesced into particularly dense layers of meaning, that were particularly thick, or were what Geertz calls "a stratified hierarchy of meaningful structures" . . . "piled up structures of inference and implication" (Geertz, 1973, p. 4). In keeping with Geertz's advocacy of the literary critical view of the world-as-text, I looked for the dominant rhetoric, the recurring themes that I found occurring again and again in this movement: not just in terms of accounts people gave, but in terms of the symbols of the movement. However, I illustrate how my use of a Gadamerian hermeneutic critique of textual analysis, as well as the "low-brow" content of the subject matter itself, hopefully enable my particular use of this methodology to transcend the historical tendency of this methodological tradition to claim that only certain kinds of texts are worthy of analysis.

There were several places where meaning became "piled up" or symbolically overdetermined in the New Age. This is apparent not only in terms of my analysis of written works (i.e., my own transcripts from conversations, interviews, at meetings, or of New Age magazines and books), but also in the dominant symbols of the New Age. For instance, the New Age is rife with illustrations depicting the unified earth, different races holding hands, the unity of "man" and "nature," the timelessness and therefore connectedness of all living things, and so on. Thus, textual analysis does not mean (as it is frequently misunderstood to mean) that I am only looking at the written words (i.e., New Age literature, my own transcripts), but rather that the New Age as a broad cultural phenomenon is to be approached in terms of the tropes, metaphors, and rhetorical devices it employs: In other words, through modes of interpretation established through literary criticism. For instance, New Age rhetoric contains clusters of meaning occurring particularly around themes such as wholeness, unity, oneness, harmony, balance, integration. As well, dominant New Age symbols such as the crystal, are perceived as symbols of connectedness, continuity, oneness, wholeness. Thus, I frequently use an interpretive methodological approach called Semiotics, borrowed from film and literary criticism whereby, the interpreter searches not just for the manifest but also the latent content(s) behind every chain of significations. This "depth" analysis of the multiple layers of meaning ascribes to the position that "a sign does not simply exist as a part of reality—it reflects and refracts another reality" (Volosinov, 1973, p. 13). I have tried to look for the "other realities" to which these significations point.

Although there has been a huge proliferation recently of essays on popular culture, there is by no means a consensus within the field of cultural studies as to what particular methodological approach is most effective. For example, in the introduction to *Cultural Studies,* a compilation of essays by contemporary cultural theorists, the authors deny that cultural studies has some stable or clearly defined disciplinary base, theoretical paradigm, methodology, or domain of objects (Grossberg, Nelson, & Treichler, 1992). Rather, they claim it is interdisciplinary, that its approach to theory is alchemic (in that it borrows from many major bodies of theory such as Marxism, feminism, psychoanalysis, poststructuralism, postmodernism, etc.). Methodologically, they claim that they do not formally adopt any particular disciplinary practices, but borrow, as needed, from "textual analysis, semiotics, deconstruction, ethnography, interviews, phonemic analysis, psychoanalysis, rizomatics, content analysis, survey research" (Grossberg et al., 1992, p. 2), sometimes employing a multimethod approach, a bricolage, to escape inscription within whatever tradition each method is associated. However, they do claim that cultural studies does express a shared commitment to analysing relations of power, to self-reflection, and to moments of self-clarification.

To some degree I ascribe to this type of "methodological bricolage." However, in this work I make strong use of psychoanalysis. A psychoanalytic interpretation of the New Age illustrates that the continual recurrence of these themes reveals not belief in wholeness, in connectedness, in continuity, but a profound anxiety about fragmentation, disconnection, heterogeneity. At this level of analysis I take from Freud and Lacan the psychoanalytic model of how fears and desires become projected and transferred onto the Other. Thus, the New Age is a repository for our desire for reconciliation with various others: with the developing world, with Nature (Haraway, 1991), with the divided parts of the self (Zizek,

1989), and other Others with whom the New Age claims we existed in an original unity.

First, in reaction to the colonialist impetus to consume or annihilate the Other, the New Age has responded by identifying with, or in Irigaray's (1988) terms *consummating* with the Other, a strategy that ironically replicates the same denial of difference found in colonialist narratives of the Other. Second, the New Age desire to "protect" nature through its program of "cleansing," "detechnologising," and "decivilising" nature constructs nature as the site of some idyllic, preindustrial past that is as much a commentary on the dissatisfaction with the antagonism of the social as it is a fear of environmental destruction. Third, New Age self-help technologies that stress achieving "inner balance," "harmony," and "oneness" represent the New Age fantasy of the unified, accessible, and coherent subject devoid of conflicting desires or a chaotic unconscious. Thus, what gets coded as the Other in the New Age through the figures of the "alien," the crystal, and the "aura" all reveal how the realms of the developing world, nature, and the spiritual are all sites in which fears and desires, projection and transference regarding difference and sameness are played out. In this way, a psychoanalytic interpretation of the manifest content of the analysis of the speech of the New Age reveals the perception of the self, the ego, community, identity, as balanced, unified, whole, but of course the latent content is that this is not the case, and the New Age represents the attempt to "suture" this lack, this hole.

Thus, a psychoanalytic reading of the New Age tries to answer the question "What is the New Age desire?" in order to develop an interpretation of these themes around which there was a particular density of meaning. As well as a desire for reconciliation with an antagonistic Other, based on psychoanalytic and existentialist models I make the claim that the New Age expresses a desire for self-determination, for some form of resistance to conventional scientific, medical, political, and cultural authorities. Although the diversity of the various strains of this movement indicates that this movement is neither self-conscious, nor politically unified, the fact that New Age philosophy and rhetoric have a certain visibility, a certain cultural currency, indicates that the New Age desire for self-determination, for some form of resistance to dominant forms of cultural authorities, has struck a common chord.

Thus, a psychoanalytic interpretation of the semiotics of the New Age, which reveals that the New Age desire is the desire for self-determination illustrates at a more abstract level what social theorists such as Ross (1991), Laclau and Mouffe (1985) and Habermas (1975) are calling a crisis of cultural authority. This interpretation of the semiotics of the New Age leads me at a higher level of abstraction to posit the New Age as a "symptom" of more general social tendencies and processes, as a sign of other things happening, and in a way, as an exaggerated but clear illustration of a societal reaction to what some people are calling postmodernism. Thus, my overall orientation is to take it as a kind of a code language for larger social trends and processes.

This approach is consistent with Ross' approach to the New Age as a "sign of the times" or with Hall's approach to the New Age as an indicator of various aspects of social change:

> How new are these "new times"? Are they the dawn of a New Age or only the whisper of an old one? What is "new" about them? How do we assess their contradictory tendencies—are they progressive or regressive? . . . If we take the "new times" idea apart, we find that it is an attempt to capture, within the confines of a single metaphor, a number of different facets of *social change*. (Hall, 1989, p. 22)

This treatment of the New Age also has a precedent in the sense that members of the Frankfurt school treat art in a similar fashion. "We interpret [art] as a kind of code language for the processes taking place within society, which must be deciphered by means of critical analysis" (Lowenthal, in Jay, 1973, p. 177). If we take seriously the postmodern acknowledgment of the breakdown between high culture or art, and mass culture, and acknowledge the extent to which the New Age is omnipresent in contemporary culture, we could make the claim that the New Age is one particular and prominent lens through which culture was refracted in the 1990s. Saying this, I am treating the New Age as Hall treats it, as a representation of facets of social change, and as the Frankfurt school treats art, as a "code language" for processes taking place.

In criticizing the tenet of objectivity (at least in terms of the classical sense of its meaning) for failing to recognize the inevitably interpretive character of the study of culture, I am forced to take the position that accounts I give of the New Age are simply my accounts, my fictions, my interpretations. Geertz highlights the perspectivality of cultural analysis in his claim that all ethnographic accounts, writings, translations are what Geertz calls "fictions," fictions not because "they are false, unfactual, or merely 'as if' thought experiments" but rather that ethnographic accounts or cultural interpretations are actively fashioned, are made, which as Geertz points out was the original meaning of the word fictio (to fashion, to make) (Geertz, 1973, p. 15). This involves much more active process than simply the claim that knowledge is socially constructed, which caricatures the cultural theorist as a passive conduit for historically and culturally specific "truths," but rather entails the idea that ethnographic accounts are actively constructed, created. Thus, the process of interpretation is about unravelling, peeling layers of meaning that are particularly dense or thick, like a knot on a yarn or peeling the skin of an onion, but it is also about theorising, rewriting, producing accounts, or reweaving our interpretations of these "webs of culture" into another pattern or unravelling or transcribing of meaning in one site or field and reweaving or translating it in another.

Recognizing that all knowledge is interpretive in character does not mean that this perspective is anti-empiricist, or not concerned with the "real" world. Nor does it mean that within this perspective, all knowledge is subjective, and empirical phenomena like starvation and poverty do not exist, and is merely a representation, a discourse that exists purely at the level of signification. Rather, this perspective holds that the "existence" of this phenomenon is inseparable from how it becomes intelligible to us, from the various means by which it becomes represented to us, and the sense we make of it.

However, accepting this "interpretive turn" does inevitably lead to the question: if objectivity is no longer possible, is every interpretation as valid as the next? For instance, Charles Taylor, one of the contemporary proponents of this interpretative position claims there are "no verification procedures we can fall back on. We can only continue to offer interpretations" (Dreyfus, 1979, p. 75), a claim echoed by some more relativist social theorists who believe that to establish hard and fast verification procedures is tantamount to adopting a foundationalist position whereby one has to resort to an overarching metanarrative or transcendental claim in order clearly distinguish between a true and a false claim, a good and a bad account, and so on. Habermas (1987), for instance, attempted to solve this foundationalism–relativism dichotomy by articulating a position whereby the criterion for verification is arrived at through the collective decision-making processes of a communicative community. Various theorists who have taken this interpretive turn have tried to find ways of dealing with the impasse that results from with the inevitable "hermeneutic circle" that one ends up caught in, for, in the words of Rabinow (cited in Rainbow & Sullivan, 1987):

> Ultimately a good explanation is one that makes sense of behaviour. But to agree on what makes sense necessitates consensus, what makes sense is a function of one's readings; and these in turn are based on the kind of sense one understands. (p. 8)

Although it is beyond the scope of this volume to explore that issue in full, suffice it to say that I would side more with Taylor's claim that a superior position would be one that could encompass its opponent and make it stick (Rabinow & Sullivan, 1987). On these grounds, it is up to you to decide if the positions I take are sufficiently persuasive; if they "encompass" and "stick" in your mind after you put these pages down.

Two

The New Age Industry: Consumption, Ideology, and the New Age

Despite the fact that the New Age movement has become increasingly influential in shaping various political, religious, and popular discourses in the last decade, the literature on this phenomenon is mostly limited to four general themes: (a) theological critiques that perceive New Ageism as a threat to Christian values (Groothius, 1986, 1988), (b) positivist scientific critiques that view New Ageism as a flight from reason (Hunt & McMahon, 1988), (c) detached journalistic skepticism (Basil, 1987; Gardner, 1991) and (d) uncritical "how-to" books on New Age philosophy and practices (Ferguson, 1980). Very little of the literature on this movement examines New Ageism in terms of the social, historical, political, and cultural context in which this movement has emerged.

Of the literature that does examine the New Age movement from a social scientific perspective, the predominant tendency is to view the New Age movement as ideological. For example, Ross (1991) implies this movement is ideological in his claim that it is "an alternative, though not necessarily in opposition, to the dominant paradigms of scientific and technological rationality" (p. 19). Zizek (1994) argues that the New Age understanding of the polarities of reason–emotion, active–passive, intellect–intuition, and so on, as "cosmic opposites" that must be balanced is ideological. Coward (1989) argues that the alternative health focus on individual bodies that has the effect of individualizing and de-collectivizing versions of social transformation.

Ross' and Coward's use of terms such as *transformation, opposition, collectivity* illustrates their underlying commitment to a perspective that conceives of the New Age as an impediment to emancipatory social change, a perspective predicated on a fundamentally Marxist critique of capitalism. In Marx's understanding, ideology is an attitude that is functional to social domination (Zizek, 1994). Although Marx specified particular forms of culture such as religion and the philosophy of German idealism that are complicit in causing ideological distortion (Giddens, 1971), he said little about the specific mechanisms, or cultural forms through which ideology operates. His main concern was with the effects of ideology: the failure of the working class to recognise their common exploitation. Although theorists such as Althusser have developed his notion of ideology with regards to how it becomes materialised, or how it is embedded in various structures such as the family, the educational system, and the state (Giddens, 1979), and Gramsci has articulated ideology in terms of power, or its use by the dominant classes to maintain hegemony over subordinate classes (Hebdige, 1979), it has been theorists such as Horkheimer and Adorno who have looked specifically at ideology in terms of its relationship to popular culture, a relationship that is the focus in this chapter on the New Age movement.

In accordance with the Western Marxist tradition of engaging in "ideology critique," in this chapter I will examine the New Age movement in terms of the various ideologies that underpin it. For instance, the incorporation of the New Age into corporate business seminars and into wide-scale consumer outlets expresses a corporate ideology, the creation of a whole new range of health food and holistic health products ranging from cosmetics, books, oils, and so on, expresses the ideology of conspicuous consumption, and as Ross (1991) points out, the proliferation of regenerative brain machines, isolation tanks, and other such commodities that enable one to instantly achieve a state of relaxation is consistent with the "Yuppie work ethic" (p. 32) that enforces high-productivity leisure time. Despite a certain degree of overlap between the membership, rhetoric, and agenda of Western Marxism and the New Age movement, this movement can be seen as in some ways evoking various ideologies more compatible with the New Right than the New Left. Based on observations of dominant themes derived from Toronto bookstores and New Age Groups, but generalizable elsewhere, I show how fundamental aspects of ideology such as holistic health, Harmonic Convergence, and self-help therapy all express an ethic of individualism that is in some ways incompatible with a socialist agenda. For instance, the New Age emphasis on personal transformation, on "energy," and its holistic health picture of the self-regulating body–mind–spirit reflects and expresses, respectively, the ideology of possessive individualism, of industrial efficiency, and of the free market economy.

However, what I also wish to demonstrate in this chapter is that in the wake of recent revisions and critiques of Western Marxism, ideology has come to mean many different things to many different people. This lack of unity has caused theorists to claim that contemporary Marxist theories of ideology are currently in crisis, or in a state of disorder (Abercrombie et al., 1994). On one hand, there is a consensus amongst Marxists that ideology must have a relative autonomy from the economy (Abercrombie, Hill, & Turner, 1994) and must resist a reductionistic based superstructure model. On the other hand, however, current critiques of distinction between appearance and essence and between false consciousness and true consciousness (Zizek, 1994) underpinning Marxist versions of ideology have had the effect of reducing ideology to discourse (Zizek, 1994) and of blunting the critical edge of ideology (Abercrombie et al., 1994). What I hope to do in this chapter is to engage in an ideology critique of the New Age that takes account of these various challenges to the notion of ideology, while still retaining the notion of ideology as a means of social critique.

MARX AND IDEOLOGY

Although Marx only explicitly developed his notion of ideology in *The German Ideology*, in Althusser's (cited in Zizek, 1994) words "everything seems to lead Marx to claim a theory of ideology" (p. 120). Marx's understanding of ideology in his early works can be characterised as "the system of the ideas and representations which dominate the mind of a man or a social group" (p. 120), but later came to take on a much more complex and all-encompassing meaning in his work. The notion of ideology underpins his entire critique of capitalism, a mode of production that he claims in *The Communist Manifesto* simultaneously clarifies and obfuscates relations of power. To Marx, capitalism is an accentuation of the antagonism between oppressor and oppressed, yet it has made visible relations of exploitation that were hidden in other epochs. Whereas in premodern times relations of exploitation were legitimated in religious and political illusion, capitalism has "pitilessly torn asunder the motley feudal ties that bound man to his 'natural superiors' and has left remaining no other nexus between man and man than naked self-interest, than callous 'cash payment'" (Marx, 1985, p. 24). Although capitalism has its own unique forms of ideological illusion, such as most notably, commodity fetishism, what Marx illustrates here is that in some ways capitalism is less reliant than previous modes of production on ideologies, understood here as illusions, that obfuscate mechanisms of power underpinning existing productive relations.

Marx's claim that the mechanisms of calculation accompanying this capitalist organization of production have rationalized traditional worldviews previously based on religious and political illusion thus implies at one level that relative to other modes of production, capitalism involves a process of demystification of such illusion. In other words, capitalism has shattered the ideological foundation for traditional forms of authority. He invokes metaphors of sobering intoxication and cooling passion to describe how this process of rationalisation has drowned the "heavenly ecstasies of religious fervour, of chivalrous enthusiasm, of philistine sentimentalism" in the "the icy water of egoistic calculation" (Marx, 1985, p. 24), substituting "cold callous cash payment" for ecstasy, fervour, and sentiment. These processes of rationalization have stripped the halo off traditional authority, and unveiled premodern forms of religious and political exploitation. Although capitalism demystifies traditional forms of religious and political authority, however, it re-institutionalizes exploitation in another form. Marx illustrates how one of the central paradoxes of capitalism is that the highly specialised division of labor "has created more massive and more colossal productive power than have all previous generation put together" (Marx, 1985, p. 25). But also is predicated on the degradation, dehumanisation, and alienation of man's labour and has reduced him to "slaves of the bourgeois class, and the bourgeois state" (p. 27). Thus, capitalism is both oppressive and liberatory in that it has on one hand unleashed colossal, unprecedented productive power, yet on the other is predicated on the degradation of human labor.

Although capitalism unveils ideological illusion justifying traditional forms of religious and political authority, it reproduces such self-justificatory illusions in another form. In *The German Ideology* Marx clearly understands ideology not simply as illusion that obfuscates reality (as in the Manifesto) but as false ideas that legitimate a particular set of power relations, or material relations of inequality. In his view:

> The ideas of the ruling class are in every epoch the ruling ideas, i. e. the class which is the ruling material force of society is at the same time its ruling intellectual force. The class which has the means of material production at its disposal, has control at the same time over the means of mental production, so that generally speaking, the ideas of those who lack the means of mental production are subject to it. The ruling ideas are nothing more than the ideal expression of the dominant material relationships grasped as ideas; hence of the relationships which make the one class the ruling class, therefore the ideas of its dominance. (Marx, 1965, p. 64)

In this understanding, ideology is the representation of the particular interests of the ruling class as the general interests of the broader society. Through the operations of a self-legitimating ruling class, the capitalist organization of production comes to be seen as natural, inevitable, and legitimate. As a result, the possibility of an alternative to this essentially exploitative system remains hidden.

This passage has come to represent one of the understandings of ideology as ideology has come to be associated with the (at times intentional) propagation of ruling class ideas, as "social cement," or the "dominant ideology" thesis. This understanding sees ideology specifically as class ideology. In this view, it is in the interest of the ruling class to legitimate the existing social hierarchy, and they exert their control over the means of mental production to present the capitalist organization of production as eternal, natural, and legitimate. This process is also facilitated by the division of labor itself: Our capacity to recognize the exploitative character of the social conditions in which we live is inhibited by that very division between mental and manual labor that gives rise to these conditions. He argues that the division between mental and manual labor characteristic of capitalism allows the ruling class control over intellectual culture or mental production (including the state, the media, the education system, etc.). Thus, paradoxically, the highly specialised division of labor characteristic of the capitalist mode of production that is responsible for the exploitation, alienation, and degradation of the workers is also responsible for the ideological distortions which obscure this exploitation:

> The division of labour, which we already saw above as one of the chief forces of history up till now, manifests itself also in the ruling class as the division of mental and material labour, so that inside this class one part appears as the thinkers of the class (its active, conceptive ideologists, who make the perfecting of the illusion of the class about itself their chief source of livelihood), while the other's attitude to these ideas and illusions is more passive and receptive, because they are in reality the active members of this class and have less time to make up illusions and ideas about themselves. (Marx, 1965, p. 65)

This formulation of ideology characterizes it as "ruling class ideas," which are deliberately manufactured by the bourgeoisie to ensure class reproduction. However, Marx also implies that the bourgeoisie's role as "active conceptive ideologists" is only made possible by this division of labor that frees them from socially necessary labor.

One of his strongest examples of ideology in practice is apparent in his analysis of commodity fetishism. Under capitalism, social relations come to be regulated by the seemingly autonomous interactions of commodities that human beings produce. This fetishism of the commodity ensures that real human relations appear as relations between things. This has several ideological effects, which Eagleton (1991) elaborates as follows:

> By virtue of this "commodity fetishism," real human relations appear, mystifyingly, as relations between things; and this has several consequences of an ideological kind. First, the real workings of society are thereby veiled and occluded: the social character of labour is concealed behind the circulation of commodities, which are no longer recognisable as social products. Secondly . . . society is fragmented by this commodity logic: it is no longer easy to grasp it as a totality, given the atomising operations of the commodity, which transmutes the collective activity of social labour into relations between dead, discrete things. And by ceasing to appear as a totality, the capitalist order renders itself less vulnerable to political critique. Finally, the fact that social life is dominated by inanimate entities lends it a spurious air of naturalness and inevitability: society is no longer perceptible as a human construct, and therefore as a human alterable. (p. 105)

In this understanding, Marx's version of ideology is that which fragments our perception of social relations among ourselves, and thus distorts our perception of our place in the social totality. This includes all ideas that misrepresent, or obscure existing social relations, and hides the "real" relationships behind objects, as in the case of commodity fetishism.

To Marx, consciousness is materially and socially conditioned and is thus derived from (and exists in a dialectical relationship to) one's conditions of existence. He also claims that social circumstances at times can present themselves thus in distorted form:

> Consciousness can never be anything else than conscious existence, and the existence of men is their actual life-process. If in all ideology men and their circumstances appear upside down as in a camera *obscura*, this phenomenon arises just as much from their historical life process as the inversion of objects on the retina does from their physical life-process. (Marx, 1965, p. 37)

This implies a much more abstract version of ideology as emerging out of and sedimented in social relations, particularly if these relations are fragmented and alienated, such as those characteristic of capitalist relations of production. Because these relations divide us and de-collectivise us under capitalism, we fail to recognize our individual and collective place in the social totality. This implies a notion of ideology that emerges spontaneously from our social conditions. In this understanding, ideology is present when reality appears to us in bits and pieces, in reflections of echoes, like fragments of a looking glass, the distorted reflections inside a house of mirrors, or even upside down, like the inverted images on the retina.

Thus, ideology to Marx is a very complex and all-encompassing concept. It refers to and has been interpreted to mean illusion, ruling class ideas, the deliberate representation of the particular interests as the general, the misrepresentation of one's relationship to the social totality, ideas that hypostatize social reality and present the current organization of production (i.e., capitalism) and the social relations that comprise this system as natural and inevitable, and as ideas that present social reality in inverted form. Its effects are both intentionally (i.e., ruling class ideas) and unintentionally orchestrated (i.e., a "spontaneous" outcome of the division of labor). Whether illusory worldview, camera obscura, or ruling class ideas, this notion of ideology in Marx implies something that can be unmasked or stripped away. Ideologies were to be treated as illusory worldviews, and to criticize such ideologies meant to "unmask" any position that emphasises ideals and spirit as the driving force in history (Malesevic, 1997, p. 2). In Gidden's (1979) words, "the diagnosis of ideology became a mode of penetrating beyond the consciousness of human actors, and of uncovering the 'real foundation' of their activity, this being harnessed to the end of social transformation" (p. 166).

To engage in ideology critique presumes a clear distinction between appearance and essence, between true and false beliefs, and between pathological and healthy interests. Furthermore, it implies that the ideology critic occupies a position somehow outside of the very ideology the critic sets out to unmask. In Zizek's (1994) words "does not the critique of ideology involve a privileged place, somehow exempted from the turmoils of social life, which enables some subject-agent to perceive the very hidden mechanism that regulates social visibility and non-visibility?" (p. 3). Furthermore, he claims this assumption is itself the clearest example of ideology, asking "is not the claim that we can accede to this place the most obvious case of ideology?" (p. 3). Zizek contends that "these distinctions are based on an outdated epistemological assumption that there can be a direct correspondence between thought and reality" (p. 4).

As well as these problems, theorists of ideology are also currently under fire for ascribing to the dominant ideology thesis, or the notion that "dominant ideology creates an acceptance of capitalism in the working class", a thesis shared by Habermas, Marcuse, Miliband, and Poulantzas (Abercrombie et al., 1994, p. 1). Several theorists have challenged the assumption that a "dominant ideology" incorporating subordinate classes is either present or required in late capitalism. As Abercrombie et al. (1994) put it, the contemporary state of ideology is characterised by the "paradox that in late capitalism the ideological apparatus is greatly extended, while the economic and political subordination of people makes ideological incorporation increasingly redundant" (p. 164). As well, both Therborn's (1980) *The Ideology of*

Power and *The Power of Ideology* and *The Dominant Ideology Thesis* by Abercrombie, Hill, and Turner (1980) strongly challenge this dominant ideology thesis by arguing that "existing order/ domination is not maintained to any significant extent, by a belief among the ruled in the ruler's right to rule." Rather, they stress "the crucial importance of non-normative constraint, the different relations of different classes to the same ideology, and the lack of coherence and consistency of most ideologies" (Abercrombie et al., 1994, p. 169). Moreover, Therborn resists the totalizing image of ruling class ideology, and emphasis instead the power and complexity of various "alter-ideologies" in interpellating subjects, and thus that ideologies vary in their contents and their effects (Abercrombie et al., cited in Zizek, 1994). Such attempts to establish the complexity, indeterminacy, contingency, and polyvocality of ideology have been very helpful in illustrating the problems with the dominant ideology thesis.

Moreover, the Marxist paradigm within which the notion of ideology is inscribed has been criticized on several bases. In short, postmodern critics have posed a strong challenge to Marxism by critiquing the Enlightenment representations of social totality, of the emancipatory subject, and of a logic of history that Marxism relies on (Laclau, 1991). First, postmodernists have critiqued the Marxist notion of society as a rationally graspable totality represented by relations of production (Laclau, 1991). Secondly, psychoanalytic critiques of the subject have challenged the Marxist notion of the emancipatory subject (Young, 1990) Third, the postmodern critique of the metanarrative, or "overarching narratives of history" propagated by theorists such as Lyotard (1979) has called into question the Marxist story of the forward march of history and increasing level of self-actualization of humanity through the dialectic between consciousness and social conditions (Fraser & Nicholson, cited in Nicholson, 1990) and thus the legitimacy of the concept of ideology.

As such, the critique of the concept of ideology forms but one thread of the complex tapestry that forms the current debate between those concerned with critical theory and emancipatory political action and who want to preserve categories such as ideology, resistance, the emancipatory subject, and those who take seriously postmodern critiques of these categories and want to challenge them. This debate has become polarized into a struggle between what has become known as critical theorist versus the postmodernist positions, or, in the philosophy of the social sciences, as foundationalism–relativism, or absolutism–perspectivalism, with the former wishing to retain, and the latter, to reject, a transcendental notion of "truth" as a way of distinguishing between valid and nonvalid, oppressive and nonoppressive knowledges (Hekman, 1986). Thus, these two positions are also split on whether ideology is still a meaningful concept.

At first glance, the other option would appear to be the postmodern recognition of the impossibility of the extra-ideological position, or the response that we have reached the "end of ideology" as a useful concept. This postmodern position argues that because there is never a correspondence between reality and representation, attaining the extra-ideological position is impossible. One conclusion of this critique of representation, then, is that uncovering ways in which this relationship is specifically, dramatically or intentionally distorted is a meaningless exercise, because all knowledge is distorted anyway. In short, this critique of ideology critique is in danger of invoking the relativist position that because everything is ideological, ideology is no longer a meaningful concept. For example, Zizek (1994) cautions us against the "quick, postmodern solution" of merely reducing ideology to discourse. To him, this position entails concluding "that the only non-ideological position is to renounce the very notion of extra-ideological reality and accept that all we are dealing with are symbolic fictions, the plurality of discursive universes, never 'reality'" (p. 17). In its relativism, this position is complicit with those very power interests ideology critique intends to make transparent. Thus, this position "slides into ideology under the guise of stepping out of it" (p. 17), and ends up acting in accordance with various power interests while pretending to be outside them.

However, embracing the postmodern turn in social theory does not necessarily mean that critiques such as those of the Frankfurt school are outdated or pointless, or that ideology critique as a form of cultural criticism should be abandoned, for such a position is itself ideological. We must recognize the impossibility of an extra-ideological position. However, while acknowledging our own immersion in ideology, we must also keep alive the tension, the critical vantage point that animates ideology critique. However, this vantage point must not be fixed, or inscribed within a specific metanarrative. In Zizek's (1994) words, "although ideology is already at work in everything we experience as 'reality'. . . it is possible to assume a place that enables us to maintain a distance from it but this place from which one can denounce ideology must remain empty, it cannot be occupied by any positively determined reality-the moment we yield to temptation, we are back in ideology" (p. 17). Furthermore, all we can hope to do is stake out a vantage point that exists at a distance from the phenomenon we are describing as ideological, but this distance is itself an ideal. In line with what is variously called the "discursive," "linguistic," or "interpretive," or "hermeneutic" shift in social theory, that acknowledges that there is no objective reality distinct from the languages, discourses, interpretations, and symbols in which this "reality" is inevitably embedded, we should conceive of ideology critique more generally as the attempt to identify particular discursive formations that may have particular power effects, rather than as distinguishing between true and false knowledges.

Despite the efficacy of the postmodern critique in illustrating the totalizing assumptions inherent in Marxist categories, the notion of ideology critique is still a crucial one when critically examining popular culture. In particular, Horkheimer and Adorno's critique of the culture industry remains a useful template for ideology critique as long as it is recognized that the effects of such ideology is not totalizing, that ideological phenomena are overdetermined with a plurality of meanings, and that alter-ideologies persist alongside ruling class ideologies and interpellate subjects in a variety of ways. Horkheimer and Adorno themselves believed in the relative autonomy of the economic base from the superstructure, and in the power of culture to incite "nonidentity thinking" as well as "harmonizing illusions". However, the ideology critique of the New Age elaborated here emphasises the placatory function of popular culture, for even though the postmodern critique of ideology critique must be noted, an understanding of culture cannot be reduced simply to discourse and deprived of its critical edge.

POPULAR CULTURE AND IDEOLOGY CRITIQUE

Although many theorists in the 20th century took a Marxist approach to popular culture, Horkheimer and Adorno's analysis of the culture industry represents the first major attempt and in many ways the most influential attempt to analyse popular culture through the lens of a Marxist ideology critique. In their analysis, they examine how aspects of popular culture serve a placatory function by distorting one's perception of their relationship to the social totality. Their analysis takes on board various aspects of Marx that are associated with ideology including the relationship between ideology and commodity fetishism, the role of ideology in legitimating the capitalist system, the idea of ideology as reconciling social contradictions, and the ideological character of religion and idealism. In general, their analysis of culture documents how culture is designed to promote light distraction, wish fulfillment, and the intensification of passivity (Jay, 1973). The central theme in their analysis of culture is that mass culture decollectivizes and atomizes individuals, which serves to hypostatize and legitimate existing social relations and to quell any potential revolutionary spirit.

The clearest example of the Frankfurt school's understanding of the ideological character of culture in terms of its commodification is perhaps contained in the essay "The Culture Industry: Enlightenment as Mass Deception" in *Dialectic of Enlightenment* (Horkheimer & Adorno, 1972). Although this text was first published in 1947, it has been tremendously influential in academic circles and is still regarded as a benchmark text on themes of Enlightenment reason, instrumental rationality, and the culture industry. In the essay on the culture industry the authors argue that interdependence between cultural production and industrial interests results in the production of a homogenized, monopolistic, "affirmative" culture because this kind of culture can be easily produced and mass-consumed. This level of analysis is concerned with the extent to which the production of culture has become an industry, a money-making enterprise instead of an artistic process. They emphasize infrastructural interdependencies, showing how the culture industry's dependence on industrial sectors, the broadcasting industry on the electrical industry, the movie industry on the banks, ensures that innovation, spontaneity, or individual style has been purged through selective recruitment only of those willing to succumb to these standardizing and homogenizing processes. In this fashion, recruitment and membership into cultural production demands conformity to its agenda of prioritizing mass consumability over quality.

Ironically, this type of critique of the culture industry has itself become an industry, as much a money-making enterprise as an intellectual process wherein cultural theorists can themselves benefit from rapid production of critiques of the culture industry that become standardized, formulaic, and mass-produced, resulting in what one could call the "commodification of the critique of the culture industry." In the spirit of the postmodern trend toward self-reflexivity, this commodification of critique has also itself been critiqued and parodied by writers such as David Lodge in his book *Small World* wherein he humorously portrays cultural critics as petty, competitive, egotistical (predominantly) men for whom the content of their work is inextricably bound up with concern over their popularity, the size of their publication records and research grants. Lodge intentionally and self-mockingly obfuscates the difference between the system of production that the cultural critic is critiquing, and the system in which his or her own work is produced and consumed, thus challenging the idea that the cultural critic lies outside of this commodification process. To add a further twist to this analysis, Lodge's work, which in a sense represents "the critique of the commodification of the critique of the culture industry" that itself has been commodified and was shortlisted for the Booker Prize in 1984 and was adapted as a major television serial by Granada TV, illustrates the impossibility of remaining "outside" this position.

To return to Horkheimer and Adorno's original analysis, their work of the commodification of culture emphasizes that the production of culture had become an industry whereby aesthetic taste or experimental variation has become eradicated in favour of a standardized, homogenized form designed to appeal to all, arguing, for instance, that movies, television, novels, and magazines all adhere to a standard formula in order that the works they produce can be easily mass consumed. In their words, "Not only are hit songs, stars, and soap operas cyclically recurrent and rigidly invariable types, but the specific content of the entertainment itself is derived from them and only appears to change" (Horkheimer & Adorno, 1972, p. 125). For this reason, Horkheimer and Adorno claim that the term *popular culture* is a misnomer, and is neither popular nor democratic, because the necessity for its stylistic unity, and homogeneity are based on the needs of the producers, not the consumers themselves. Thus, this dimension of their analysis is an essentially Marxist critique of the processes of commodification whereby profit motive outweighs the consideration of artistic merit, a critique that resonates in many analyses of popular music, television, film, and videos even today.

Another dimension of their critique of mass culture is focused around the theme of how mass culture serves the function of legitimation. Specifically, it illustrates how the culture industry produces forms of culture that are compatible with the demands of alienated labor in that they afford light amusement, distraction, and that legitimate the existing social hierarchy. This theme that is particularly apparent in their essay on the culture industry, but is also apparent in Adorno's critique of music. For instance, in their essay on the culture industry, they claim that mass culture is designed to provide light distraction and amusement, as an escape from the drudgeries of everyday life, but this escape must be an afterimage of the work process itself, because anything beyond the worker's everyday reality would remind them of their alienation. In their words, "one can only escape their work if their time off is an approximation to it" (Horkheimer & Adorno, 1972, p. 122). Similarly, Adorno claims that popular music took on a homogenized, formulaic form that induced "atomised listening" (Jay, 1973, p. 192). Despite the "spiteful resentment of passivity" that the liveliness and innovation integral to modern jazz expresses, Adorno believed that it merely induced a "pseudo activity" rather than a true "negation" of existing reality (Jay, 1973, p. 192).

Furthermore, Horkheimer and Adorno critiqued the placatory function television, radio, and print media perform in advocating light amusement and distraction. Amusement to Horkheimer and Adorno (1972) represents merely the sublimation of pleasure, for "jovial denial take the place of the pain found in ecstasy and asceticism" (p. 133). This analysis emphasizes the extent to which movies, television, and radio programs follow predetermined formulas that audiences can easily follow, and use conventions such as applause signs and canned laughter that even tell us how and when to react. They claim that this industry is oriented to produce a state of passivity and compliance, an effect that is prescribed, predetermined, calculated by the industry to placate the consumer, and to compensate for an exploitative division of labor and what they perceive as a spiritual and intellectual vacuousness and a hypermaterialist ethos. This renders the individual a passive consumer rather than an active interpreter of culture; it provides distraction, amusement, rather than social critique, and hence supports or legitimates the current organization of production and all its attendant hierarchies through quelling any spirit of revolt.

The third usage of ideology, which is related to the second, is the way in which the culture industry fosters a premature reconciliation of social contradictions that eliminates the possibility of praxis, agency, or critical reflection in consumers. To them, the culture industry inhibited the possibility of dialectical or critical reason—reason that was capable of reflecting on the gap between the "is" and the "ought," the real and the utopian, or the way things are and the way they should be. At this level of analysis, they see the culture industry as ideological in that it artificially imposes harmony or the reduction of tension between the particular and the universal, or the premature reconciliation of the part with the whole (Jay, 1973). This analysis is in many ways more compelling and less overtly materialist than their critique of the functions of commodification and legitimation that culture performs, analyses that tend to be too inscribed within a base–superstructure model whereby culture emerges purely from economic interests. As several cultural studies critics have noted, the application of Marxist categories of ideology has often had the effect of producing overly reductionistic, economistic analysis of culture. For instance, some writers in the field of cultural studies have rigorously contested elements of Marxism that have "imprisoned" Marx: "its orthodoxy, its doctrinal character, its determinism, its reductionism, its immutable law of history, its status as a metanarrative" (Hall, cited in Grossberg et al., 1992, p. 279), challenging more simplistic versions of the relationship between the base and superstructure.

This broader usage of the term is what enables Horkheimer and Adorno's relatively coherent juxtaposition of Marx's ideas with a Weberian critique of instrumental rationality, as well as more psychoanalytic analyses of culture. Their usage of ideology in this third fashion enables them to reconcile their Marxist concern with the commodification of culture with a more Weberian critique of the processes by which this industry renders individual consumers objects of rational administration and calculation. For instance, the Weberian influence can be seen in their emphasis on how viewers become the passive objects of calculation, categorization, and administration, in audience research studies that calculate consumer response to minute detail in order to manufacture future cultural production and ensure its salability. Media programming is rationally organized and planned to correspond to the public's taste. In short, rationalization ensures commodification. However, they also emphasize how both these processes distort the individual's view of the social totality, both in terms of how they are objects of the dual processes of rationalization and commodification, yet this is not recognized, because this homogenous, reified form of culture that is produced her or his capacity for critical reflection, and encourages what Marcuse (1964) calls "one dimensional thought" (p. 1).

This definition of ideology as that which entails the reconciliation of social contradictions allows them to engage in an ideological critique of the role of popular culture in a way that is compatible with their more general project of critiquing the dual character of the enlightenment reason, a critique that is performed in a predominantly Weberian tradition. In *The Dialectic of Enlightenment*, they conclude that the worst excesses of recent history, namely the domination of nature through science, and of humans through fascism, have shown us that there is nothing inherently liberatory about Enlightenment reason. Taking from Kant the notion that reason both comprises the "idea of a free, human social life in which men organise themselves as the universal subject" but also "constitutes the court of judgement, of calculation, which adjusts the world for the ends of self-preservation and recognises no function other than the preparation of the object from mere sensory material in order to make it the material of subjugation" (Horkheimer & Adorno, 1972, p. 83) they conclude that in fact modernity illustrates the ascendancy of the negative side of the dialectic of the Enlightenment, or reason as domination.

The Frankfurt School illustrates how the ethic of domination or mastery over nature inherent in positivist science is one instance of the ascendancy of reason as domination, for, in defining matter as a possible object of manipulation, leads to the conclusion that "people embodying the natural are also potentially controllable" (Marcuse, 1964, p. 155). Their concept of reason as domination is derived from Weber's understanding of domination as the inexorable logic of purposive or instrumental reason, a reason that "does not lead to the concrete realisation of universal freedom but to the creation of an 'iron cage' of instrumentally rationalised acquisitiveness or "bureaucratic rationality from which there is no escape" (Bernstein, 1985, p. 5).

Marx and Weber have different understandings of ideology both of which influence the Frankfurt school: To Marx, what needs to be "unmasked" are relations of underlying relations of production, whereas to Weber, it is the mechanisms that render us objects of rationalization, bureaucratization, and administration. The Frankfurt school's incorporation of both, rather than a strictly Marxist understanding of modernity allow these two concerns to both be addressed in their more general work on culture. Thus, their most important analysis of the ideological character of culture is that which is concerned with the tendency to misrepresent the social totality, or in Jay's (1973) words, that which falsely harmonises the particular with the universal (p. 216).

For instance, Adorno's work on music, astrology and the occult all illustrate how these cultural forms produce the social effects of distraction, wish fulfillment, and the intensification of passivity, all of which serve to divide and de-collectivize the individual. For example, Adorno critiques the "tendency towards atomised listening" which he sees as "perhaps the most universal feature of the present-day's musical consciousness" (Jay, 1973, p. 192).

Thus, the most important aspect of Horkheimer and Adorno's view of culture was the utopian or critical role they saw art as playing in keeping open the contradictions of daily life, or the Other dimension. To them, art works that shock and provoke, which reproduce the abyss between the individual and the environment (Held, 1980) are the only forms of art that constitute resistance. Only works of art which preserve this abyss, this space, this gap between the is and the ought constitute the Great Refusal. Moreover, the role of works of art in social transformation or resistance is not purely to represent resistance or revolution, but rather to invoke it in another medium. To Horkheimer (cited in Held, 1980):

> The works in which the subject cut off from his own development still manages to find expression are those in which the abyss between him and the barbaric environment appears most insistently: poems such as those of Trakl, the Guernica of Picasso, a composition of Schoenberg. The sorrow and the horror which adhere to such works do not correspond to the experience of a subject who turns away from reality, for understandable reasons, or revolts against it; the consciousness to which these belong is cut off from society, thrust back on distorted, outré figures . . . The latest works of art . . . relinquish illusion of an existing community, they are memorials of a lonely and desperate life . . . Insofar as they still represent communication they denounce the dominant forms of intercourse as tools of destruction. (p. 104)

Thus, the preservation of this abyss, this gap, this space, between the "is" and the "ought" or the real and the utopian is crucial.

THE FRANKFURT SCHOOL AND THE NEW AGE

Adorno is one of the few well-known social theorists who wrote about the New Age movement, and wrote two very influential essays on how astrology and the occult perform the function of reconciling social contradictions based on a Marxist concept of ideology. However, Adorno's analysis also contains strong elements of a psychoanalytic critique of the emergence of "authoritarian personalities" as well as a Weberian critique of the totalitarian possibilities inherent in Enlightenment rationality. In his analysis of astrology, he illustrates how astrology is a symptom of an administered society, a desire on behalf of the collectivity to be told what to do, to be subjugated by an overarching paradigm, and as such, compares astrology to Fascism: "Just as those who can read the phony signs of the stars believe that they are in the know, the followers of totalitarian parties believe that their special panaceas are universally valid and feel justified in imposing them as a general rule" (Adorno, 1994, p. 121). In this fashion, an essentially Marxist view of popular culture in terms of how it dupes the consumer by artificially reconciling the contradictions of daily life is inscribed within a more general concern with what he sees as the eclipse of the emancipatory possibilities of Enlightenment reason, encapsulated in what he calls "identity thinking," and what Marcuse calls "one dimensional thought."

One aspect of his analysis of astrology is his claim that the separation of production from consumption integral to the economy of astrology allows for ideological distortion. First, Adorno argues that astrology is based on a radical separation of the sites of distribution and consumption whereby the "primary group," the astrologers who interpret astronomical data regarding the location of the stars and planets, and translate them into astrological advice are radically separated from the "secondary group," the consumer, from the sites of distribution and consumption, the reading of the column at the breakfast table, the coffee shop or commuter train. This separation leaves unchallenged the particular kind of "expert" advice that is given. As Adorno (1994) phrases it, astrological column readers "don't even see the sorcerers at work any more nor are they allowed to listen to their abracadabra" (p. 37). Furthermore, this type of mystification of the mechanisms of authority is by no means an isolated case but rather is characteristic of the more general "irrationality" of contemporary life, and is a clear example of how culture reproduces individuals who obey authority.

Furthermore, the separation of the site of production of astrological advice from its consumption covers over the illogic behind the process by which the science of astronomy becomes translated into the "pseudo-science" of astrology. In his terms, astrology derives its claims to authority by "piggybacking" off the legitimacy claims of its scientific corollary, astronomy, yet the process by which these claims are appropriated is hidden (Adorno, 1994). The specific mechanics and justificatory foundations of astrology are never themselves discussed, but rather, the astrological advice seemingly emerges in consumable, pop-psychological form out of the science of astronomy. Thus, it is not entirely rational nor entirely irrational, but rather is a paradoxical "pseudo-rationality" that ascribes anachronistically to two contradictory worldviews: the astrophysician's knowledge of the complexity of the mechanical laws governing the movements of stellar systems that inevitably entails the recognition of the cosmic insignificance of the earth, and the geocentric and anthropocentric view concomitant with astrology. Furthermore, the separation of production and consumption that characterizes (cultural) production enables astrology to suppress its own irrationality and the contradictory nature of its own claims to legitimacy. This tendency is evidence of a broader tendency of mass culture to repress paradox and contradiction.

Adorno's main criticism of the ideological aspects of astrology focuses on the extent to which it exploits "ego weaknesses," narcissistic defenses, and other vulnerabilities of its readers in order to reproduce their dependence on its advice. For instance, he focuses on the internal contradictions of astrological advice, which simultaneously advise readers to conform but "be yourself"; to take charge of your life, but to be ruled by the advice of the stars; to enjoy leisure, but only insofar as it fits into the rigid pattern of work. To Adorno, these contradictions are exemplary of its more general tendency toward the suppression of the contradictory nature of its own claims to legitimacy.

As well, Adorno tries to point out that the contradictory character of astrological advice also results from the necessity for the columnist to reconcile contradictory demands. This advice is sufficiently general to apply to a mass audience, but not so vague as to be transparently mass produced. One way in which this is achieved is that the columnist adopts a strategy of what Adorno calls "pseudo-individualization" whereby he or she must provide advice that has the appearance of being individually tailored enough to satisfy the reader, yet is "non-committal enough so that he cannot be easily discredited" (Adorno, 1994, p. 51). This balance is achieved although the projection of general attributes onto the reader such as a "keen mind," "intuition," and so on, attributes that are general enough to not invalidate the columnist's advice, yet which flatter the reader.

Another example of how the columnist negotiates contradictory requirements in the astrological column is the strategy of pitching the column at a level that both allows the readers to imagine themselves as active and powerful social agents, but also takes account of the real lives of the readers, who are in Adorno's words, basically "frustrated." This is achieved by tendering advice oriented at one level toward a young professional, occupationally and romantically successful, typically male reader, apparent in the columns advocacy of what Adorno calls "pseudo-activity" whereby "continuous advice is given to take some action, to behave as a successful go-getter," in terms appropriate to such a subject. On the other hand, however, the columnist must also take account of the fact that the reader is most likely to be lower middle class, and thus must adopt a compromise position whereby advice is targeted toward a reader whose level of class and occupational success is at a level midway between the actual reader, and the idealized person this reader would like to be. Thus, the columnist must tender advice that acknowledges a reality that is near enough to the real life of the addressee, the lower middle class reader, yet still allows a feeling of vicarious pleasure in the fate of the reader's idealized image of him or herself: This advice must continuously address the column to a fantasy reader in which "the addressee's ego ideal and his realistic experience of his actual place in life are somehow fused" (Adorno, 1994, p. 62).

As well as the Marxist and Weberian elements of the Frankfurt school critique of popular culture and of the New Age movement, Adorno takes the Freudian concept of reaction formation to explain how astrology achieves its purpose of pseudo-agency. In order to do a content analysis of the *Los Angeles Times* astrology column, Adorno adopts what he calls a biphasic approach, an approach based on Freud's concept of the biphasic reaction-formation apparent for example in the behavior of the Ratman who "felt compelled to remove a stone from the road because it might hurt somebody, and them felt compelled to put it back again" (Freud, cited in Adorno, 1994, p. 71). For instance, Freud used this reaction to describe a compulsive symptom in neurotic patients whereby a positive action, such as the turning on of a gas jet, is immediately followed by negative action, a direct reversal of the first, such as the turning off of the jet, this is a biphasic reaction. Adorno abstracts this concept of its specific psychological context, conceiving of it as any generalized situation in which a positive action is cancelled out by a negative action, the result of which gives the illusion of action or progress but really results in impotence.

In adopting his notion of the biphasic reaction to astrology, Adorno claims that the columnist advocates his biphasic behavior in order to give readers the illusion that they are active, self-determining, self-responsible social agents, but that doesn't actually necessitate that they challenge their basically subordinate positions on the social hierarchy. For example, he illustrates how a particular columnist advises readers to seek pleasure, but only insofar as it is "integrated into a rigid pattern of life" compatible with the demands of alienated labor; he advises them to express their individuality, but only insofar as this expression complies with the requirement that this expression does not conflict with their adjustment to the hierarchical and competitive organisation of the social order. This biphasic approach is most evident in the suggested manner of treating superiors, "higher-ups," referred euphemistically as "friends," who are characterized simultaneously as the source of considerable conflict, anxiety, and criticism, and as people who must be humored, placated, "played up to," and toward whom readers should adopt a "clever meekness," an attitude "reminiscent of that of the woman who wants to get the better of the man on whom she depends" (Adorno, 1994, p. 112).

In this manner, Adorno claims that astrology inhibits autonomous thought and action and reproduces the reader's dependence on authority:

> The column aims at promoting conventional, conformist, and contented attitudes and that any insights into negative aspects of reality are kept under control by making everything dependent on the individual rather than on objective conditions. The individual is promised the solution to everything if he complies with certain requirements and avoids certain negative stereotypes. He is prevented from really acknowledging the very same difficulties which drive him into the arms of astrology. (Adorno, 1994, p. 65)

Thus, Adorno's overall view of astrology in particular, and by extension much of the related phenomena that constitutes the New Age in general is that it is a symptom of the alienation, the lack of subjectivity, the absurdity of contemporary life. "The real absurdity is reproduced in the astrological hocus-pocus, which adduces the impenetrable connections of alienated elements-nothing more alien than the stars-as knowledge about the subjects" (Adorno, 1994, p. 130).

This conclusion that astrology reproduces dependent personalities is reiterated in stronger form in Adorno's analysis of the regressive character of occultism, in an argument that resembles a psychoanalytic version of Marx's critique of religion as "the opiate of the people." To him, the occult is the "metaphysic of dunces" (p. 130) wherein the "mediocrity of the mediums is no more accidental than the apocryphal triviality of the revelations" (Adorno, 1994, p. 130). Furthermore, in this essay, Adorno illustrates how both the occult and astrology are a "reflex action to the subjectification of all meaning," and as such are complicit with the potentially dominating effects of reason. In other words, these forms of what he calls "irrationality" foreshadow the larger crisis of authority that is entailed in the tendency for so-called rational forms of authority to take on an instrumental form. In his words, "The horoscope corresponds to the official directives of nations, and number-mysticism is preparation for administrative statistics and cartel prices" (Adorno, 1994, p. 129).

To Adorno, this advocacy of pseudo-agency, and the strategy of pseudo-individualization are profoundly ideological, in that they address the reader's desire for agency and individuality, but sublimate these desires harmlessly by only granting them at the level of fantasy. Astrology thus reconciles the contradictions of daily life through vicarious pleasure and wish fulfillment, rather than allowing individuals to confront their lack of autonomy and change their lives. As such, Adorno's claim that the occult and astrology are forms of "unreason" are themselves complicit in the dominating effects of reason must be placed in the context of his neo-Weberian concern that the emancipatory possibilities of reason have been eclipsed through the ascendancy of instrumental reason as domination. It must also be looked at in the context of his neo-Freudian interrogation of how sublimation, wish fulfillment, and fantasy allow for the reproduction of "authoritarian personalities." In this fashion, Adorno's version of ideology critique contains Marxist, Freudian, and Weberian elements, and attempt to reconcile analyses of ideology, rationality, and psychoanalysis.

THE NEW AGE AS IDEOLOGY

Adorno and Horkheimer were writing in a very different social context than that of critics of popular culture today. The most active years of the Institute for Social Research in Germany, the home of the Frankfurt School, coincided with the prominence of Fascism and the rise of Nazism (Held, 1980). Not surprisingly, the central agenda underpinning the Frankfurt School's work, whether critiques of both Enlightenment Reason or of popular culture, was to explain the rise of Fascism and the historical, social, and psychological elements responsible for the creation of the "authoritarian personality." However, despite the particular social context in which their critique of popular culture emerged, and the particular motivation underpinning their analysis, their essay on popular culture still exerts a profound influence on critiques of popular culture today.

In accordance with the understanding of the concept of ideology in Marx, and its application to popular culture in the Frankfurt School, the following section engages in an ideology critique of the New Age. Specifically, I illustrate that the New Age movement expresses various ideologies that run counter to its own avowed intent. The main elements derived from Marx that I use in my analysis are Marx's critique of the abstract, other worldly, anti-materialist aspects of religion, and of the tradition of German idealism, as well as his more general understanding of commodity fetishism. From Horkheimer and Adorno, I derive their critique of the culture industry in terms of how it illustrates the merging of industrial interests and processes of artistic or cultural production. I also heavily rely on Adorno's critique of the irrationality of astrological or occult cosmologies, and how the popularity of astrological or mediumistic advice is yet another example of the willingness of the masses to be dominated and reproduced as authoritarian personalities. As well as their work on the culture industry, Adorno's work on the complicity of astrology and occultism in reproducing authoritarian personalities is also relevant to my investigation of the relationship between ideology and popular culture.

I illustrate how the New Age reflects particular ideologies that its proclaimed affiliation to "the left" does not acknowledge. First, I examine specific aspects of New Age thinking such as the Harmonic Convergence version of abstract spirituality, the holistic health emphasis on unity, and the integration of self-help seminars into business and executive training courses. I look at these in the context of Horkheimer and Adorno's claim that aspects of mass culture and popular music impede the development of a dialectical consciousness by misrepresenting the particular as the general, the "is" as the "ought to be" by decollectivizing individuals and hypostatizing social reality through strategies such as pseudo-individualism, pseudo-agency, the promotion of escapism, the advocacy of abstract spirituality, and the manipulation of consumer desires through wish fulfillment.

THE IDEOLOGY OF HARMONIC CONVERGENCE

My own personal interviews with subjects attending at Toronto's 1994 and 1995 psychic fairs consolidated my belief that certain aspects of this movement's orientation toward reading the future encourages the intensification of passivity that Adorno describes. Many aspects of the psychic fair such as telephone vibration readings, aura readings, palmistry, and tarot readings were oriented toward reading the future, and also drew what appeared to be a predominantly lower middle-class audience. Some of these "readings" promised "pleasant surprises," and "good times ahead," types of wish fulfillment that advocate an intensification of passivity whereby nonaction is seen as a virtue, implicit in the saying "all good things to those who wait." These types of readings also inspire in the customers a vicarious pleasure toward their fortunate, future self. Other types of readings advocated a "lottery mentality" whereby it appeared to be luck rather than class privilege or individual agency that determines whether or not one's life "works out," yet claimed that because of the reading, at least one was prepared for good or bad luck, and could organize one's life accordingly. Most of these readings targeted their prophesies midway between that of the actual class and occupational level of the subject, and that of who they would like to be. Whether advocating passivity or luck as their dominant cosmology, they were self-reproducing in that they encouraged a dependence on their form of advice, and hence secured their market. According to a research subject, a third-generation Indian woman, in her mid-30s, "I'm addicted to it—it is wonderful to find out what is going to happen this week."

This intensification of passivity is also strongly apparent in the theme of Harmonic Convergence, which some feel is the quintessential New Age doctrine. For instance, in the New Age section of Yorkville and Annex bookstores in Toronto, Marilyn Ferguson's book *The Aquarian Conspiracy* held pride of place. This doctrine is based on the premise that we are entering into a new age, a new era, and are poised on the brink of a global transformation, a theme apparent in the popular 1960s song we are entering into "the Age of Aquarius," and that is elaborated in Ferguson's 1980s book *The Aquarian Conspiracy*. This theme recurs throughout New Age thinking today. For example, the magazine *Magical Blend*, a popular journal among the Toronto New Age community who share an interest in Shamanism, claims in its statement of purpose:

> The transformative journey . . . *Magical Blend* accepts the premise that society is undergoing a fundamental transformation. A new world is being born, and whether this birth is an easy or difficult one will depend largely on the individual. It is our aim to chart the course this transformation is taking, and to assist the individual to cope with and contribute to the birthing process. We believe that people's thoughts influence their reality; if this is true then the world we live in is a combination of our highest hopes, our deepest fears, and the whole range of experience that falls in between. Our goal is to embrace the magical behind the mundane. In this way we hope to act as a catalyst to encourage his or her spiritual awareness. We endorse no one pathway to spiritual growth, but attempt to explore many alternative possibilities to help transform the planet. (*Magical Blend*, p. 1)

Both Adorno's commentary on his use of content analysis and his description of the biphasic strategy used by astrological columnists are useful in analyzing how this phenomenon of Harmonic Convergence expressed in *Magical Blend's* statement of purpose simultaneously posits its members as both active and passive. On one hand, this "manifesto" invokes some of the central rhetoric of Marxism, implying the inevitability of transformation, of the birth of a new world, positing the new Age community, or its readers as catalysts, or vanguards, who will aid in this tranformatory process. However, this desire for transformation in Magical Blend's call for change is channeled harmlessly into individualistic expressions that place the responsibility for transformation ambiguously both onto the individual, then vaguely into "time" itself.

In Adorno's (1994) opinion, this faith that individuals have that "time" itself will make everything right is exemplary of a weak ego, a stymied personality, an infantile attitude by necessity adopted by children, an example of ideological illusion par excellence, which "absolves them of their failures and promotes their hope as though they could expect relief from all their ills from the very simple fact that things move on and more particularly that most sufferings are likely to be forgotten" (p. 70). Erich Fromm (cited in Adorno, 1994) captures the self-deluding character of this relationship to time in his essay "The Feeling of Impotence" when he claims:

> Faith in time lacks the sense of sudden change. It substitutes expectations that "in due time" everything will come out all right. Conflicts, which one feels unable to resolve oneself, are expected to be resolved by time without one's having to take the risk of deciding. Faith in time is found especially frequently with respect to one's own

> achievements. People not only console themselves over their unperformed performances, but also over not preparing for the performance by persuading themselves that they have so much time left and that there is no reason to hurry. An example of this mechanism is the case of a greatly gifted author who wanted to write a book which, in his opinion, would rank among the most important of world literature All he did was to pursue a series of thoughts about it, to indulge in fantasies about the epoch-making effect his book would produce and to tell his friends that it was almost finished. Actually, although he had "worked" on the book for seven years, he had not yet written a single line. As these people get older, they must cling even more stubbornly to the illusion that time will take care of things. Many, when they reach a certain age, usually the early forties, either sober up and abandon the illusion and make efforts to utilise their own power or have a neurotic breakdown because life without the consoling illusion of time as a benefactor becomes intolerable. (pp. 69-70)

Arguably, this ideological illusion characterizes the cynical protagonists of Coupland's (1994) book *Generation X* who believe that by accident of birth as Post-Baby boomers they have missed the historical boat, the post-World War II promise of affluence, yet are still subject to such overinflated parental aspirations. In a variation of Fromme's description of the belief that "time will take care of things," Coupland's Gen-X-ers not only perceive themselves as "victims of time," but also justify their self-marginalized, "slacker" identity on the basis of this ideological self-understanding.

The New Age doctrine of Harmonic Convergence invokes what Adorno calls the "pseudo-agency" by the strategy of positioning its members in a space that vacillates between agents and passive witnesses; as vanguard and bystander, a strategy that divests its manifesto of any potential revolutionary import. It characterizes its readers as occupying the ambiguous status as both catalysts and midwives, as both initiators, and mere facilitators of the "birth" of the New World. For example, the writers of *Magical Blend* aim to "act as a catalyst" in the birth of this new world, but also to "chart the course this transformation is taking," and to "assist the individual to cope with and contribute to the birthing process," and don't really position either themselves or their readers as active agents in this birthing process. Rather, their role in this "birth," is less that of midwife, and more of that of the journalist or of the spectator.

The agency of the imperative to be a catalyst in this transformation is undermined by the subsequent retreat to the position of spectator or journalist who either charts or assists, but does not really take part. Implicit in this formulation is the idea that agency is not necessary, the notion that time itself is the most active agent, since the New Age will come anyway, if nature takes its course. This positioning of the New Age member as both active and passive, as agent and then spectator, bears resemblances to Adorno's characterization of the biphasic strategy of the astrological columnists: The positive action, encapsulated in the rhetoric of transformation, is undermined by the negative action, the de-emphasization of agency in favor of the transformational effects of time. As such, we need only be historians, passive witnesses to history, rather than agents ourselves.

Similarly, this movement simultaneously politicizes and depoliticizes the realm of the individual, the private, the personal by obfuscating the specific relationship between the individual and the collective. This results in a contradictory logic, a biphasic loop that advocates both moral imperatives regulating individual conduct, and the freedom to repudiate these rules; moral imperatives for commitment to an alternative community, and the freedom to be completely immune from any collective surveillance. For example various New Age magazines, ranging from *Common Ground*, *Vitality*, *Magical Blend*, and the *New Age* vacillate between an advocacy of individual moral responsibility, and a complete moral relativism, by advocating, on one hand, self-development and personal responsibility as one's moral obligation to the collective, and on the other, relativist, liberal pluralist advocacy of an "anything goes" posture toward ones moral responsibility, the attitudinal corollary of laissez-faire of the market, which does not preclude embracing an ethic of anarchic hedonism. Similarly, glimmers of a collectivist ethos are apparent in the advocacy of alternative community with a political agenda based around feminist, environmental and anti-racist concerns, yet strategies of responsibility are vague, esoteric, and apolitical—"find your inner self," "seek spiritual transcendence," "buy crystals." Ultimately, these contradictory imperatives and the failure to articulate the connection between the personal and the political undermine any transformational agenda the editors may pretend to have.

Furthermore, the *Magical Blend* manifesto for change lends itself to a critique that its version of transformation is formulated in vague, abstract, idealistic, ahistorical terms that emphasize the spiritual at the expense of the material, a critique reminiscent of Marx's critique of Hegel. In this critique, Marx problematizes the man–God, real–divine relationship as it appears in both Hegelian idealism and religion. The problem with religion, according to Marx, is that, as Feurbach has shown, "in religion, men participate vicariously in an unreal, fantasy world of harmony, beauty, and contentment, while living in a practical everyday world of pain and misery" (Marx, cited in Giddens, 1971, p. 5). He raises a similar objection to the Hegelian idealists, whom he calls ideologists, whose dialectic he inverts in order to develop what we have come to know as his materialist method. "In direct contrast to German philosophy which descends from heaven to earth, we will ascend from earth to heaven" (Marx, 1965, p. 37).

In Hegel's formulation mankind is a product of an alienated God, of the real as emanating from the divine, a dynamic that recurs in Christianity. In contrast, Marx inverted Hegel's man–God, real–divine relationship in a materialist reworking of this dialectic that argues, following Feurbach, that "thought proceeds from being, not being from thought" (Giddens, 1971, p. 3). He thus argues that both Hegelian idealism and religion misrecognize the relationship between the material and the ideal. This critique that forms the basis of his claim that Hegelian Absolute Spirit, and his formulation of man's self creation through labor, remains arrested at the level of the ideational, and hence is abstract and idealistic. This critique of the material–ideational relationship also forms the basis of his critique Christianity is an "opiate of the people" (Giddens, 1971).

Clearly, a similar charge can be levied against the notion of Harmonic Convergence. This manifesto claims "We believe that people's thoughts influence their reality; if this is true then the world we live in is a combination of our highest hopes, our deepest fears, and the whole range of experience that falls in between." Thus, this formulation of the dialectic between the ideational and the material resembles the Hegelian one, which Marx critiques as falsely claiming that the material is created out of the ideational. To Marx, individuals must act, not just think, to transform existing reality, by consciously altering the natural material world through labor—thinking is not enough. As such, the *Magical Blend* manifesto resorts to this same idealistic, escapist spiritualism Marx and Feurbach challenge in both Hegelian idealism and Christianity, an idealism that defers liberation in favor of some sort of abstract transition to another dimension, to Geist, to God, or to the age of Aquarius, wherein we passively accept our fate rather than create it ourselves. This tendency eschews any concrete formula for either resistance or social transformation. For instance, one of my interview subjects who had tried a variety of New Age therapies and philosophies anticipated a future transformation in which she would "explode in an ecstasy of light and sound." Many more materialist formulations of the necessity for a utopian "social imaginary" or "vanishing point" (Mouffe, 1992, p. 379), for the "ought" rather than the "is" argue for the need to invoke the idea of another dimension as a space in which to inspire the imagination to bring about social transformation, but rightfully argue that transformation should not become arrested in the realm of the imaginary.

Furthermore, this model of Harmonic Convergence advocates a type of transformation that envisions us "exploding in an ecstasy of light and sound." Adorno's description of the biphasic agenda of the columnist claims that the columnist is complicit in tying the reader to the system of instrumental rationality wherein astrology co-opts the body into a regiment of work under the guise of pleasuring it. As in other aspects of the New Age, the body in Harmonic Convergence is repressed, is subsumed under the category of "consciousness" in order to avoid dealing with the problem of agency, and of difference and particularity. This explosion invokes intense oral and aural imagery, yet imagines a subject who is a passive witness to this spectacular event, but has no materiality. Thus, this subject is disembodied, immaterial, purely an incorporeal imaginary spectator, but not an agent herself. This formulation of the subject as an abstract, disembodied consciousness is pervasive in Western philosophy, and is one that recent postmodern attempts to reembody the subject have vehemently critiqued (see Butler's *Bodies that Matter*, 1993). Not only does this abstract, idealistic formulation of the subject dispense with the practical dilemmas of the precise role of the individual in this transformation, but this repression of the body does away with the problem of difference—if we are all just abstract consciousnesses, differences between male and female bodies, Black and White bodies, young and old bodies need not be addressed. Thus, the ideological trick of Harmonic Convergence is that it renders us conveniently all the same.

THE MIND-BODY-SPIRIT AT ONE WITH ITSELF: THE IDEOLOGY OF HOLISTIC HEALTH

Other images of the body that recur in New Age culture aside from the transformational subject of Harmonic Convergence could be said to be "affirmative" as well. For instance, the holistic health emphasis on individual responsibility for health reflects an emergent critical posture toward mainstream biomedicine, and the medicalization of the body. This critique has incorporated elements of Chinese herbalism, Japanese Reiki, and other Eastern and folk medicines, in response to the social critique of the medicalization of health that argues that Western medicine is "of all industries, the most wasteful, polluting, and pathogenic (Gortz, cited in Ross, 1991, p. 49). In Andrew Ross' (1991) words:

> Biomedicine has been held responsible for an explosion in iartrogenic illness—the diseases generated by institutional medicine (poisoning, infection, and unnecessary surgery in hospitals, which are the site of most accidents)—and the general appropriation of people's bodies by professionals dependent on megatechnology. (p. 49)

Often holistic health remedies employ counterrational notions of healing "energy" that encourage visualization, concentration, and a harnessing of the powers of the mind to heal the ailments of the body. Thus, the holistic health practitioners reject what they see as the artificial separation between mind and body, and separation of both from "spirit," advocating instead a model that integrates these three sites.

However, the radical end of the spectrum that sees the body as self-curing could ultimately claim that illness is the result of negative thinking, a position that Ross claims is already apparent in radical holistic health response to AIDS as a voluntary succumbing to the virus. In her book *The Aquarian Conspiracy*, Ferguson (1987) clearly illustrates this voluntaristic position (although not in direct reference to AIDS): "Health and disease don't just happen to us. They are active processes issuing from inner harmony or disharmony, profoundly affected by consciousness . . . This recognition carries with it implicit responsibility and opportunity. If we are participating, however unconsciously, in the process of disease, we can choose health instead" (p. 257).

Although this critique of biomedicine is potentially empowering for the New Age community, this emphasis on personal transformation, on "energy," on the holistic picture of the self-regulating mind-body-spirit reflects, and expresses, respectively, the ideology of possessive individualism, of industrial efficiency, and of the free market economy, and as such, are imbued with bourgeois ideology, or the ideology of the ruling class. Although the ethic of "self-help, self-healing, self-equilibrium and self-transcendence" (Ross, 1991, p. 49) constitute a powerful populist critique of the medical expert, and reappropriation of what were once everyday knowledges, the underlying ideology of holistic therapy, one of self-responsibility, can also be interpreted as perfectly consistent with the ideology underpinning the dismantling of Medicare and the welfare state, that has been systematically occurring in Britain, America, and now Canada.

Furthermore, the self-help ethic of personal empowerment and the holistic heath ethic of individual responsibility is perhaps an exaggerated representation of ultimately potentially relativist possibilities of a postmodern "politics of the local." In Ross' (1991) formulation, the New Age marks the replacement of health with sexuality as the new moralising category for power to exercise its hegemonic oppositions. Despite its sophisticated critique of the centered subject, the postmodern formulation of politics as local and imminent (which emerged in part from the antifoundationalist critique of the totalizing and exclusionary tendencies of the Marxist politics of class) may not be far off from the relativist "anything goes" politics of this dimension of the New Age.

THE HEALTH AND WELLNESS INDUSTRY: THE CORPORATIZATION OF THE "FRINGE"

Frequently, theorists of the left take the position that alternative ideas lose their oppositional power once they become incorporated into mainstream marketing and popular ideology. For instance, Ross (1991) describes the unfortunate fate of many "oppositional impulses" of the left, of the New Age, and of countercultures of recent years as the process of absorption, recuperation, then commodification, which deprives these impulses of their oppositional character. In contrast, some theorists of subcultures describe how one perceived response to this commodification, this assimilation of oppositional ideas to "mainstream society" is withdrawal (from conventional politics and structures), and "reassessment (from the extreme fringes of society)" (McKay, 1996, p. 53). Both formulate the emancipatory possibilities of any countercultural idea as inversely proportional to their position to the "center" of power.

Although equation of oppositionality with marginality is problematic, clearly the commodification of certain ideas or products can at times lead to a subjugation of its political intent to its salability. For instance, the incorporation of once marginalized or "alternative" philosophies or practices such as natural foods, self-help therapies into mainstream marketing, industry, and popular culture has undoubtedly been accompanied by an increase in false advertising. One of the store managers of a Toronto health food collective told me that many of their products sell better simply if they are accompanied by a description as "natural," although he also said there was often no significant difference between products that claimed to be "natural" and those which did not. "Natural," "whole," "green," and "traditional," "organic," and "old-fashioned"—signifiers that detone an affinity to New Age ideals of wholeness, of reconciliation with nature, the past, and the primitive—themselves cease to be descriptions of products, and have become actual brand names: a yeast supplement I was recently given by a health-conscious New Age relative (which ironically was synthetically produced selenium) carried the the misspelled brand name "Old Fashion."

This commodification of the New Age has also resulted in their homogenization, their reduction to the "lowest common denominator" whereby they will appeal to the largest number of people. For instance, the radical, populist impulse of self-help therapy is undermined by the formulaic, repetitive structure of books with titles such as *The Dance of Intimacy* (Lerner, 1989), and *Feel the Fear and Do it Anyway* (Jeffers, 1991). Although such books encourage reflection on identity, relationships and career goals, and thus promote self-reflexivity, the interspersal of "advice" with numerous examples of the author's (or some other probably mythical subject's) marital problems, breakdowns, and moments of humiliation can at times be more voyeuristic than therapeutic. As well, self-help rhetoric includes such trite suggestions that one should regularly take one's "psychic temperature," take a "reality check," and so on, which reflects the language of science and of of a corporate organizational thinking, undermining claims that this advice is oriented to self-discovery and self-understanding reflecting instead an agenda of integration into existing corporate structures.

Furthermore, the New Age has been strongly assimilated into business interests by various New Age organizations that merge self-help therapy and corporate thinking. Warner Erhard's well-known seminar called in conspicuous lower-case letters, "est" (Erhard's Seminars Training), has been hugely popular in America; an estimated 1 in 9 college-educated young adults in the San Francisco area in the 1970s, and 1 in 34 in Boston by the mid-1980s participated in est (Heelas, 1996). Since Erhard's initiation of Transformational Technologies in 1984, est has been working strongly with companies such as Cunard Ellermen and Guinness in Britain (Heelas, 1996). Scientology, an est-like organization, has been running WISE (World in Scientology Enterprises) and has been associated with Sterling Management Systems (for dentists), David Singer Consultants (chiropractors), the Concerned Businessmen's Association, and Uptreads (concerned with marketing), as well as a multitude of other businesses with seminars entitled things like "Managing Accelerated Performance," "Corporate Breakthrough," and "The Leadership Program" (Heelas, 1996). Other non-est New Age groups are involved as well; Bhagwan Shree Rajneesh runs a seminar for IBM, and Transcendental Meditation now offers MBAs at its new University of Management in the Netherlands (Heelas, 1996).

The proliferation of business seminars and television talk shows that espouse the New Age self-help rhetoric of "potential," "growth," "energy," "personal space," the phenomenon of the Reagan's reputed consultation with various psychics and astrologists, the rapid expansion of the once marginal health food stores into large-scale consumer outlets, the blurring of boundaries between mainstream medicine and homeopathic and naturopathic practices are examples of movements that were originally oppositional that then became deprived of their original intent.

Such phenomena would confirm Marcuse's (cited in Jay, 1973) claim that the pervasiveness of technological or instrumental rationality successfully subverts any forms of opposition to the "existing apparatus" that arise, ultimately co-opting them into the system. In his words, "dominant economic and social organisations do not maintain their power by force . . . they do it by identifying themselves with the faiths and the loyalties of the people, and the people have been trained to identify their faiths and loyalties with them" (p. 144). To Marcuse, the health food industry, holistic health medicine, and so on is not an example of the triumph of popular resistance over mainstream industry, but rather an example of the incorporation of rebellion into the existing apparatus of technological rationality, an example of how forms of protest that he sees in philosophies such as Zen, existentialism, and "beat ways of life" are quickly "digested by the status quo as part of its healthy diet" (p. 149). As such, the New Age movement is a characteristic example of how technological or instrumental rationality "is by no means confined to the subjects and objects of large scale enterprises, but characterizes the pervasive mode of thought and even the manifold forms of rebellion" (Marcuse, 1964, p. 149). From this point of view, the New Age is yet another example of how what originates as opposition or resistance can become incorporated, and then assimilated. Insofar as it abhors mediation, masquerades as revolution, and presumes to directly represent utopia, New Age spiritualism is ideological and affirmative rather than a form of resistance.

IS THE NEW AGE THE NEW RIGHT?

Another analysis somewhat consistent with that of Marcuse is Ross' (1991) claim that the New Age is an example of the absorption, recuperation, and commodification of the countercultural impulses of the sixties. In Ross' words:

> It is a narrative about how promises of post scarcity that once encouraged a glut of cultural transgressions now sanction the culture of Yuppie gluttony; how a liberatory revolution in individual rights became a privatised cult of self-interest; how the feminist watchword "the personal is political" was inverted to become "the political is personal"; how the bohemian rejection of materialism became an acceptance of corporate transmaterialism; how the radical otherness of Eastern spirituality was distilled into radical Protestantism, fully aligned with the American work ethic; how the medium of transformation evolved from outlawed psychedelia to corporate high-technology; how the collectivists experiments in co-operative community living became experiments in small-scale entrepreneurship; how radical libertarianism became neo-liberalism; how the hunger for collectivism was taken up in the concept of social networking, a parody of the idea of participatory democracy; how respect for E.F. Schumacher's small-scale economics turned into enthusiasm for John Naisbitt's "megatrends"; how Blakean innocence became social mystification; and how the semiotic gestures of disaffection from a dominant culture became incorporated into the business of marketing lifestyles. (p. 66)

Thus, many dimensions of the New Age movement could be described as ideological or "affirmative." The New Age trend of futurology—tarot card, palm, and aura readings, psychic prediction, and the like—are oriented toward wish fulfillment and the vicarious pleasure derived from contemplating our more fortunate, "future" selves. Harmonic Convergence resorts to an abstract spiritualism, and idealistic, disembodied, depoliticized version of social transformation. The New Age emphasis on personal transformation, on "energy," and the holistic health picture of the self-regulating mind–body–spirit reflects, respectively, the ideology of possessive individualism, of industrial efficiency, and of the free market economy. The health food industry, the mass opening of New Age bookstores, crystal shops, and music outlets, is a form of commodification of countercultural impulses, an example of their assimilation into dominant forms of commercial and industrial production.

Thus, the Frankfurt School's critique of popular culture as ideology, Adorno's content analysis of astrology, critique of the occult as illusion, provide ways to how to look at the New Age as ideology. One perspective on New Age version of transformation encapsulated in the phenomena of Harmonic Convergence, is that it sublimates practical material concerns for abstract spirituality. From this perspective, the holistic health ethic of self-responsibility and the merging of corporate interests with self-help seminars also clearly signifies the dislocation of the New Age from the sentiments characteristic of their leftist associations of 1960s counterculture. In fact, they are more in line with an orientation to the welfare state, to political unrest characteristic of the New Right.

However, this determination of popular culture as ideological precludes the possibility of a phenomenological investigation of the meanings individuals attach to forms of culture such as the New Age, meanings that may not be consistent with the Frankfurt School conclusion that they are "cultural dupes." For instance, this hierarchy overlooks the extent to which the reader may actually read the astrology column ironically, critically, or for entertainment. For example, one of my research subjects in Toronto who had a library full of astrology books, and engaged in weekly astrological readings where her own "personal" astrologer interpreted complex "star" charts, claimed that she did not "believe" in astrology, but rather saw it as an opportunity to reflect critically and self-reflexively on her life. Many recent analyses of popular culture emphasize that despite the intent of advertisers or culture "industrialists," individuals are much more critical, creative, and active in their consumption and interpretation of culture that this "cultural dupe" hypothesis would suggest. For instance, Baudrillard (1983) challenges this view of the consuming public as cultural dupe or as the couch potato and claims instead that individuals "decode messages in their own way . . . They intercept them . . . and transpose them . . . contrasting the dominant code with their own particular sub-codes, finally recycling everything passing into their own cycle" (p. 42). This description of cultural consumption as characterized by resistance, innovation, and redirection strongly contrasts with the patronizing depiction of consumers as passive mindless masses Baudrillard claims is still adopted by American sociology.

In other words, perhaps Adorno's critique of astrology as reflective of the rise of the authoritarian personality, of the desire of the masses for domination, and thus of the symptom of an administered society is not applicable to all, or even the majority of New Age consumers. In Zizek's (1989) words, "The very concept of ideology implies a kind of basic, constitutive naiveté" (p. 28) where individuals follow the formula as he puts it "they do not know it, but they are doing it" (Zizek, 1994, p. 8) Adorno's sort of ideology critique presumes a "naive consciousness" that sees New Age consumption as evidence of the consumers' unself-reflexive acquiescence to clever advertising and marketers' deliberate exploitation of consumer's unconscious desires. Such a view does not accurately describe the large number of New Agers who approach aspects of the New Age with ambivalence and even cynicism, but as an option of encouraging their own "alternative rationality," or a more cynical position that he describes as "they know every well what they are doing, but they are doing it" (Zizek, 1994, p. 8). In other words, not all consumers can be simply characterized as cultural dupes, for even in buying into consumer culture individuals can be seen as asserting a great deal of agency and active choice.

For instance, the woman I interviewed who got weekly readings in astrology did not uncritically accept the advice she received, but rather viewed these readings as an interpretive device in order to encourage her to become more self-reflective about her identity, her past, and her relationships to other people. In her words, "I treat my astrologer like a therapist—I may take his advice, or I may reject it, but either way I am forced to reflect on who I am." In this fashion, this person is not treating the astrologer as the Lacanian "subject presumed to know" (Zizek, 1989, p. 185), but rather as offering a perspective from which she can critically reflect on her own life. Similarly, another woman with whom I spoke claimed that she used astrology as a conversational gambit to initiate conversations with others about their personal lives. The advice from the astrological columnist, the persona of the Goddess, or even the guru may not be embraced as authentic, but merely as the vantage point of externality, of an almost arbitrary other from which to view the self. Ideology critiques that presume that reading astrology columns are tantamount to believing them are overlooking the fact that subjects may engage with these "authorities" playfully, ironically, disbelievingly, or cynically, or as Baudrillard (1983) puts it, how individuals redirect, and salvage "the material diffused by the dominant culture" (p. 42).

Furthermore, many of the people I spoke with who practiced alternative medicine including Reiki, acupuncture, aromotherapy, rebirthing therapy, and other fringe medicines did not express an uncritical belief that such alternative therapies work simply because New Age authorities say so, but rather judged therapies as either useful or unhelpful based on their own experience. Contrary to the perceived image of holistic health clients as flaky, bohemian, and predominantly middle class, and often female, several of the clients with whom I spoke who attended an alternative health clinic were working-class laborers who had suffered work-related injuries, and found mainstream medical pain relief treatments limited or unhelpful (particularly in the case of one man who was concerned about becoming addicted to the painkillers his doctor prescribed). These men were by no means "cultural dupes" of the New Age, but rather had a strongly utilitarian view of holistic health, and had heard about the clinic by word-of-mouth by co-workers. When speaking of acupuncture, for instance, one man said "I don't know what the hocus-pocus is behind it, and I don't care, but I do know it works." Nor did he ascribe to an essentialist view of experience, for he was aware of the possibility that his recovery could be due to the placebo effect, but claimed in a "strategic essentialist" fashion, that if he got rid of his pain, the way in which the cure worked did not matter.

Most importantly, an application of such an ideology critique to the New Age movement overlooks the extent to which some dimensions of the New Age movement could be interpreted as forms of resistance to, rather than affirmation of various mechanisms of power. For example, holistic health can be seen as a strong resistance to conventional science, medicine, and thus to technological rationality. Alternative religions and philosophies, even when esoteric and "flaky" can be viewed as symptoms of a more general crisis of rationality of which these forms of alternative thinking are an expression. Contrary to the "cultural dupe" hypothesis, some of my research subjects who dabbled in New Age philosophy that could justly be critiqued as abstract spiritualism were not fully indoctrinated into beliefs, but rather expressed disillusionment at the lack of any mainstream alternative. As such, critiques of popular culture cannot presume that the consumption of popular culture is itself an indication of a lack of agency, rebellion, individual expression or critical thought on behalf of individuals: what is important is the particular meanings that are associated with their consumption.

Despite the fact the *Dialectic of Enlightenment* definitively marks Horkheimer and Adorno's shift from a critique of political economy to a critique of instrumental reason (Benhabib, 1994), and has a much more sophisticated version of ideology than I was able to represent here, their essay on the culture industry still reveals a fundamental preoccupation with the processes of commodification and manipulation, a preoccupation that is shared by many contemporary analyses of the media. Although articulating the way in which relations of power are sedimented through deliberate manipulation of ideas is a valuable and meaningful project, critiques of contemporary popular culture are coming to terms with the fact that social actors can have complex, diverse, and self-reflective relationships to their own patterns of consumption, relationships that transcend the notion of "cultural dupe."

As Zizek (2000) puts it, the contemporary preoccupation with "conspiracy theories" that characterizes both media studies and media content (i.e., *The X-Files*) paradoxically illustrate the strength of our desire to believe their actually is a "Really Existing Big Other" (p. 5) more than they tell about any actual existing conspiracy. Zizek demonstrates how the appeal of films such as *The Matrix* (1999) and *The Truman Show* (1999) is based on the desire for a Big Other who pulls the strings, such as the ominous artificial intelligence posing as Agent Smith who operates the computer program that animates *The Matrix*, and who films the subject and is responsible for constructing Truman's fabricated universe in *The Truman Show*, a desire that illustrates our desire for some sort of "cognitive mapping" in the context of the "empty place of power," the indeterminacy of the future, and the impossibility of a coherent social totality. As Zizek illustrates, the emphasis Beck and other "Risk Society" theorists place on democratic discussion and consensus building overlooks the extent to which in the context of the crisis of expert knowledge and the proliferation of incommensurable private languages, decision making will be arbitrary. Thus, To Zizek (2000), "the recourse to 'conspiracy theories' is a desperate way out of this deadlock, an attempt to regain what Fred Jameson calls 'cognitive mapping'" (p. 9) in the context of these various crises of communication, of legitimation, and of community.

In conclusion, the idea of ideology critique has recently been challenged by many theorists for ascribing to the fantasy of the "extra-ideological position," yet as I have tried to illustrate, examining the New Age from the lens of ideology critique is still a valuable exercise in showing the extent to which the New Age expresses the ideology of conspicuous consumption, operates as wish fulfillment, and is compatible with the demands of alienated labor. However, I also wanted to demonstrate the extent to which New Age consumption is not simply passive: Even in its more ideological guises, aspects of the New Age such as holistic health and self-help therapy represents a desire for agency and control that illustrates more generally the crisis of confidence in medical, scientific and other experts, a desire that is shared by social theorists, technophiles and New Agers alike. Paradoxically, the recent internet craze cyberspace illustrates this desire for control and for a community as well, for as Zizek (2000) puts it, "cyberspace was supposed to bring us all together in a Global Village, however, what effectively happens is that we are bombarded with the multitude of messages belonging to inconsistent and incompatible universes—instead of the Global Village, the big Other we get a multitude of 'small others', of tribal particular identifications at our choice" (p. 8). Thus, the reification of cyberspace and of Nature/the Mystical are two sides of the same coin. In this fashion, the New Age is a symptom of social processes that transcend this particular example, and although can be better understood through ideology critique, cannot be dismissed simply as ideology.

III

New Age as Subversive

Three

New Age Environmentalism: The New Age as a Micropolitics of Resistance

In chapter 2 I looked at how certain aspects of the New Age movement such as Harmonic Convergence advocated an abstract spirituality that sublimates desires for social transformation into the realm of spiritual transformation rather than concrete political change, how the holistic health ethic of individual responsibility advocates the liberal ethic of individual responsibility, and how the holistic health/health food movement represent the commodification of the desire for good health. These analyses are consistent with Adorno, Zizek, and Coward's analysis of the New Age movement as individualistic, abstract, and ideologically confused. Although certain elements of the New Age tend toward a version of social transformation that is individualistic, abstract, and anti-materialist (Harmonic Convergence), toward the New Right view of individual responsibility (i.e., the more conservative versions of holistic health) and toward the commodification of the politically correct emphasis of inclusivity, other aspects express a much different ideology or orientation. Although this analysis of the New Age does adequately capture certain elements of this movement, this perspective fails to do justice to the extent to which the New Age movement shares similar aspirations, histories, and desires with what we call "the left" that may be instructive. It also does not acknowledge the extent to which certain aspects of the New Age movement strive toward a liberation from domination of scientific, and medical authority.

Although many aspects of the New Age version of social transformation are too oriented toward the abstract realm of consciousness, like Marxism, they do express a strong desire for a "break with history," and for social change. Although New Age "manifestos" are characterized by their high level of abstraction, their reification of the "spiritual" and their failure to articulate concrete or collective strategies to accomplish their goal of transformation, they express a spirit of resistance to the dominant scientific, medical, and governmental authorities. For similar reasons, Ross (1991) has said that in the New Age in America "we can find at least one version . . . of a politics of identity and subjectivity that has not been entirely subsumed by the New Right's picture of individualism, aggressively protective of its privatised will to consume" (p. 68).

The New Age encompasses a broad spectrum in terms of its degree of politicization. As well as those aspects that are ideologically confused or even reactionary, there are also several aspects to the New Age that have tried to elicit positive social change. Central to the New Age ethic of self-responsibility regarding the environment, and self-empowerment in terms of one's own mental, physical (and some would say spiritual) health, is reclaiming of individual agency that cannot be entirely reduced to the ideology of the New Right. This ethic of self-responsibility and self-empowerment is a strong reaction to perceived loss of individual control regarding on one hand, the place that science, technology, and modernization has taken us, and on the other, the processes of political decision making that would allow individuals to intervene. Thus, this loss of control, is clearly related to what some theorists call various crises of modernity, of the "political," of "science," of the environment; crises that I explore in much more detail in chapter 6.

What I argue in this chapter is that despite aspects of the New Age consistent with New Right ideology apparent in New Age tendencies toward commodification, individualism, and corporatism, various trajectories of this movement do share aspirations with "the left." Specifically, I wish to show how aspects of the New Age such as the holistic health and self-help therapy movements represent a populist challenge to scientific and medical authority, even when such practices take the form of a commodified leisure activity. As well, not all New Age practices have been thoroughly commodified: Unlike the Yuppies living in metropolitan centers such as Toronto who only practice the New Age after work, on weekends, or when shopping, some New Agers deliberately place themselves on the margins of society, and attempt to live their New Age beliefs as a total way of life. For instance, New Age Travellers living in the west of Ireland who attempt to live off the waste or excess of modernity can be seen as internalizing New Age environmentalism as a practice that governs all aspects of life rather than simply as a commodified leisure activity. Thus, in this chapter, I look at New Age ethics in some of the more separatist New Age communities in order to ascertain how the New Age can be seen in some guises as a continuation of the project of the "left."

HOLISTIC HEALTH AND SELF-HELP THERAPY AS "LIBERATORY"

The proliferation of alternative nutritional, health care, and mental health specialists directly challenge several aspects of scientific and medical authority. Holistic health dimensions of the New Age movement often express a strong critique of biomedicine or mainstream medicine is based on the caricature that biomedicine treats the body like a machine that occasionally breaks down (due to entirely physical causes), and requires the ministrations of a mechanic/physician. This New Age critique of the medicalization of the body has also joined forces with environmentalist critiques that have challenged biomedicine for failing to take account of social and environmental contributors to illness, critiques of the interdependence between medicine/psychiatry and the pharmaceutical industry, and the recent exposure of the political, rather than purely medical, hindrances to development of AIDS research (p. 50). All of these critiques combined have given credence to the holistic body as an appropriate replacement for the impoverished model of the body perceived to dominate biomedicine.

The increasingly popular holistic body of the New Age movement challenges the biomedical focus on illness as due to physical breakdown, and focuses instead on "wellness," a concept that sees the body and indeed the self, as requiring continuous care and maintenance, rather than just sporadic and drastic attention in times of crisis (a philosophy articulated, for instance, in the journal *Vitality: Toronto's Monthly Wellness Magazine*). Indeed, proponents of this model are often overtly hostile to surgical and mainstream pharmaceutical intervention. Although some of the more radical critics of bio medicine see the body as virtually self-curing, in its more moderate forms, this holistic health philosophy espouses a view of the body that empowers the individual, and that challenges the modern practice of giving over authority to the physician. Such a view is both informed by and has inspired the contemporary feminist critique of obstetrics and the revival of "natural childbirth" methods, the contemporary critique of the subjugation of patients to biologistic categories, inhumane practices and profit-oriented pharmaceutical intervention in psychiatry, and other such critiques of Western medicine.

These critiques of obstetrics, of psychiatry, and Western medicine in general are not unrelated to debates on contemporary social theory that argue that the contemporary crisis of Western science and medicine is integrally related to the dualistic thinking in Western philosophy that opposes male–female, nature–culture, and mind–reason (Butler, 1993; Haraway, 1991; Hekman, 1990). In fact, some New Age texts that critique biomedicine and the medicalization of the body claim explicitly that it is this mind–body split in Western philosophical thought that has resulted in the inadequate medical model of the body. New Agers who embrace holistic health see this split between mind and body characteristic of Western philosophy as the root of the problem, and embrace instead a unitary view of the mind–body–spirit. Such practitioners view the body as an efficient, smoothly circulating system of energies, an integrated organic whole, a self-sufficient, self-contained unit where a disturbance in one dimension will have ramifications in another.

Such a notion of the body is clearly liberatory to those whose personal experiences have told them that their mental health and their physical health are inextricably interconnected. As well, the populist, "do-it-yourself" dimension of holistic health movements shifts authority over one's health from the medical expert or the conventional, science-informed doctor to the self, a move that Heelas (1996) calls "epistemological Selfism" (p. 82) or Wallis (1984) calls epistemological individualism. This gesture expresses a profound lack of confidence both in mainstream medical practices, and in the capacity of health care programs in Britain and America (and increasingly, in Canada) to meet the needs of the people, and expresses a strong critique of the authority structures of both our political and scientific institutions. In this fashion, holistic health therapy does reflect the ideology of competitive individualism and of a free market economy as is argued in chapter 2, but from another perspective represents a new kind of reflexivity and a democratized relationship to authority that is in some ways potentially empowering.

One of the dominant aspects of the New Age is the extent to which it challenges individuals to reject aspects of authority associated with established orders. For example, for New Age writers, the final arbiter of the "truth" is always the self, one's personal experience, and intuition. This is apparent in advice such as "Only accept what rings true to your own Inner Self" (Perry, cited in Heelas, 1996, p. 21), "Always feel free to follow your own inner guidance at all moments" (Linn, cited in Heelas, 1996, p. 22), and "inner listening makes clearer to us what we really want" (Ferguson, 1973). As early as the 1920s Theosophist Annie Beasant (1920) wrote of the "inner government" (Beasant in Heelas, 1996). As Heelas (1996) summarizes:

> Truth, not surprisingly for those who see themselves as spiritual beings, must—at least first and foremost—come by way of one's own experience. For this alone provides direct and uncontaminated access to the spiritual realm. "Truths" provided by the dogmas of religious traditions, or by other people—parents, scientists, even putatively-spiritual masters—might well be erroneous. A particular religious doctrine might have developed for reasons of political expediency; scientists, as history has shown use, often get it wrong; a spiritual master might have lapsed into his contaminated ego-mode of functioning. "Truths" coming from beyond the Self, that is to say, cannot be relied upon. They can only be taken into account when they have been shown to be right, something which involves testing them by way of one's own experience or (spiritually informed) intuition. (p. 21)

In this manner, the New Age tries to replace the authority of traditional religious, scientific, and political leaders with the authority of the Self, experience, and intuition.

Some of the aspects of the critique of Western medicine and science which is woven through the New Age impetus to holistic health and self-help share commonalties with such critiques in the work of Michel Foucault. His work focused on the particular ways in which Western science and medicine participated in the objectification of individual subjects and bodies. Through an examination of clinics, hospitals, prisons, and asylums, Foucault argued that the role of science in the objectification process has changed historically, but has taken predominantly three forms or modes: The first mode, "dividing practices," concerned that whereby science sanctioned the manipulation of individuals by practices of spatial and social exclusion, a conclusion drawn from studies done on the isolation of lepers in the middle ages; the confinement of the poor, the insane, and vagabonds in Paris General Hospital in 1656; the new classifications of disease and other practices of medicine in nineteenth century France; and the rise of psychiatry and its entry into hospitals, prisons and clinics in the late 19th and early 20th century France (Rabinow, 1984). The second mode, that of "scientific classification," was concerned with the role of science in constituting us as subjects through the processes of classification, categorization, and containment integral to the various disciplines of linguistics, economics, and biology (Rabinow, 1984). The third mode, "subjectivization," was concerned with how the individual becomes active in the process of self-monitoring, internalization of the collective gaze (Rabinow, 1984). Although all three illustrate the prevalence of disciplinary technologies in society, the third is perhaps the triumph of the modern imperative toward normalization, regulation, and civilization, because it represents the internalization of the panoptic mechanism itself.

Although their critiques of science originate from a practical rather than intellectual concern, holistic health and self-help therapy thinking does in fact share Foucault's critique of the way in which "dividing practices" and the "scientific classification" objectifies individuals. For instance, one member of a "Holism and Mental Health" meeting I attended put on by the local *Friends of Schizophrenics* chapter in Saskatchewan put forward the familiar argument that schizophrenia is a catch-all phrase for doctors unable to diagnose mental illness, and then proceeded to critique the process of labeling and segregation of those suffering from mental illness in favor of a more humane, holistic, and communitarian approach to mental illness. The speaker conceded that in extreme cases, those suffering from mental illness should seek advice from a physician or psychiatrist as well as a holistic therapist, and may need the help of drugs like Haldol, Prozac, or Lithium. Nonetheless, she emphasized that individual empowerment, regular self-assessment, and control over medication was still possible in serious cases, and a greatly preferable over the historical stigmatization, segregation, and objectification of the mentally ill. This more widespread use of natural therapies and self-medication techniques to treat even acute cases of mental illness shows a new orientation to pharmaceutical control and illustrates the trend away from conventional psychiatric models and power structures.

Although the New Age emphasis on self-empowerment is profoundly liberating, it does at times espouse a problematically essentialist notion of the self and sexuality. For instance, the New Age frequently formulates "liberation" from mainstream science and medicine as the agenda of New Age technologies, invoking a liberal humanist notion of our essential "humanity" that has been lost under a veneer or authoritative medical regimes. In the New Age, the "recovery" of this "humanness," this "self" is the ultimate goal of the practices of self-care. Many New Age technologies available in Toronto illustrate this tendency toward posing holistic health therapy as a means to recover the essential self. For instance, scheduled seminars for "the Carrot Common," a health food collective based on the large Toronto health food store "The Big Carrot" in 1996 included "Reclaim Your Personal Power Through Deep Blockage Removal," "Regression and Past Life Therapy: Remembering and Releasing the Past is Proving to be the Most Concise Method of Reclaiming Your Power in the Present and for the Future," and "Deep Tissue Body Work." All of these seminars posit the recovery of an essential "self" that is merely "blocked," overwhelmed by the past, as "deeply submerged."

Some New Age seminars focus on liberating sexuality. For example, a seminar entitled "Empowering the Heartwomb: Exploring Women's Sacred Longing," promised to open up a "sacred space" that will promote "sensitivity" and "self-honoring." This seminar was run by a woman who claimed to be offering an alternative sexual therapy that was a reaction to the medicalization of sexuality and overly rigid quantification and normalization of sexual behavior apparent in the research of Masters and Johnson, Kinsey, and other "sexologists" who emerged in the 1960s and 1970s. Such sexologists had the avowed intention to accumulate data that could increase knowledge about sexuality that would enhance our sexual pleasure, but as Steedman (1987) has pointed out, such expert advice nonetheless advocated an oppressive, constraining, and often masculinist version of normal sexuality. However, the assumption of the "naturalness" central to the self or of the sexual subject in the New Age counterdiscourse ignores the complexity of ways in which we acquire our (sexual) subjectivity.

In contrast, Foucault is very critical of both this notion of our essential humanness, and the idea that resisting one form of domination will in itself free us. For instance, his critique of sexuality illustrates the discourses we think will sexually "liberate" us are complicit in mechanisms of normalisation and surveillance from which we are trying to escape. From a Foucauldian point of view, "self-discovery," "unity," "health," and "wellness" could be seen as replacing sexuality as the new privileged discourse of bodily truth and inner essence (Coward, 1989). Ross (1991) summarizes Coward's Foucauldian argument that claims, "Health has become the new moralising category for power to exercise its hegemonic oppositions. Bad health is a sign of moral failing only recently attributed to repressed sexuality" (p. 54). Put another way, the holistic health impetus to "be healthy" could itself invoke disciplining and normalizing procedures that are as oppressive as those of mainstream biomedicine. The big question is what particular version of health is it we are supposed to embrace? Many technologies of the New Age advocate not just health, but a "new and improved" version of vitality, memory, concentration, and relaxation that are perfectly consistent with a Yuppie work ethic, and the compartmentalization of time whereby we make the most of our time off to "regenerate" our bodies to work again in a few hours.

Other versions of "health" espouse a rhetoric that is perfectly consistent with those very practices of ordering, classifying, and categorizing that the New Age claims to be so strongly opposed. Most New Age claim to "purify," "clean," "expunge" the "toxins," the "debris," ironically illustrating the same obsession with sanitation, the same dichotomy between clean and unclean, as that of the very civilising processes they are pretending to subvert. Paradoxically, the modern obsession with sanitation is so strong that this subtext appears in New Age rhetoric even when talking about forms of counselling such as rebirthing therapy. For instance, New Age rhetoric is riddled with references to psychic waste, psychic toxins, personal garbage, and metaphors that imply a sort of "psychic constipation" such as that used in "deep blockage removal" therapies such as colonic irrigation.

Foucault's critique of the "repressive hypothesis" in *The History of Sexuality* can attune us to the fact that New Age holistic health and self-help therapy's emphasis on "liberation" from conventional authorities does not ensure the freedom and self-determination of the subject. As Foucault (1988) says "the act of liberation alone is not sufficient to establish the principles of liberty" (p. 3). Put another way, decolonization alone does not in itself ensure that those previously colonized are "free." His critique of the discourse of sexual liberation is based on the notion that "liberation" alone cannot ensure that the reinstitution of other forms of domination does not occur. In this fashion, Foucault is critiquing both the Marxist and Freudian models of liberation, and their assumption that when oppression/ repression is lifted, and the self is liberated that the problem is solved. Foucault asks instead what types of disciplinary discourses replace the ones from which the body has been liberated. The Foucauldian approach to the New Age would ask if the liberation of the New Age from dominant medical and scientific modes of discourse ironically reinscribes the subject back in more subtle forms of domination. As Foucault (1988) puts it, "this ethical problem of the definition of practices of freedom is more important than the affirmation (and repetitious, at that) that sexuality or desire must be set free" (p. 3).

For instance, some feminists have critiqued the radical/cultural feminist characterization of men as war-like and women as peaceful for being ahistorical (in assuming that male responses to this biology or spirituality will be uniform across cultures and throughout history), for being dualistic, and for failing to recognize that supposed differences between the genders have themselves been used by patriarchal discourse and are thus damaging to women. Alcoff (1988) points out, the effect of essentialism is to "reflect and reproduce dominant cultural assumptions about women" (p. 413); assumptions that tie women to a particular set of characteristics defined as "female." She asks: "Do feminists want to buy another ticket for women of the world on the merry-go-round of feminine constructions ? Don't we want rather to the merry-go-round and run away?" (p. 414).

The feminist critique of essentialism has emerged in part from the influence of postmodernism: Alcoff claims in particular from poststructuralist or "postessentialist" theorists such as Foucault who hold the common theme that "the self-contained authentic subject conceived by humanism to be discernible below a veneer of cultural and ideological overlay, is in reality a construct of that very Humanist discourse" (p. 415). Under the influence of this poststructuralist formulation, some feminists have attacked the category of women, claiming in Foucauldian terms, that to even attempt to define *woman* forces the individual back on [herself] and ties [her] to [her] own identity in a constraining way (Foucault, cited in Dreyfus & Rabinow, 1982, p.

212). This poststructuralist critique of essentialism claims that the cultural feminist attempts to define woman constitutes a discourse that is itself harmful to women because it reinvokes the primary "mechanism of oppression" (Alcoff, 1988, p. 415) namely, a definition of women, in its alleged solution. Riley (1983) asks: "Can it be argued that the only way of avoiding these constant historical loops which depart or return from the conviction of women's natural dispositions, to pacifism for example, would be to make a greater gesture—to stand back and announce that there aren't any women?" (p. 2).

However, as several feminists have argued, essentialism perhaps is in some ways politically necessary. Although feminists are nervous about invoking essentialist notions of women, they recognize the double bind in which they are caught—to denounce the category of women on the basis that it essentializes and falsely universalizes the concern of a particular group of women renders feminists unable to demarcate who they are emancipating, and from what. As a result, what Alcoff (1988) recommends is a sort of "strategic essentialism" (p. 417), where feminists strategically assume a commonality or essential identity when engaged in particular political struggles against a common enemy while recognizing that this unitary identity of woman does not exist. Riley (1983) captures this ambivalence, claiming "both a concentration on, and a refusal of, the identity of 'woman' are essential to feminism" (p. 1).

In this fashion, perhaps New Agers, like feminists should practice strategic essentialism: the use of essential notions of self to strategically guide transformation, while recognizing that these notions are only provisional, temporary, and contingent. As Alcoff (1988) claims when speaking of the effect of deconstruction on the left, "you must have a positive alternative, a vision of a better future that can motivate people to sacrifice their time and energy toward its realisation" (p. 419). Although the search for sexual liberation, for the submerged past, for the self behind various mental blocks, clearly ascribes to essentialist and in some ways problematic categories, the journey toward these goals is strongly empowering to individuals. Although sexology manuals do in fact accede to a constraining version of "normal" sexuality, and invoke a male sexual norm against which the female is portrayed as abnormal (Steedman, 1987), the availability of these manuals enables conversations, discussion, and experimentation with various sexual techniques that are not entirely reducible to "disciplinary technologies." In a similar way, the search for an essential self when institutionalized as an ongoing practice can lead to increased self-reflexivity regarding recurring patterns and frustrations in one's relationships and in the pursuit of one's goals.

THE FOUCAULDIAN CRITIQUE OF THE MARXIST CONCEPT OF LIBERATION

Although I am making the claim that the use of essentialist categories of self and sexuality in the New Age can in some instances be empowering to individuals, essentialist notions of "liberation" have been widely critiqued in the field of the philosophy of Marxism. In particular, some theorists have employed a Foucauldian notion of discourse in asking from what is the subject liberated, as well as what types of discourses may be put in the place of the old totalitarian discourse that may simply reinstitutionalize oppression but in a subtler way. For instance, Laclau (1991) critiques the totalitarian dimensions of Western Marxism emerging out of their univocal notion of truth (p. 2). Feminists such as Flax (1990) have argued that the assumption of the centrality of class as a variable of oppression is exclusionary and ahistorical to women, people of color, and others who experience class as of secondary concern to other variables of oppression. Similarly, feminism has been challenged for presuming a unity on the basis of sisterhood, which like the Marxist category of class presents an overly homogenized view of these commonalities. The poststructuralist critique of Marxist, feminist, or any other liberatory discourses (including the social sciences) takes the position that such discourses rely on a notion of an "essential human" that is in all probability as coercive as the discourse from which they are trying to become "liberated." For instance, Foucault's (1983) critique of these supposed emancipatory discourses is that they formulate a version of the humanist subject that "forces the individual back on himself and ties him to his own identity in a constraining way" (p. 212). In other words, he illustrates that the assumption of an essential core that is natural to us can itself constitute a mechanism of coercion, which for feminism is the notion of biological femaleness, and for Marxism is our inherent productive capacities, or our "species-being."

Whereas the Foucauldian position that the Marxist version of liberation may simply reinstitutionalise oppression in another form is frequently considered to be "poststructuralist" (see Alcoff, 1988; Weedon, 1987), other theorists considered to be "postmodern" have challenged Marxism for relying on a unified subject who is fully aware of a coherent social totality from which one becomes liberated or emancipated. To the postmodern critic, the representation of the subject and the social totality in Marxism misunderstand the perspectival nature of all knowledge claims (see Haraway, 1991; Hekman, 1990). This postmodern critique of truth is influenced by the claims that truth is representative of a specific will to power (Neitszche, 1967), and internal to the traditions of modernity (Lyotard, 1994). Lyotard, for instance, argues that Marxist theory of liberation advocates a totalized, self-legitimating narrative of history that leads to an "entire morality and an entire politics" that in a postmodern era is no longer credible (Lyotard 1994). Although he is still committed to working for social change in the Marxist tradition, Laclau (1991) claims, neo-marxist theories of emancipation rely on "a single privileged agent of historical change defined by a historical and social totality which can be rationally grasped" (p. 57).

The Foucauldian critique of liberation that challenges the Marxist assumption of "essence" is thus related to the contemporary critique of ideology that challenges the notion of "social totality." For instance, Zizek (1994) criticizes the Marxist notion of ideology because it relies on such a notion of a social totality as well as the idea of an "extra-ideological position" from which one can grasp this social totality, "a privileged place, somehow exempt from the turmoils of social life, which enables some subject—agent to perceive the very hidden mechanism that regulates social visibility and non-visibility" (p. 3). This notion of ideology implies that the ideology critic can "step outside" ideology, to "truth." However, this position misunderstands the perspectival nature of all knowledge claims. In Zizek's words, "The paradox in all cases is that the stepping out of (what we experience as) ideology is the very form of our enslavement to it" (p. 6). In other words, there is no place outside ideology from which we are immune. As he puts it, "an individual subjected to ideology can never say for himself 'I am in ideology,' he always requires another corpus of doxa in order to distinguish his own 'true' position from it" (p. 20). In this fashion, the Marxist notion of ideology relies on a problematic distinction between ideological chimera and "real life," appearance and essence, illusion and "actually existing" social relations.

From this point of view, both "liberation" and "ideology" are problematic concepts. The position taken regarding Marxism by social constructivists, postmodernists, psychoanalytic theorists, and others is that the discursive construction of reality entails that the very attempt to ascertain the "essential," the truth, the "real," is itself "ideological." In Zizek's (1994) words, "When some procedure is denounced as 'ideological par excellence' one can be sure that its inversion is no less ideological" (p. 20); (e.g., Zizek illustrates how the claim of those applying ideology critique to cyberculture). According to such a critique, "virtual sex" is "false" sex masquerading as "real" sex, and is thus ideological. In contrast, Zizek shows how the most profound illusion is not that "virtual sex" masquerades as "real" sex, but rather that there is such a thing as "real sex" to begin with. In other words, the ideology critics who are defending "real" sex are no less guilty of misrecognition of the discursive construction of sexuality than the "virtual realists" they are critiquing.

To put this another way, "what if ideology resides in the very belief that, outside the closure of the finite universe there is some 'true reality' to be entered" (Zizek, 2000, p. 3). Contemporary corrolaries of this notion of the "end of the universe" or Plato's cave (within which we all watch the the shadowy performance of what we think is reality), have been posed by "the Matrix" in the 1999 film *The Matrix*, and the gigantic studio set in *The Truman Show*. The popularity of these two films demonstrates simultaneously a widespread awareness and concern with of the media studies perspective of consumers as manipulated masses, and a millinarianist concern with what lies beyond the year 2000. As Zizek demonstrates, Lacan and the Frankfurt School would answer this question of what lies outside of the cave/Matrix/studio set in very different ways. For the Frankfurt School, the Matrix is "the extrapolated embodiment of Kulturindustrie, the alienated-reified social Substance (of the Capital) directly taking over, colonizing our inner life itself, using us as the source of energy . . . the metaphor of the Capital that colonized culture and subjectivity" (Zizek, 2000, p. 3). For the Lacanian, the Matrix is "the reification of the symbolic order as such" (p. 3). From the former perspective, it is possible to step outside ideology, but from the latter, stepping outside only places us at another level of reality, because we will merely encounter another simulated universe. However, as Zizek points out, even more Lacanian readings of the Matrix tend to be paranoid and ideological as well, because they rely on the belief in an "'Other of the other,' into another Other who, hidden behind the Other of the explicit social texture, programmes . . . the unforeseen effects of social life and thus guarantees its consistency: beneath the chaos of the market, the degradation of morals, etc. there is the purposeful strategy of the Jewish plot" (Zizek, 2000, p. 6). However, the alternative, the radical Lacanian position that there is no "outside" to the Matrix of the studio set, there is really no "Other presumed to know" is unsatisfactory, because it leads to the relativist, cynical position that that that there is no liberation or freedom from ideology at all.

Another position on this debate that attempts to avoid the dichotomies of the "conspiracy theory"/"no outside to ideology": polarity is illustrated by the claims to epistemic privilege made by Marxists, feminists, and other "oppressed groups," claims based on what is called the "standpoint position." This entails the view in the works of Harding (1990), that "The view from the perspective of the powerful is far more partial and distorted than that available from the perspective of the dominated . . . because the powerful have far more interests in obscuring the injustices of their unearned privileges and authority" (p. 24). Much New Age literature makes an appeal to the superiority of these "subjugated knowledges" over our modern rational ways of thinking. For instance, Weed's book (1989) *Healing Wise* argues that women's experience gives them superior knowledge in healing. The journal *Shaman's Drum* makes frequent appeals to the superior knowledge of First Nations people and Australian aboriginals not only of their knowledge of herbs, plants, animals, and healing, but also of modern political, judicial, and economic structures. For instance, *Vitality* magazine speaks frequently of the custom of "circling" as a means to settling any dispute where community members and elders speak in turns in a circle, a mode of reconciliation that is suggested as a means to reconcile victims of violence and their perpetrators.

Such positions resemble the position some feminists take regarding women's superior comprehension regarding the mechanisms of power in governments and universities such as Smith (1987), and Hartsock (1983). However, critics of this standpoint have in effect "decentered" this unified and coherent subject, that is the historical agent, the focal point of emancipatory political discourses, challenging the self-consciousness and self-presence of this subject, by, for example, problematizing the assumption the subject has unmediated access to its own desires. Haraway (1991) challenges the standpoint position by arguing that at times individuals are damaged by their experience as marginalised, and hence may not always use the best judgment. In a Lacanian vein, Young (1990) for instance, claims "Subjects all have multiple desires which do not cohere; they attach meaning to objects without always being aware of each layer or their connections" (p. 310). The standpoint position has also been criticized on the basis of the fact that we occupy diverse and multiple subject positions (Mouffe, 1992).

Furthermore, these critiques of standpoint feminism call into question the radical feminist assumption that women are capable of a superior form of political organization through a common "sisterhood," appeals that are often woven through many of the more politically mobilized fringes of the New Age. Such critiques point out how if the subject is unable to coherently represent its own desire, to be present to itself, subjects cannot make themselves wholly transparent to each other. As such, this psychoanalytic decentering of the emancipatory subject of Marxism challenges the notion of ideology by illustrating the impossibility of occupying a position "beyond" ideology—the veils, blinders, and illusions that obfuscate reality can never be entirely stripped away because, as psychoanalysis has shown us, the misrecognition of oneself, and hence, one's social conditions is endemic to the human condition.

From this point of view, a rigorous analysis of Marxist versions of liberation that unself-reflexively impose a notion of an authentic human who can be "liberated," and versions of ideology that conceive of ideology in terms of the possibility of an "extra-ideological position" are problematic. Although essentialist versions of the "liberated self" apparent in the New Age do lead to increased self-reflexivity, as a sustained political strategy of the left, such formulations are unsatisfactory. Poststructuralist critique of the essential subject and the postmodern recognition of the perspectival nature of knowledge have problematized both these categories, which are essential to Marxism. However, the solution is not to reject the notion of liberation or ideology altogether, and espouse a relativist version of the social, for this is equally problematic, but to pry this concept from its associations with reductionistic, economistic models frequently invoked by neo-Marxism, and from its adherence to the Enlightenment notion of the authentic human subject and of the "God's eye" view of social reality or of the social totality.

Because of these problems in Marxism, many Marxists and feminists have taken on Foucault in an attempt to integrate a more nuanced version of power into their understanding of class, gender, and other forms of oppression (see Diamond & Quinby, 1988; Hartsock, 1990; Martin, 1988; Weedon, 1987). This project has not been without problems. First of all, Foucault's construction of power has been critiqued for its totalizing, all-encompassing form that leaves little or no room for resistance (see Weedon, 1987). Second, his critique of the authentic, essential subject has problematized the projects of Marxism and feminism, both of which have been hard pressed to formulate either an emancipatory subject or a causal explanation for oppression that does not resort to essentialisms (see Alcoff, 1988; Haraway, 1989). Despite these problems, feminists in particular have been quite eager to take on board his notion of how individuals have been subjectivised through the disciplinary discourses of modernity, because these disciplinary discourses have also been instrumental in producing the sexed subject as well (Weedon, 1987).

Foucault's analysis of the power–knowledge nexus has appealed to Marxists and feminists disillusioned with dichotomous and overly materialist formulations of power characteristic of their respective traditions. Although Foucault, like Marxism and feminism, is concerned with hierarchical relations, his particular concern is the subtle and multiple ways in which the various discourses about the body have been deployed in the service of such hierarchical relations. His tactic is to use the extreme example—the prisoner, the insane, the transsexual, the homosexual—to illustrate the ways in which the various disciplines of modernity: biology, economics, psychiatry, criminology, so on have located and organized individual bodies.

However, Foucault is often accused by those concerned with various emancipatory agendas such as Marxism or feminism of espousing a relativist position. For instance, Alcoff (1988) critiques Foucauldian poststructuralists because "they seem totally to erase any room for manoeuvre by the individual within a social discourse or set of institutions" (p. 417). She argues that poststructuralism destroys any semblance of agency or intentionality of the subject by arguing that history has a "totalising . . . imprint" (p. 417). From this point of view, positive social change does not seem possible, because the only liberatory position available seems to be one of "negative struggle" whereby the subject tries to resist definition (Kristeva, 1982, p. 137), a position that precludes the possibility of collective struggle.

Although Foucault was predominantly concerned with "deconstructing everything and refusing to construct anything" (Alcoff, 1988, p. 419), in several places in his work he did articulate positive rather than simply deconstructivist directives for the reconstructive project of fighting authoritarianism in all forms. For instance, in his introduction to Deleuze and Guattari's *Anti-Oedipus*, Foucault (1983) outlines how to live a non-Fascist life, including imperatives to "Free political action from all unitary and totalizing paranoia" and "Develop action, thought and desires by proliferation, juxtaposition and disjunction, and not by subdivision and pyramidal hierarchicalisation" (p. xiii).

Furthermore, his position on self-care and self-knowledge does contain within it an element that is concerned with a positive ethics rather than simply deconstruction and critique. His general position on our various contemporary modes of self-care and self-knowledge, such as the New Age, as with psychoanalysis, would be to illustrate that even when relatively dislocated from the modes of domination characterising the confession, or modern psychiatry, these discourses become merely new "disciplinary technologies" that swarm the modern subject. He would show how such discourses merely make the agent complicit in the processes of her or his own subjectification. Despite this pessimism, he nonetheless makes a strong claim in the tradition of Socrates and Plato for the positive ethical importance of self-care and self-knowledge. Foucault (1988) says: "A city in which everyone would be correctly concerned for self would be a city that would be doing well, and it would find therein the ethical principle of its stability" (p. 7). Even though self-care and self-knowledge operate in the services of our own subjugation, and perpetually bear witness to our capacity to internalize the panoptical mechanisms of surveillance, there is a moment at which he illustrates the positive ethical character of these practices.

The most important aspect of his version of self-care and self-knowledge is also consistent with an ethical orientation to the Other. Self-care and self-knowledge is not antithetical to the care of others, at least within the context of its meaning in the Greek tradition, but rather the precondition of it. He claims "the one who cared for himself correctly found himself, by that very fact, in a measure to behave correctly in relationship to others and for others" (Foucault, 1988, p. 7). He claims that self-care and care for the Other only became disarticulated in the Christian tradition which paradoxically embraced both the ethic of self-care and self-renunciation. Although Foucault argues strongly for the understanding of self- care and self-knowledge in the Greek tradition, he illustrates that not all versions of "self-care," "self-knowledge" are ethical. Similarly, what one might call "liberation" is not in itself oriented toward the other. In his words, "is it obvious that in liberating one's desires one will know how to behave ethically in pleasurable relationships with others?" (p. 4).

The holistic health injunction to "care for thyself" embodied in its emphasis on "wellness," on healing, and the self-help therapy injunction to "know thyself" can become purely narcissistic rather than oriented toward an ethical relationship to the Other, and therefore not intrinsically ethical in the positive sense. However, other aspects of the New Age such as environmentalism that often accompany and intersect with holistic health and self-help thinking illustrate a move toward an Aristotelian notion of virtue in its attempt to establish a principled relationship to the environment. New Age environmentalism has several points of origin. For instance, Schumacher's (1974) book *Small is Beautiful: A Study of Economics as if People Mattered* marked the popularization of a New Age environmental consciousness. In this book, Schumacher claims to examine "what economic laws and what definitions of the concepts 'economic' and 'uneconomic' result when the metaeconomic basis of western materialism is abandoned and the teaching of Buddhism is put in its place" (p. 43). Similarly, Norwegian philosopher Arne Naess' claim that "nature should be valued for its own sake and not according to its utility value" (Heelas, 1996, p. 85) has been appropriated by New Age holistic health and self-help therapy and reintegrated into a cosmology of Deep Ecology that holds that "those who experience themselves as Self-actualised come to experience nature as part of an interconnected whole and value it accordingly" (p. 85). Furthermore, radical or feminist writings such as those by Daly (1979) that argue for the connectedness of a feminine consciousness to nature and the capacity of this consciousness to challenge patriarchal, destructive aspects of modernity that have harmed the earth have been influential in a strain of environmentalism called "eco- feminism" as well. In Daly's words:

> Gyn/Ecology . . . is about discovering, developing, the complex web of living/ loving relationships of our own kind. It is about women living, loving, creating our Selves, our cosmos. It is dispossessing our Selves, hearing the call of the wild, naming our wisdom, spinning and weaving world tapestries. (p. 10)

What these somewhat diverse environmentalist discourses of metaeconomics, deep ecology, and eco-feminism share in common is the claim that this notion of care for the self and care for the other can be reunited through an "environmental consciousness." On the positive side, such thinking has played a positive role in encouraging some internalization of environmental ethics into corporate thinking, and encouraging what Gerzon (1977) calls "the new entrepreneurs" (p. 1) such as Loblaws in Canada, or the international chain The Body Shop who have made efforts to minimise harm to the environment, to improve energy efficiency, and to avoid animal testing. However, on the negative side, New Age environmentalism very often overemphasises an abstract essentialist "ecological consciousness" at the expense of practical solutions, a consciousness that is furthermore entrapped in a set of binary dualisms that continually opposes the feminine, the peaceful, the natural or the "good" with the masculine, the war-like, the civilized or the "bad." However, as feminists have recognized, consciousness is the first stage of transformation: Such abstract, dualistic, essentialist versions of the relationship between humans and nature have still managed to persuade many people toward political action.

For instance, there is a clear commonality between the rhetoric of New Age environmentalism and the more politically active wing of the Greens. Green political thought in Germany, Britain, and America clearly transcends the abstract rhetoric of consciousness characteristic of much New Age Environmentalism insofar as it advocates concrete political strategies to combat the global crisis, However, the Greens are still guilty of operating on the basis of conceptual dualisms similar to the New Age. In their book *Green Politics: The Global Promise* spokespeople Capra and Spretnak try to articulate a manifesto for the Green movement in terms of how it encapsulates a "new paradigm":

> It is an ecological, holistic, and feminist movement that transcends the old political framework of left versus right. It emphasises the interconnectedness and interdependence of all phenomena, as well as the embeddedness of individuals and societies in the cyclical processes of nature. It addresses the unjust and destructive dynamics of patriarchy. It calls for social responsibility and a sound, sustainable economic system, one that is ecological, decentralised, equitable, and comprised of flexible institutions, one in which people have significant control over their lives. In advocating a co-operative world order, Green politics rejects all forms of exploitation—of nature, individuals, social groups, and countries. It is committed to non-violence at all levels. It encourages a rich cultural life that respects the pluralism within a society, and it honours the inner growth that leads to wisdom and compassion. Green politics, in short, is the political manifestation of the cultural shift to the new paradigm. (pp. xix-xx)

Although these simple dichotomies could of course be intended purely rhetorically, that is, to enhance the persuasive power of the document, this aspect of the Green's thinking seems to presume a strong and clear distinction between what is destructive, exploitative, and centralized, and what is cooperative, flexible, and nonviolent. It also presumes a "top–down" notion of power whereby a unified party or mobilized resistance is necessary to counteract the ill effects of postindustrial society. Although this Green version of power and resistance is crucial in the struggle to make environmental concerns an aspect of political action within the structure of participatory democracy and formal party politics, such a discussion lies outside the concerns of this chapter. What I emphasize rather is the extent to which this "top–down," party politics notion of power that clearly juxtaposes the violent, patriarchal, and exploitative aspects of industrial society with the nonviolent, feminist, and communitarian aspects of its Green politics is not the only model of power and resistance available to those concerned with the environment. Rather, there are forms of New Age environmental resistance that are more in line with Foucault's concern with the micropolitics of struggle, and his emphasis on the contextual, subtle, and multiple dimensions of power.

In contrast to Marxist and Green politics that tend to locate power in a central point (the state, the entrepreneur, the industrialist) and to focus on large-scale resistances or "revolutions," Foucault (1980) sees both power and resistance as operant through a "number of centres and mechanisms" (p. 217). In this version, neither power nor resistance arise from a single point, but rather involve a "multiplicity of force relations, the interplay of various discursive fields with their immanent necessities and developments" (Martin, cited in Diamond & Quinby, 1988, p. 212). This micropolitics of power suggests a mode of resistance substantially more personal and subtle than the Marxist version.

THE POLITICAL ECONOMY OF NEW AGE TRAVELLERS: LIVING OFF MODERNITY'S EXCESS AS AN ENVIRONMENTAL ETHIC

As well as my research conducted in Canada, specifically metropolitan Toronto, I have also had the opportunity of experiencing New Age culture in Ireland. Approaching this movement from these two very diverse contexts provides two contrasting vantage points from which to look at the New Age. It is not my intention to comment at length about the cultural differences between Canada and Ireland. Rather, my use of two different settings was intended to look at the particular forms this movement takes in two very different contexts. Nonetheless, examining the New Age in Canada and in Ireland means taking into consideration substantial differences between these two cultures. For instance, Canada is a relatively "new" country, whereas Ireland has a long history and tradition. Canada is a relative heterogeneous nation, whereas Ireland is quite homogeneous. Canada as a developed "first world nation" would be located firmly in the center according to the core–periphery model of development theory, whereas Ireland's level of modernization is slightly more ambiguous, generally being called by Irish scholars a "late industrialising peripheral economy" (Mahon, 1994), despite its recent emergence on the world economic scene as a "Celtic Tiger." Conceived as a "cultural mosaic," the symbolic order of Canadian identity is based on indeterminacy, openness. In contrast, Irish identity is strongly associated with Irish language, literature, and music, sites at which the Irish can assert their particularity as a form of resistance to both British colonialism and to the homogenizing possibilities of both European and American popular culture.

In the New Age discourse of both these cultures, much of the New Age perceives itself as recuperating "folk knowledges" that were lost, forgotten, or distorted through modernization. In both Canada and Ireland, there are aspects of this movement that involve a New Age colonizer and the colonized "Other" whose folk knowledges the New Age is trying to recover. For instance, in the Canadian New Age, First Nations music, paintings, clothing, dance, and culture figure centrally. New Age shamanism in Canada, is an example of the appropriation of First Nations music, culture, and philosophy by Canadians who are often descendants of European settlers, or "White." In Ireland, Irish people often find themselves the target of an enthusiastic but misguided New Age "Celtophilia" by British, North Americans, and Germans in search of authenticity. Such cultural colonization not only involves a very exploitative and problematic appropriation of certain aspects of an "Other's" history or culture and a reinscription (and often commodification) into another context for which they were never intended, but also allows the colonizer to speak for the colonized, and to recreate and caricature the colonised in whatever image they desire.

Despite these differences regarding how these two nations experience the New Age movement, between these two nations, the high visibility of the New Age movement is shared in common. Like Canada, Ireland has a large number of holistic health, and counseling services available, as well as many environmental animal rights, and alternative religions groups. The *Alternative Ireland Directory* lists holistic health therapies ranging from acupuncture, Chinese medicine, homeopathy, herbal medicine, reflexology, therapeutic massage and counseling available in most of the 32 counties, and in both the larger cities and the smaller rural areas. Ireland also has several communities who practice a range of "alternative spiritualities" such as Tibetan Buddhism, Japanese Zen Buddhism, Vipassana meditation, as well as more esoteric, multidenominational centers such as Lomanlu Centre for Healing and Creative living, the Lios Dana Natural Living Centre, the Fellowship of Isis, and the Amethyst Resource for Human Development, all located in relatively small towns in counties Kerry, Wexford, Wicklow, and Cork. There are also many environmental groups such as Friends of the Earth Ireland (Earthwatch), Greenpeace, ECO, Environment Link, and others. It also has many types of counselling and therapy available such as hypnotherapy, Gestalt, and addiction therapy.

However, whereas my New Age observations in the Annex and in Yorkville were largely examples of practices engaged in by what Heelas (1996) calls "New Age Yuppies" (p. 2), a phenomenon relatively unique to Ireland is the large numbers of English New Age Travellers. These New Age Travellers in the words of McKay (1996), are the "gloriously downmarket end of the commodification spectrum" of the New Age (p. 51). New Age Yuppies treat the New Age as a leisure activity, a commodity, and tend not to look at the contradictions between their way of life and their beliefs. In contrast, New Age Travellers see New Age as a total way of life that requires commitment, discipline, and at times asceticism. Whereas for New Age Yuppies, the New Age can in some ways be seen as yet another dimensions of a lifestyle organized around conspicuous consumption, for New Age Travellers, the New Age is integrated into their lifestyle organized around anti-consumerism.

NEW AGE TRAVELLERS IN IRELAND

When I first moved to Ireland I was struck by the large number and high visibility of people called New Age Travellers in the city streets and in travelling encampments around the country. Unable to accept the settled or sedentary way of life in cities and towns of Britain, these young men and women have taken to the roads of Britain, and more recently Ireland, travelling often in convoys of converted vehicles. This lifestyle originated during the free festivals in Britain in the 1960s, and is thus strongly associated with hippy counterculture, but also is derived from the traditional gypsy or Traveller way of life (Hetherington, 1996; McKay, 1996). The New Age Travellers in Ireland and in England has been becoming more numerous in numbers, and more visible in recent years, with an estimated 100,000 now living in Britain (Hetherington, 1996).

Although they are associated with hippy counterculture and with the gypsy way of life, New Age Travellers have an extremely diverse and eclectic set of countercultural beliefs and philosophies from which they derive their lifestyle. For instance, many Travellers adopt a style that is an often bizarre and sometimes colourful amalgamation of various countercultures in the past 40 years including from hippie 1960s, punk 1970s, grunge 1980s, and rave 1990s. The hippy and punk influences are perhaps most apparent in the combinations of tie-dye and army fatigues, denim and leather, beads and studs, flowing locks springing up Mohawk-style from shaved heads, flowery dresses and army boots, love beads and pierced eyebrows. However, New Age Travellers also show traces of grunge, wearing bright striped jumpers over waif-like figures, wrinkled, loose-fitting Kurt Cobain-style sweaters in dull collars, faded, second-hand shop jackets with 1970s and 1980s cuts. The odd, and more likely younger Traveller will wear black and white Adidas sweat pants considered to be rave gear because, I have been told, they are suitable for extended periods of dancing, and provide a "trippy" color contrast under the laser lights. Although there is a high premium placed on how innovatively and creatively these styles are put together, there is an even higher emphasis of economy, because most Travellers are not engaged in the formal economy: Most styles come from bargain basements, secondhand shops, and rubbish bins: The cheaper the outfit, the more highly esteemed the wearer.

However, this strong affiliation with the various youth subcultures in the last 40 years is strongly cross-cut with a commitment to many aspects of New Age thought. Heelas (1996) claimed "There might well be a sense in which these travellers are 'New Age'—namely that they are seeking an alternative way of life—but few would appear to be committed to the spiritual quest within" (p. 17). However, both the centrality of sites like Stonehenge, stone circles, and other ancient or pagan sites to New Age Traveller culture, and the commitment of most Travellers to some form of environmentalism, holistic medicine, or self-help therapy proves him wrong. In contrast to Heelas, Hetherington (1996) argues that paganism, mysticism, and other characteristics posed as antithetical to modernity characteristic of the places like Stonehenge are in fact central to New Age Traveller identity. Travellers imaginatively combined the styles and the ideas of youth subcultures with New Age ideas drawing on sources as diverse as "hippy and punk youth cultures, eastern mysticism, Native American traditions, environmental and pacifist beliefs, the Diggers and the Levellers, Anarchism, Gypsy lifestyles, communal living, Celtic Paganism, and Earth Mysteries beliefs" (p. 42).

One of the characteristics that unifies the diverse New Age Traveller community and sets them apart from the broader community is their attitude and relationship to the formal economy. Although some New Age Travellers work for wages or even own small businesses, work within an informal economy (such as the LETS program in which skills are traded), or operate on an alternative economy (i.e., vending, juggling), many subsist by collecting the dole. For some, "dropping out" was a response to the meaninglessness they experienced in their previous jobs or professions. For instance, some expressed reluctance to participate in reproducing a system they perceived was based on the exploitative division of labor. Others preferred not to participate in what they perceived as an unethical system designed to create false needs. Still others were disillusioned with the alienation, the lack of autonomy they were given in their jobs or professions where they experienced themselves, literally or otherwise as that of an "appendage to the machine." As I outline here, the reluctance some express toward participation in the formal economy was generally not based on an unreflexive desire to "freeload," but at times a thoughtful, self-reflexive ethical position based on a critique of exploitation, commodity fetishism, and alienation.

Of more than 50 New Age Travellers I interviewed in detail, a minority of them (about 10%) worked for a wage, either permanently or sporadically in mostly shops, restaurants, cafes or pubs. Some of them defined themselves as self-employed, and did odd jobs, carpentry, taught various skills such as languages or music lessons when they could get the work. A larger proportion claimed to be seasonally employed, and relied on the sale of artwork, jewelry, clothing, or other crafts during the tourist season in art fairs. Of these Travellers who did have some sort of engagement in the economy, there was a strong preference for undeclared over declared wages, for self-employment over working for someone else, for part-time, temporary or seasonal employment over permanent employment, or selling wares over hourly wages.

Furthermore, some of the Travellers have a marginal relationship to the formal economy, but a strong relationship to some version of an "alternative" economy. One very interesting example is LETS' attempt to entirely eliminate the commodity form altogether, a system originally developed in Canada. Several Travellers on the Beara Peninsula participated in alternative economy that was not based on a money system but was based on a system of exchange. What is called a LETS scheme (Local Economic Trading System) whereby an estimated 200 participants can work for credit–barter system, administered from an office in Castletownbere, a system that does not interfere with those who wish to sign on the dole. In this system, members exchange services based on a currency called a Hag (after the Hag of Beara), services that range from carpentry, plumbing, child care, Irish and photography classes, to herbalism and holistic healing, all listed in a central Hag directory. This system is a barter economy that replaces government recordkeeping and cash transactions through private record keeping coordinated through the central LETS office, and mediated through Hags rather than pounds. According to the staff at the LETS' office in Castletownbere, the philosophy behind it is based on an ethical, rather than simply an explicitly political economy whereby to keep the "value" of services that have been performed for you on par with the services you provide for others, or to keep your deficit on par with your credit. Members are sent monthly invoices that state which contributors are operating with a deficit or credit. As such, several travellers do participate in an alternative economy. As well as this system on the Beara Peninsula, there are similar schemes in most counties in Ireland, including Cork, Kerry, and Clare.

Often, their participation outside this economy is both substantial and complex. Many also participated in a broad range of activities that may not directly contribute to the formal economy, but contribute tremendously both to the cosmopolitan ethos and alternative sensibility of cities like Galway and fair and festivals all over the country. Some Travellers often made jewelry, crafts, art, music, selling their wares year round in Dublin or Galway, and in the summers in fairs and festivals around the country. Some live off the proceedings of often makeshift sidewalk stalls, braiding hair, selling Celtic, Indian, or other third world jewelry or clothes, or selling paintings, candles, crystals, and other items. Others are in a sense, entertainers for a living, busk, playing music, juggling, breathing fire, walking on stilts, and so on. This community is somewhat integrated into the arts community in Ireland, and as Michael D. Higgins recognized by his official endorsement of the New Age Traveller contribution to the Galway Arts Festival, they bring an air of unconventionality, a challenge to dominant conventions, an alternative spirit that is the lifeblood to artistic subcultures, and one of the less traditional but nonetheless colorful threads in the tapestry of culture that Irish tourism relies on. They may have no discernible relationship to the formal economy, but insofar as their contribution to street culture in the cities, and carnival culture in the country fairs, their contribution is visible and appreciated as an integral part of the myriad of spectacles that are the mainstay of Irish tourism. As such, more in-depth inquiry into the "inner mechanisms" of the New Age Traveller economy reveals it is very complex.

However, most Travellers self-admittedly subsist by drawing the dole, and are condemned on that basis. For instance, in my discussions with some of the non-Travellers in the surrounding areas of Traveller encampments in Dunmanway, Crosshaven, and the Beara Peninsula, many people characterized the Travellers as "leeches," "spongers," "knackers," "parasites," and "vermin." These characterizations were imposed on the basis of a particular moral code where participation in the formal economy through farming, wage labor, or (if unemployed) the active pursuit of wage labor is seen as a moral obligation to one's community, and failure to do so is evidence of a lack of discipline, or moral fiber. This tendency to view participation in the formal economy as the only significant type of labor is reminiscent of Marx's critique of the non-dialectical character of political economists who also refuse to acknowledge other types of labor. "In political economy labor occurs only in the form of wage-earning activity" (Marx, 1964, p. 72). Any type of labor performed outside of the system of exchange production is invisible, valueless. Thus, to political economists, any one existing system of commodity production, anyone engaging in work outside the formal economy was invisible, and hence did not exist. In Marx's (1964) words:

> Political economy thus does not recognise the unemployed worker, the working-man so far as he is outside this work relationship. Thieves, tricksters, beggars, the unemployed, the starving, wretched and

> criminal working man, are forms which do not exist for political economy, but only for other eyes, for doctors, judges, grave-diggers and beadles, etc.: they are ghostly figures outside its domain. (p. 72)

As such, Marx's critique of the field of political economy is based on its tendency to view the real objects of analysis, humans, as peripheral to the operations of the market.

This anxiety is somewhat understandable in Ireland because of the relatively undeveloped economy and high rates of unemployment. However, this characterization of Travellers as "parasites" reflects a familiar New Right ideology in Britain and North America until the mid-1990s—the idea that if an adequate social welfare system or unemployment scheme is provided, or if immigration laws are relaxed, most will "abuse the system" in this parasitic fashion.

Although participation in the formal economy is to many a symbol of adulthood, of integration into the community, of one's fulfillment of a moral obligation to the collective, to the Travellers it is often a symbol of submission. For instance, many refuse to "work" in the sense of participation in the formal economy, because they feel they would be complicit in a system that perpetuates their own exploitation. Such claims at times resemble Marx's critique of political economy whereby he claims that one of the paradoxes of the capitalist system is that the worker's participation in wage labor results in the devaluation, and commodification of her or his own labor, and hence themselves. He says:

> On the basis of political economy itself, in its own words, we have shown that the worker sinks to the level of a commodity and becomes indeed the most wretched of commodities; that the wretchedness of the worker is in inverse proportion to the power and magnitude of his production; that the necessary result of competition is the accumulation of capital in a few hands, and thus the restoration of monopoly in a more terrible form; and that finally the distinction between capitalist and land renter, like that between the tiller of the soil and the factory worker, disappears, and that the whole of society must fall apart into the two classes—the property owners and the propertyless workers. (p. 106)

Marx's primary critique of commodity production then, is based on the devaluation of the worker relative to the objects he produces. "The worker becomes an ever cheaper commodity the more goods he creates. The devaluation of the human world increases in direct relation with the increase in value of the world of things" (Giddens, 1971, p. 121). Thus, the paradox of capitalism is that the more capitalism advances, the more impoverished the worker becomes. This impoverishment, however, is not simply in terms of the worker's material conditions, but rather in a spiritual sense.

Other Travellers advanced a critique of the division of labor under capitalism that ensured that certain people did the socially necessary labor in society, whereas others accrued the surplus accumulated by that labor, a critique that again resembles Marx's argument regarding the labor theory of value. As one Traveller from Newcastle put it, "I woke up one day and realised I had worked 14 hour days for sixteen years selling time share vacations in order that someone else could get rich." Others claimed that they felt themselves dehumanised by the work they used to do, and that their own "productivity" was seen as much more important than their "humanity."

Although these Travellers were not referring explicitly to Marx, what they articulated, with varying degrees of coherence was a Marxist critique of the alienating conditions of the capitalist division of labor. Although the objectification of the worker is a necessary characteristic of all work according to Marx, this objectification takes on a specific, distorted form under capitalism whereby the worker is unable to realize himself or his species being in the labor process, or in the product he produces. To Marx, the relationship between the worker and the object he produces always involves a process of objectification, whereby in modifying the world of nature, the worker interacts with the external world in creating a product that comes to stand outside him. However, under capitalism, this process of objectification becomes distorted in that the worker becomes subordinated, negated, in favor of the object; the process of production, objectification, thus takes the form of "a loss and servitude to the object"; the worker "becomes a slave to the object" (Marx 1964, pp. 122-123). The material objects the worker produces come to be treated as more important than him or herself.

It is this inversion of the relation between subject and object, between producer and product, that forms the basis of Marx's critique of alienation. In his critique of religion (derived from Feuerbach), he describes how the qualities attributed to God in Christianity come to take on an agency themselves whereby they appear imposed by another agency. Similarly, the product of the worker under capitalism becomes "alien to him and . . . stands opposed to him as an autonomous power. The life which he has given to the object sets itself against him as an alien and hostile force" (Marx, 1964, p. 123). Moreover, this process of alienation has a significance that goes far beyond merely signifying his oppression. Rather, this process degrades the very thing that separates us from animals; dehumanizes us, degrades us to the depths of our souls. To him, this subordination to the object destroys man's spiritual life, and serves, in Marx's words, to "mutilate the worker into a fragment of a man, degrade him to the level of an appendage of a machine, destroy the content of work by his agony, and alienate him from the spiritual potentialities of the labour process" (Marx, cited in Giddens, 1971, p. 57).

Marx's theory of alienation is based on a conception of the centrality of labor in realizing our humanness, or our "species being." In this view, political economists, in their advocacy of private property and wage labor, are advocating processes that deny rather than recognize our humanity:

> under the semblance of recognising man, political economy, whose principle is labour, rather carries to its logical conclusion the denial of man, since man himself no longer stand in an external relation of tension to the external substance of private property. What was previously being external to oneself—man's externalisation in the thing—has merely become the act of externalising—the process of alienating. (Marx, 1964, p. 129)

The New Age Travellers seemed to espouse a critique of participation in the formal economy that was based on such a critique of capitalism. Although none made references to Marx or other philosophers or political economists, and spoke of their position using the rhetoric of "common sense," many did use Marxist terms such as *alienation*, *dehumanization*, and so on. In this way, their nonparticipation in the formal economy was not out of "laziness," but rather was a part of a well thought-out ethical stance. Furthermore, life in the countryside with no modern conveniences is hardly a life of luxury: As one Traveller living in an abandoned house on the Beara Peninsula put it, "They hate us because we don't work, but I work all the time to stay dry, warm and fed. They think we are lazy, but do you think it is easy to live this way?" Another Traveller who rents a shack with a few conveniences set me straight when I asked what he did with his extra time. "What do you mean extra time?" He said. "I'm up early every day. I pick herbs, flowers, berries, I cook everything I eat myself, and make jewelry to sell in the summer. There isn't any extra time left." Another self-proclaimed "surfer Traveller" from Lahinch who lived a much less minimalist life had a more hedonist view of work claiming "I work all the time, but just not at one particular thing—writing songs, playing guitar, organizing dance parties. What I do I do well—I just don't get paid for it." What these accounts share in common is their rejection of a compartmentalized notion of a profession or occupation, and a commitment to a non-reductionist version of work that associates it with pleasure and agency rather than duty.

Some Travellers had an explicit critique of the narrow version of "skill" the modern organization of production allows, as well as the division between mental and manual labor. For instance, many claimed they moved to the country to develop a broader array of skills than they could in the city engaged in wage labor. Many took pride in acquiring a broad number of skills such as carpentry, cookery, efficient fire lighting, the mechanics of rain-proof housing, skills that are not just an option in the country, but rather are crucial to long-term survival. In this sense, they were refusing to conceive of "skill" and "work" in the narrowly defined, dehumanizing terms dictated by the highly specialized division of labour characteristic of capitalism. In *The German Ideology* Marx writes:

> For as soon as the division of labour begins to come into being, each man has a particular, exclusive sphere of activity, which is forced upon him and from which he cannot escape. He is a hunter, a fisherman, a shepherd, or a critical critic, and must remain so if he does not want to lose his means of livelihood.

As well, they were implicitly challenging the division between mental and manual labor characteristic of capitalism. Many claimed that various forms of mental labor were also a strong aspect of their identity: reading, writing, creating, painting. However, they deliberately chose a lifestyle that does not allow them to escape responsibility for their day-to-day bodily needs. In a sense then, they refuse to disembody the mental laborer, to glorify or pamper the artist, the writer, the musician, to artificially divide mental and manual labour. Most importantly, perhaps, these Travellers were attempting to resist the narrow division of labor under a capitalist organisation of production and to engage in the active self-construction of "well-rounded" selves, striving to be "jack-of-all-trades." As well as feeding and clothing herself and her two children in her ambulance with no electricity, heat, or running water, one Traveller, for instance, picked herbs, did carpentry, was a mechanic, cared for a horse, two dogs, and many other assorted injured animals she was rehabilitating, made jewelry, and did some writing. Such an effort at self-creation is more in line with Marxist vision of the division of labor under Communism:

> in communist society, where nobody has one exclusive sphere of activity but each can be accomplished in any branch he wishes, society regulated in the general production and thus makes it possible for one to do one thing today and another tomorrow, to hunt in the morning, fish in the afternoon, rear cattle in the evening, criticise after dinner, just as I have a mind, without ever becoming hunter, fisherman, shepherd, or critic. (Marx, 1965, p. 45)

In this fashion, the New Age Traveller advocacy of a lifestyle on the periphery of the formal economy is not based on a "lazy," or "parasitic" ethos, but rather is an attempt to pursue a non-alienated life. It is also an attempt to conceive of work as a more poetic and creative endeavor than that imposed by the formal economy. But what I hope to show here is that the Traveller lifestyle is not entirely based on self-concern, but rather also on a strong ethical concern with the other that is most clearly illustrated in my case study of a Travelling encampment on a place called Cúl Mountain, known locally as "Cool Mountain." This translation from the Irish spelling to hippie vernacular is perhaps reflective of a tendency in the New Age movement.

This example will illustrate that although on one level, the New Age Travellers are not "productive" in terms of their relationship to the formal economy, on another level, they are very productive in terms of their relationship to the global economy. Although Travellers do not "work," they are committed to subsisting purely on the refuse, the leftover, the garbage, the excess of modernity, to making the unproductive productive, the unusable usable, and see recycling rather than "working" as the basis of their moral economy and of their assessment of personal skill. For instance, New Age Travellers pride themselves on their capacity to recover a "use value" out of objects perceived to be superfluous—fixing vehicles given up as useless, retrieving thrown-out tablecloths for clothes, and junked appliances for furniture. In one way, the New Age Traveller economy can be seen as a much more imaginative form of productivity than participation in the local economy, which the locals are condemning them for not doing.

However, what this example will show is that the New Age Traveller ethic of living off the waste of modernity can be seen as a much more principled relationship to the environment than middle-class environmentalists who "think green," recycle, and buy biodegradable products, and can be seen as having a much more symbolically complex orientation to the economy than conventional environmental politics. It illustrates what Foucault would see as an ethical orientation to the "Other." Thus, unlike many of the practices involved in New Age environmentalism that reduce environmentalism to "consciousness," or "buying green," this New Age Traveller lifestyle is intended to make the commitment to environmentalism into a way of life rather than simply a commodified leisure activity. From this point of view, New Age Travellers are very "productive" in terms of their relationship to the global economy, in the sense that they monitor their own consumption and live off that of others. Their lifestyle shows us the extent to which production and consumption are artificially dichotomized in the modern world.

BETWEEN THE MOUNTAINTOP AND THE MARKETPLACE: NEW AGE TRAVELLERS IN IRELAND

In my research in Ireland, I have spoken with New Age Travellers in Crosshaven, Cork city, the Beara Peninsula, and Dunmanway, in order to determine how these communities could be perceived as symptoms of the crisis of community, and the crisis of meaning that some theorists claim characterize contemporary society. Because of its reputation in New Age Traveller circles as a desirable destination, I focused particularly on the community in Cool Mountain in the Bantry/ Dunmanway area in order to see precisely how this community negotiated this tension between unity and difference, between shared common values and internal diversity that theorists such as Young claim characterize contemporary communities.

Like other communities, the Cool Mountain community is characterized by internal divisions, conflicts, and antagonisms, largely focused around the issue of how to synchronise individual conduct and collective welfare. This conflict expressed itself in the formation of three different geographically distinct divisions within this community based on different opinions regarding what constituted an alternative lifestyle. First, the "bogfield" community located several kilometres away from the mountain that was where new initiates began their experience as Travellers. Second, the foot of the mountain, where initiates could settle if they "graduated" from the initiate community and established their credentials to those on the mountain. If accepted by the community, they then had the option of moving up toward the top of the mountain to the more "communitarian" group. The differential ethics of these three grades were expressed in a different type of housing: the bogfielders lived mostly in caravans and were more mobile and temporary; the foot-of-the-mountaineers were much more sparse, eclectic, and functional in their choice of habitat, living in rusty lean-tos, caves, wigwams, abandoned vans, and self-made shacks; and the mountain-siders whose elaborate gardens, greenhouses, windmills, manicured sod roofs marked them as more overtly and conventionally "green." Despite their shared commitment to a particular lifestyle, this community is very diverse. Thus, the New Age Traveller community is an expression of these tendencies between diversity and identity evident in local, national, and global experiences of community today, and as such can be seen as a microcosm of these tendencies.

As well, these three distinct groups exhibited varying degrees of commitment to a collectivist ethos and an ideal of community involvement that characterizes conventional politics of the left. In terms of their relationship to a community ethos, the more transient bogfielders were relatively peripheral to the Cool Mountain community, because most bogfielders either went back to where they came from, left Cool Mountain to live in other New Age Traveller caravan sites, or began their ascent, so to speak, up the mountain as members of the more permanent community. As such, the name new age traveller is a misnomer, because it only really applies to the transient bogfielders. In contrast, the mountain community call themselves "settlers," perhaps revealing a utopian desire to break ground on a "new frontier." Of the more permanent mountain community, several community members who tended to live near the top of the mountain worked arduously at organizing several community projects such as the running of the community center and restaurant, youth groups, various art, craft, and educational classes, and supply runs, often canvassing the others to elicit volunteers.

Others who tended to live near the bottom of the mountain by the side of the road experienced these attempts as overly totalitarian, an infringement on their autonomy they were trying valiantly to maintain, and thus, as an uncomfortable reminder of the overregulated life they had hoped to leave behind. Thus, the strongest division amongst the "settlers" was regarding tension between the communitarians and the more libertarian mountaineers, which expressed itself in a mutual antagonism regarding their respective versions of community—the communitarians felt that the libertarians were apathetic and not appropriately civic-minded, and the libertarians felt that the communitarians were imposing unnecessary conventions, and thus, merely paying lip service to getting away from suburban values of conformity.

However, despite these ideological and geographically observable differences, what bound these somewhat disparate communities together, what the New Age Traveller sought in the Cool Mountain lifestyle, was the freedom to pursue their own life in conditions of their own choosing. The theme of recovery often recurred in my discussions with this community. Although some of the Travellers I met were German, Dutch, French, Spanish, or American, most of them were English, self-proclaimed refugees from Thatcher's Britain, and perceived the possibilities for self-determination as much greater living on the side of a mountain in Ireland in a lean-to than in a council flat in Britain.

Others chose life on the mountain to find a quiet space to "recover" from city life, having suffered some sort of personal crisis, trauma, or assault immediately prior to moving to Cool Mountain. Furthermore, they were quick to dismiss the idea they were engaged in some pursuit of the "common" good, or "higher purpose" and were cynical regarding the notion of an "alternative" lifestyle, claiming, "we are all just getting on with it really." Thus, most exhibited a skepticism toward the possibilities of community in effecting some sort of social change or transformation in the broader society. Thus, what was expressed was not so much the desire for the recovery of some sort of agrarian idyllic, mythical past, a mechanical solidarity, a *Gemeinschaft* community, but rather the recovery of some sort of agency, to the right to self-determination that they felt had been eroded through the combined effects of the dismantling of the welfare state, the introduction of the public order acts in Britain, and the excesses of modern life. In a sense, they were refugees from modernity, from the increasing complexity and erosion of personal freedoms that characterizes modern cosmopolitan existence.

This New Age community also expressed a strong ambivalence toward their retreat to the mountain. Most made no claims to seeing themselves as gurus or role models for how to organise an alternative community, or made any pretense of moral superiority. Unlike Neitzsche's prophet Zarathustra, who advises his friend to flee up the mountain into solitude to escape the "poisonous flies" and the "solemn buffoons" of the marketplace, these mountain dwellers did not feel antagonistic toward or superior to the local farmers and members of the surrounding community. Despite their desire for solitude, they were not separatist in orientation. Most were friendly, if noncommittal to me when conducting my research, several had children in the local school, and most had amicable, if minimal relations with local farmers. Neither did they imagine that their mountain dwelling solitude was preparing them to be prophets of the people or philosopher kings. Rather, several were self-mocking, quick to condemn their "escapism" from "reality," and felt torn between the life they had carved out for themselves on the mountain and the lives they had left behind, ambivalent about staying, ambivalent about returning. In a sense, they were caught between their previous homes and the mountain, between two worlds, and were aware that their "escape" was only illusory, temporary, and that there is really no refuge, no utopia, no place outside the social, outside of the complexity and fragmentation of modernity in which to heal.

Nonetheless, New Age Travellers are often criticized by the broader community for their lack of participation in the formal economy. In my experience, New Age Travellers have been characterized as "parasites" and "freeloaders," as "wasters" and as "knackers." This anxiety expresses a very legitimate concern that the already overstretched welfare state cannot withstand more strain. However, the vehemence with which some of these negative sentiments are expressed would indicate that New Age Travellers are sometimes feared and disliked not because of the potential drain on the welfare state, but because of the possibility that they will further destabilize traditional values already eroded by modernity. In a sense then, some of the critiques of their potential drain on the welfare state are merely give a rational, economic veneer to a more generalized fear of difference, change, and diversity.

From this point of view, Travellers are not necessarily consumptive, hedonistic, freeloaders "living off the dole," but rather have attempted to live off the waste of others, to establish a principled relationship to the global community, an awareness of the complex and abstract political economy of modernity in a broader sense, an environmental ethic at a complex level that more abstract versions of New Age Environmentalism that focus on developing an environmental "consciousness." By living off the garbage heap, they are inverting the structure of modernity that would designate themselves as welfare recipients, as useless, unproductive, as waste products themselves.

In a sense, their choice to live long term in temporary dwellings is a literal expression of this identity crisis, of what Lucaks (1971) calls "transcendental homelessness," a condition of modernity whereby we want to recreate our origins, to rewrite or rediscover our roots, yet know this cannot be done. To Lucaks, this transcendental homelessness emerges out of the tenuousness of identity, the experience of identity as "kaleidoscopic and changeable" "nefarious and evasive," and hence is a symptom of the postmodern skepticism toward origin myths and skepticism toward the dissolution of grand narratives. In the words of Lucaks, we are both "secular, but yearning for the sacred, ironic, but yearning for the absolute, individualistic, but yearning for the wholeness of community, fragmented, but yearning for imminent totality" (p. 189).

This ambivalence towards utopias, this appreciation of paradox, this tolerance of contradiction was itself the basis of the production of meaning in the lives of the Cool Mountain residents. For example, they found humor in the discrepancy between the highly specialized, responsible positions many of them had previously held (engineer, teacher, computer scientist) and the mundane nature of their current struggle to stay dry, warm, and fed. Several had self-consciously and ironically fashioned habitats for themselves that were emblems of those very aspects of modernity they were anxious to escape, and that were seriously at odds ideologically with the lifestyle they had produced: an old ambulance, a tourist information booth. To interpret this merely as an aesthetic gesture or as postmodern pastiche, however, is to miss the political economy of the Travellers; for this recycling of the artefacts of modernity has a much more central significance to the Traveller lifestyle than this.

However, subsisting purely on the waste of modernity was what gave New Age Traveller's lives meaning, what they prided themselves on, the focus of their creative and aesthetic sensibilities, their definition of skill, and what unified them as a community. Making the productive unproductive, the unusable usable was the basis of their shared relationship to the environment and their role in the political economy of modernity. For example, they would diligently scour dumps for material for housing, clothes, furniture, and anything that could be recycled, a practice they called "seagulling." Supermarket rubbish bins were routinely searched for bags of thrown-out food, although apparently some had taken up the practice of dying food unpalatable colors such as blue to discourage this practice. To New Agers, the challenge of mountain life is based on refining one's skill, regarding how to create a use value out of what is abandoned, thrown out. Who is designated an informal community leader is often dependent not on sociability, intelligence, or other abstract values, but rather on who is most accomplished at this process. As such, the New Age Travellers are not consumptive, hedonistic, freeloaders, "wasters," "living off" the dole, as they are sometimes characterized, but are attempting to establish a principled relationship to the global community and to the political economy of modernity.

Thus, the simultaneous unity and division within the New Age Traveller community in Ireland is illustrative of the tensions between difference and identity, between the need for the tolerance of heterogeneity, and the necessity for some common "unifying principle" that characterize the contemporary "crisis of community." These tensions have emerged historically from the process of social differentiation imposed by the increasing heterogeneity of modernity, the increasing fragmentation of the social along the lines of class, race, ethnicity, gender, and whole other ranges of "differences" currently under discussion in debates and struggles around the politics of representation. Feminists, postcolonialists, and other Others have shown how unitary, essentialist versions of community can be experienced as totalitarian by voices from the margins. However, this politics of difference, this recognition of the heterogeneity of community, this sensitivity to voices from the margins has caused a crisis of community, insofar as in our scramble to accommodate difference, what binds us together, what constitutes us as a community at a neighborhood, a local, or any other level of abstraction, is increasingly elusive. In short, we can no longer locate a notion of "the common good." As such, the challenge to contemporary communities, is, according to Hegel, to "cancel the opposition but preserve the difference".

However, the New Age Traveller community is unified in its commitment to the possibility of some sort of utopian imaginary. These travellers are unified in their shared experience of living the tension between the "is" and the "ought", experiencing the paradox of life midway between, in Nietzsche's words, the market and the mountaintop. The disparate factions of this community are not, however, unified in their capacity to successfully negotiate this tension. The Bogfielders, as the most recent and traumatised refugees of Thatcher's Britain, live perhaps a little too close to the marketplace, and are in a sense, "damaged goods." Their more frequent crises, their higher rate of substance abuse (or so it appeared from my discussions with a group of extremely friendly but troubled core bogfielder group who would often get themselves into a state of obvious intoxication on weekends in the local pubs) indicates they are still inextricably bound up in the excesses of modernity they hoped to escape. The mountaintoppers are perhaps a little intoxicated by the possibilities of reconstructing an alternative community in their own image, and perhaps it was a reflection of their own somewhat authoritarian tendencies that they chose to live on the top of the mountain.

In conclusion, the New Age Travellers are united in their search for meaning that Jameson and others claim characterizes postmodernity.

They attempt to preserve, in the face of overwhelming resistance, the utopian possibilities of some sort of ethical life based on a new relationship to the land, a broader notion of ecology, of the global community than that which characterizes the political economy of "normal life," or even a conventional environmental politics. The collapse of the range of utopian possibilities, however, to the refining their skill at living off this waste is perhaps indicative of the extent to which the realm of possibilities for the pursuit of an ethical life narrowed in contemporary life, to a postmodern "politics of the local." In the words of Hegel (1967), "By the little that now Satisfies the Spirit, we can measure the extent of its loss" (Hegel, 1977, p. 110).

NEW AGE ENVIRONMENTALISM AS A WAY OF LIFE

Undoubtedly, the New Age movement's orientation to holistic health, self-help therapy, and other "technologies of the self" do contain moments that are individualist, self-preoccupied, and that do espouse self-knowledge as an end in itself. However, aspects of New Age Environmentalism that advocate "Green Consumption" and more "environmentally friendly" forms of industry are most definitely positive developments. Nonetheless, the example of New Age Travellers, the less commodified end of the New Age spectrum, reveals to us that there are other ways of adopting an ethical position to the environment that in many ways transcend most of our capacities to think of how to deal with the environmental crisis. Although not all Travellers who are trying to reject the values of consumer society by living off the waste others are strongly politicised, but all of them have a general notion of the importance of reusing, recycling, and re-invigorating these "dead" objects.

Although the New Age Travellers on Cool Mountain had a strong critique of capitalism and the state, their politics are much more consistent with the Foucauldian "micropolitics of resistance" than a more centralised and state focused Marxist or Green model of political organization. Nonetheless, I have tried to illustrate how this model is effective as well. What New Age Traveller life on Cool Mountain ascribes to is a version of human excellence or of virtue in a classical sense that values frugality over consumerism, control over consumption rather than the Yuppie work ethic, living off waste rather than producing it, and conservation rather than sanitation. More importantly perhaps, this locates the realm of the political in everyday practices rather than simply large-scale political action: an attempt to live a unified life in the face of the inevitable fragmentation of the self that MacIntyre (1981) claims characterizes modernity.

This unusual notion of virtue that characterizes the New Age Traveller community on Cool Mountain is one attempt to live life as a unity, a whole, and to establish an ideal of "the good life" that preoccupies MacIntyre in *After Virtue*. As such, it is a response to what MacIntyre characterizes as "the partitioning of human life into a variety of segments, each with its own norms and modes of behaviour" (p. 190). It is an attempt to construct a moral community in the face of the moral incoherence of contemporary society that MacIntyre attributes to both the failure to recognize that contemporary moral theory is a series of disconnected fragments displaced from their original contexts, and to the moral vacuousness of instrumental rationality.

Despite our best efforts, the centrality of cleanliness and order to the modern psyche that Foucault, Elias, and Bauman point out may mean that our psychological capacity to deal with the disorder that strong versions of environmentalism may require is limited. We have internalized the panoptic imperative to have clean, sanitary, germ-free bodies, kitchens, and houses, all things that require the use of chemicals, the creation of garbage, that no amount of recycling depots, emissions regulations, or green-friendly products can change. Although many may disagree with the New Age Traveller's way of life, at the very least, they present an alternative that seems to elude the reinscription of modes of domination Foucault is so fond of pointing out occurs with any hopes of "liberation." They provide another way of conceiving of a strong, rather than reformist view of an "environmental imaginary."

Four

New Age Travellers in Britain and Ireland: The New Age as Subculture

New Age Travellers are perceived by some as the fringe of the New Age movement, and occupy an interesting position as "the fringe of the fringe." For instance, in his very comprehensive book on the New Age movement, Heelas (1996) claims "There might well be a sense in which these Travellers are 'New Age'—namely that they are seeking an alternative way of life—but few would appear to be committed to the spiritual quest within" (p. 17). In some ways, New Age Travellers have more in common with subcultures of resistance such as punk, grunge, rave, and can thus be seen as the 1990s version of what Hebdige, Hall, and others would see as youth subcultures of resistance rather than as a manifestation of the New Age.

However, in my view, there are three aspects of New Age Travellers that qualify them as "New Age." First, most Travellers are sympathetic to or actively engage in New Age practices such as holistic health, wicca, and paganism, and espouse "alternate" rationalities and "spiritualities." Second, most are strongly influenced in particular by environmental issues and adopt a "deep green" attitude of living lightly on the land by living off the waste of modernity, as illustrated in my case study of Cool Mountain, or living in travelling tipi encampments in Britain (Hetherington, 1996). As Hetherington documents, those who live in travelling encampments have a strong ecological consciousness, and see their lifestyle as "not a dropping out from society, but an alternative way of living more 'naturally'" (p. 41). Third, the identities of New Age Travellers' in both Ireland and Britain are strongly connected to stone circles, Stonehenge, New Grange, and other ancient or pagan sites that are regularly visited during the winter solstice, the spring or autumn equinox, or other times considered by ancient calendars to have spiritual significance.

What I show in this chapter is how New Age Travellers integration of New Age beliefs with subcultural politics of resistance represents the latest, hybrid form of the New Age movement. To presume, as Heelas does, that the New Age is analytically separate from subcultures of resistance is to express that very same fear of hybridity that New Age Traveller life is so anxious to oppose. My argument here is that the New Age Traveller lifestyle is based on a version of micropolitical struggle in the Foucauldian sense, but one that has two dimensions: On one hand, the New Age Traveller way of life is an assertion of resistance to increased legislation and the domestic crisis characteristic of post-Thatcher's Britain. This section makes the claim that the New Age Travellers can be seen as the early 21st-century version of what Hebdige, Hall, and others would see as youth subcultures of resistance rather than in the context of an analysis of the New Age movement. However, on the other hand, the centrality of pilgrimages to "mystical" sites such as Stonehenge to New Age Travellers is a geographical illustration of the more general aspiration of members of the New Age movement: to travel, explore, and journey to other places, spaces, and planes.

I show that the New Age Traveller destabilization of boundaries regarding identity, time, and space illustrated by their embracing of hybridity, their nomadicism, and their search for the marginalized, liminal, or magical space illustrates in an extreme or literal form what the New Age tries to do with ideas: challenge modern ordering of time and space that Foucault argues disciplines and normalizes individual bodies. In fact, I make the claim that because New Age Travellers often "live" the "New Age" in a visceral, material, embodied way, their challenge to the temporal and spatial ordering of modernity by rejecting the modern obsession with sanitation and the modern division of work and leisure, their way of life is even more subversive than more abstract versions of the New Age movement that focus purely on consciousness.

On a much more abstract level, the New Age Traveller invocation of the carnivalesque, of the grotesque, and their search for the marginal space in which they can reimagine the world and their relationship to it represent some of the more subversive elements of the New Age spectrum, and perhaps some of the more imaginative of the New Age attempt to reconceptualize the modern ordering of time and space. Thus, this chapter illustrates how the New Age Travellers' association with the land, their nomadicism, and their search for a "free space" makes them an exemplary, if more persistently hybridized example of the New Age movement.

NEW AGE TRAVELLERS AS REFUGEES FROM A POST-THATCHER BRITAIN

Although New Age Travellers have a strong commitment to the alternative spiritualities, herbal medicine, environmentalism, "alternative rationalities," and other New Age beliefs, this subculture has also been shaped by various economic, political, and legal events in Britain that have, in their perception, driven them out of Britain. For instance, many Travellers moved to Ireland to avoid becoming yet more of Britain's "urban Poor," and moved as a response to various economic crises in Britain that have occurred since the 1970s: to high unemployment rates, to even further cutbacks to the welfare state, to the introduction of Public Order acts, and to the clamp down on squatter's rights. People who were already Travellers moved because of police brutality, and New legislation that requires a place of residence, and to an increase in infringements on civil liberties of squatters, Travellers, and other voluntarily or involuntarily homeless people produced by new legislation. Whatever the reason, most British Travellers characterized themselves as "refugees" from Thatcher's Britain, from the city, and from the values of suburban life.

From this perspective, New Age Travellers are the new incarnation of what Hebdige, Hall, and other members of the Birmingham School would call Britain's youth subcultures of resistance. Hall's general orientation to youth movements such as mods and punks is to locate them in the context of various crises in Britain, particularly its high unemployment rate. He illustrates how the punk movement was an attempt to assert some sort of agency, to achieve some sort of affirmation of their "unemployedness," their "working-classness" (Hall, 1989, p. 2) in the face of soaring unemployment rates and a social system that could promise them no future. Hall emphasizes that much of the political character of punk is politically indeterminate, ideologically contradictory, a sort of a floating, generalized, but nondirected political energy, or prepolitical. However, he also illustrates how overlaying this indeterminacy is a distinct "radical thrust" (p. 2).

Although New Age Travellers used to be predominantly middle class, their class composition is now mixed. As Hetherington (1996) has noted, when this way of life emerged in the mid-1970s, Travellers were from middle-class, sedentary backgrounds. For these people, taking on this New Age Traveller identity involved a self-marginalization, an active choice toward downward mobility. For instance, some Travellers with whom I spoke, like Jane, were "deprofessionalized professionals," gave up desired professions, fed up with the poisoned air in their workplaces, and the lack of greenery in the city. For others, like Joe the ex-salesman, who was tired of working 16 hours a day for somebody else, had less autonomy, but were previously employed.

However, Hetherington (1996) acknowledges "an increasing number of young working-class people started to join the ranks of the New Age Travellers and took to a life on the road, especially during the height of Thatcherism in the late 1980's, with its clampdown on social security payments for young people and Poll Tax demands" (p. 35). Travellers like 32-year-old Joe who was unemployed and virtually homeless in Britain, decided to adopt the New Age Traveller lifestyle because its commitment to nomadism and to an "alternative" version of the economy actually celebrates this status, rather than submitting meekly to it. In Joe's words, to voluntarily choose a life of living in "a permanent recession" was more empowering than being reduced to an object of administration by Britain's welfare state. This could perhaps explain the popularity of the band "The Levellers," perceived by some as the defining spokesband of the New Age Travellers, whose recent album cover bore the subheading "Music for a Jilted Generation."

However, if the New Age Travellers challenge the conventional, the conformist, the mainstream, and are a protest, an alternative, a Refusal, and opposition, what is it they are opposing? As I tried to indicate, some Travellers were able to clearly articulate how their lifestyle was an opposition to what they perceive as a consumerist and environmentally irresponsible lifestyle. Others could only speak vaguely of how they were protesting "mainstream existence," the "status quo," "society," an existence they conceived of as an overarching system, a totalizing force so powerful and so binding that the only escape was through radical self-marginalization. The status of the New Age Traveller as oppositional often relied on a notion of a social totality that must be opposed. As such, some ascribed to a clear opposition between the binary positions of "mainstream" and alternative, center and margin that strongly informed their political identity and self-perception as radical.

Many New Age Travellers' identities were couched in terms of opposition to what they saw as "dominant values" emanating from the center of power (at least those with the most purchasing power) described as the consumerist, family-oriented values of suburbia. John, for example, an 18-year-old Traveller who lives in a tent on Cool Mountain claimed "I stay here because I have no desire to live the suburban dream." The very categories or relative privilege they used to describe as the source of this hegemonic value system—those of White, middle-class, urban, and so on, are ones that they themselves occupy. In a sense, there is an element of self-hating, of rebellion against parental authority about these young Travellers. In a sense, then, the New Age Travellers' choice of a transient lifestyle is an assertion of agency over the only category of their identity they can alter—where they live. They cannot erase their Whiteness, their Englishness, their working-class or middle-class background. Their movement from the geographical center—urban England—to the margin—rural Ireland—is their way of trying to oppose the value system of the "center" of power.

In this manner, some New Age Travellers "drop out," whereas others are "pushed out," characterizations that bring up the question of whether voluntary or forcible marginalization elicits a stronger political consciousness. For instance, Nigel Fountain (cited in McKay, 1996) views voluntary marginalization as more integrally related to a political consciousness, arguing that one of the greatest differences between the 1960s and the 1980s is that in the 1960s, "Dropping out could be seen as a critical indication of power" whereas in the 1980s, it was "passive, a symptom of powerlessness" (p. 52). Others contend that it is rather forcible marginalization that induces a critical consciousness, apparent for instance in Smith's (1987) claim that the marginalized have a clearer view of social reality than those in power, because their marginalization has enabled them to see from the view of the oppressed and from the point of view of those at the axis of power simultaneously.

At times, New Age Traveller's version of their own oppositionality resembles the self-destructive nihilism that allegedly characterized the life of Sid Vicious of the Sex Pistols, or to use a more recent example, which characterised this life of the protagonists of Irvine Welsh's book, which became a hit film *Trainspotting*. The film begins with main character Mark Renton's cynical monologue:

> Choose life. Choose a job. Choose a career. Choose a family. Choose a fucking big television. Choose washing machines, care, compact disc players, and electrical tin openers . . . Choose DIY and wondering who the fuck you are on a Sunday morning. Choose sitting on that couch watching mind-numbing and spirit-crushing game shows, stuffing junk food into your mouth. Choose rotting away at the end of it all, pishing your last in a miserable home, nothing more than an embarrassment to the selfish, fucked-up brats you spawned to replace yourself. Choose your future. Choose life . . . but why would I want to do a thing like that? (cited in the film *Trainspotting*, 1997).

By rhetorically positioning any strong resistance to a version of this "life" involving suburban drudgery, and an unhappy but duty-bound confinement to a consumption-oriented nuclear family as a Refusal, he justifies his choice of life as a heroin addict. The way he formulates these choices makes it appear that the only way to escape this life of suburban drudgery was a strong advocacy of "something else," or an assertion for a radical Otherness (an assertion that is infused with a moment of Scottish nationalist opposition to British rule) that strongly rejects this version of "life." In this fashion, Renton makes heroin addiction appear existentially heroic in comparison to the vacuousness of "adult" life confronting youth today.

Some Travellers illustrate Renton's tendency to formulate life choices in a dualistic, either–or fashion wherein chemical addiction is perceived as oppositional. For example, for some urban Travellers, nicknamed "Drongos" in England, and "crusties" in Ireland, only politics appears to be a self-destructive nihilism, apparent in their often very public alcohol and drug abuse. As Jeremy of the Levellers (a prominent Traveller band) says, "We weren't a movement, just a bunch of pissed up people, some so nasty that even I wouldn't talk to them" (cited in McKay, 1996, p. 52). However, others have a clearly worked out political agenda. For instance, Gerrard, a New Age activist and writer, argues that Traveller politics involve "withdrawal (from conventional politics and social structures), reassessment (from a standpoint on the extreme fringes of society)" (cited in McKay, 1996, p. 53). They themselves had a mixed perception about the level of political awareness among their fellow Travellers. For instance, Traveller Eddie claimed that most Travellers are simply antisocial, apolitical, and "don't want anything to do with anything." His friend said that it is now fashionable to be a "crusty," and argued that many kids are drawn to this way of life for kicks rather than political motivations.

However, most exhibited a high degree of awareness regarding the structure of British politics, the infringement on civil liberties caused by recent legislation, and other structural reasons why, in their opinion, life in Britain had become intolerable. Many claimed to be economic "refugees" from Thatcher's (and Major's) Britain, victims of a decimated welfare state, unemployment, and homelessness. After some initial optimism about Tony Blair, the Travellers I have spoken with since his election are profoundly disillusioned with Blair's leadership, claiming he is overpreoccupied with his and his nation's "Cool Britannia" image without promoting any policies that will concretely challenge social inequalities. (As some commentators have observed, Blair's entire attempt to define a "New Britain" and to fill out the empty signifier of "New Britishness" in the Millennium Dome was a commercial and a semiotic failure [see O'Neill, 1999]). However, Traveller life allowed them to voluntarily marginalize themselves rather than allow themselves to be "pushed" out. Some of them took this self-marginalization to extremes, and moved to the deserted, barren ungrowable land, for example, on Cool Mountain, living as rural homeless in shack, tents, and caves with no running water, electricity, or heat. Their belief that the possibilities for self-determination are much greater in Ireland living in a lean-to on the side of the mountain than in a council flat in Britain is just an indication of how limited they felt their options were in their previous lives. Many, like a woman named Jane with whom I spoke with on Cool Mountain, had a sophisticated and committed version of one's responsibility to oneself, to animals, and to the environment, but had grown cynical regarding the emancipatory possibilities of the "left" politics of socialism. She espoused an individualist but ethically committed postmodern "politics of the local."

Whether they are pushed out or they drop out, once they have become New Age Travellers, they are most definitely a marginalized, excluded group who encounter substantial discrimination from the media and at times, from locals. Some New Age Travellers reported that they were barred from pubs, shops, and public functions simply because they were Travellers. Such discrimination was often supported, and in some cases, openly instigated by local authorities. For instance, Mike Murphy, a counselor in Youghal, went on RTE radio arguing for the right to ban New Age Travellers from all public spaces, and admitted that he had called the guards to arrest them several times on any possible grounds whenever he saw them on the streets of Youghal, and felt fully justified in doing so. Barry Roach, a local journalist in Cork recounted to me an instance of the mass arrest of New Age Travellers in March in Fermoy and elsewhere in the year of 2000 on trumped-up charges. Despite critiques of the treatment of New Age Travellers by journalists such as Roach, several recent news stories have, by innuendo and selective reporting, contributed to negative images of Travellers, unnecessarily mentioning that individuals are New Age Travellers if they are up on criminal charges, and moralistically emphasizing that these individuals are "of no fixed abode."

The New Age Travellers themselves were acutely aware of such negative sentiments. A few claimed that when they had applied for jobs, their employers refused to hire them, even though they were appropriately suited-up and squeaky clean. Others reported feeling more subtle examples of community disapproval when, after being singled out and subjected to name-calling and taunts in a pub by inebriated local adolescents, nobody intervened. As one 15-year-old who was a second-generation Traveller put it "people make a lot of assumptions about what Travellers are like, stereotype us, but none of those people are interested in really know what we are like, or why we are living this way."

McKay (1996) reports similar abuse directed toward Travellers in England who also experience rejection and exclusion and have to deal with "being sprayed with silage . . . putting up with 'fuck off' looks . . . being harassed for 'producers' by local police, that is, to produce vehicle registration documents at the local station within seven days" (p. 47). McKay also reports that since 1993 police intelligence units in Wiltshire and Cumbria have been dedicated to the national coordination of intelligence on Travellers, known as Operation Snapshot, whose aim is to collect information on 8,000 Travellers, including details of their trucks and living spaces, friends, nicknames, and so on.

On an even more sinister note, several Travellers in Cork told me that the secret history of the mass exodus of English Travellers to Ireland originated during what they called the "bean field war" in 1984 when, after police beat them, destroyed their vehicles, and hung their 100 dogs up by the neck, many decided to leave Britain altogether. Earle confirms their story this one-way confrontation, claiming:

> Though popularly recalled as the "Battle of the Bean field," it was, more accurately, a cowardly attack by armed men on family groups including many women and children. (Earle et al., 1994, p. 18)

Such reports of police brutality toward Travellers are also confirmed by other witnesses:

> One image will probably stay with me for the rest of my life. I saw a policeman hit a women on the head with his truncheon. Then I looked down and saw she was pregnant, and I thought: "My God, I'm watching police who are running amok." (cited in Davies, 1985, p. 3)

It's no wonder a recent album cover of the Levellers was adorned with a photo of a Traveller giving "the finger" to a policeman.

As well as police harassment, negative media stereotypes and often a cool reception from the locals, Travellers also have to contend with periodic homesickness. As one Traveller who lives in a van in West Cork said to me;

> Some days I think I'm crazy to live out here. I often wonder if I should go home. There isn't a lot to hold me here. On the other hand, there isn't much to pull me home, either.

In addition to homesickness, Travellers have to contend with what McKay (1996) calls periodic "straight sickness" as well—when they ask themselves "Why aren't I in a house, with a flushing loo, running water, a telly, pubs and cinemas nearby?" (p. 47). As Donal, a Traveller who alternates life between Cork and Cool Mountain described, "Sometimes I ask myself what I am trying to prove?"

THE SEMIOTICS OF THE NEW AGE TRAVELLER

The distinctiveness of the New Age Travellers' style of dreads, dirt, pastiche, and androgyny also makes them an obvious choice for comparison to punk and other youth subcultures. For instance, Hebdige (1979) illustrates how punks deliberately and purposefully crafted a strongly oppositional "style" of dress, jewelry, music, and general demeanor designed to expose the social contradictions of post-war Britain in the unemployment crisis of the 1970s, early 1980s. In his words, "No subculture has sought with more grim determination than the punks to detach itself from the taken-for-granted landscape of normalised forms, nor to bring down upon itself such vehement disapproval" (p. 19). In Hebdige's terms, the subversive power of punk lay in its power to wage "semiotic warfare," to provoke a visual outrage, that disrupts the taken-for-granted world. It is this strategy that Hebdige believes indicates an energy, a Refusal, and unwillingness to submit meekly to their unemployed status.

To Hebdige, style is an integral part of the punk challenge to post-war hegemony in Britain. He says:

> the challenge to hegemony which subcultures represent is not issued directly by them. Rather, it is expressed obliquely in style. The objections are lodged, the contradictions displayed . . . at the profoundly superficial level of appearances. (p. 17)

Although most New Age Travellers are not engaged in a "semiotic warfare," in the strategy of visual outrage as are (were) punks, they did adopt a similar aesthetics of innovation, eclecticism, pastiche, that illustrated an attempt to recover a sense of agency they had lost through what they perceive as the erosion of personal freedoms in Britain. However, the selection of the pieces that form each personal pastiche is not arbitrary, but is rather dominated by considerations of economy and of convenience. First of all, regardless of the countercultural affiliations of each Travellers individual style, collectively their dress sense is dominated by a concern with economy. Second, Traveller style is multifunctional, and multipurpose, in order to enable the "on-the-move" lifestyle that is integral to Traveller identity.

Personal style must be tailored for extended wear and appropriate to sleeping, staying warm, and keeping relatively clean in caravans, vehicles, and, when in the cities, in parks, on floors, and wherever they can. In this way, Traveller extended wear is an implicit rejection not only of the way in which the fashion industry tries to determine style, but also the expansion of this market into artificially created categories Spring and Fall, into day wear and night wear, work wear and leisure wear that in part is simply the creation of false needs.

For instance, thermal underwear, army gear, workboots, and work socks are worn as daily wear. As well, dreadlocks, shaved heads, and braids are the dominant New Age Traveller looks, easy care hairstyles designed to withstand life often without running water.

New Age Travellers are referred to as "crusties," by some, particularly those who live in the cities and attend summer festivals. Although many Travellers work hard at staying scrupulously clean without modern conveniences, some of these Travellers take pride in their capacity to exist without running water, and wear their own dirt, sweat and bodily odors as an emblem of their rejection of the modernist conventions of sanitation, artificiality, and chemicalization, of the denaturalization of the body encouraged by the cosmetics industry. One Traveller with whom I spoke claimed that sometimes this idealization of "dirt" has a strong symbolic value in Traveller culture: It has an almost purifying function whereby it can remove, or "cover over" the ills inflicted by civilization, industrialization, technologization, and modernity. Thus, the dirty–clean dichotomy characteristic of modernity is not simply dissolved in New Age Traveller culture, it is inverted.

NEW AGE TRAVELLERS: THE "ELECTIVE ETHNICITY"

This analysis of New Age Travellers from the point of view of high unemployment and changes in legislation in Britain does explain some dimensions of New Age Travellers' lifestyle and identity, but it doesn't acknowledge the diversity of this community. The New Age Traveller community is not a community, but rather an amalgamation of various diverse ethnicities (such as Irish, Spanish, German, Dutch, American, French, Italian, as well as English), and aesthetic or countercultural impulses (1960s hippie, 1970s punk, 1980s grunge, and 1990s rave).

I encountered Dutch, German, Spanish, French, and U.S. Travellers as well as English and Irish, and members ranging in age from 18 to 60, with second-generation Travellers children from infants to teens. I spoke with punk, rave, and hippy New Agers in Dublin, Cork City, and Cool Mountain; I met New Age surfers in Lahinch, New Age jugglers, musicians, actors, and writers at the Galway Arts Festival.

The diversity of the New Age Traveller community is expressed in the diversity of musical tastes, including 1960s peace and protest songs, 1970s punk, 1980s grunge, and 1990s techno music. Furthermore, these tastes reflected not just aesthetic choices but the dominant youth subculture of the decade during which each of the Travellers "came of age." For example, 40-somethings (and over) preferred folk, the 30-somethings punk, those in their 20s preferred grunge, and those in their late teens or early 20s chose rave music, seemingly preferring to identify with the musical era and associated youth subculture that predominated during their formative teen years. Eighteen-year-old Jake, for instance, was a DJ for his own Raves that he organised around West Cork when he wasn't living in his tent on Cool Mountain. Other Travellers with whom I spoke on Cool mountain identified more with 1970s punk or 1980s grunge, naming Johnny Rotten and Kurt Cobain as their musical idols, musical tastes that are consistent with the grunge/punk revival inner-city night-club scene catering to the slightly older crowd than the ravers. For the over 40s, often nothing but Dylan would do.

Among those who admitted that some Travellers used drugs, a similar generational preference occurred: The teens preferred ecstasy; those in their 20s and 30s, cider or hashish; and the older generation, usually nothing but herbal teas and health food, having renounced drugs after flirting with acid in the 1960s and 1970s. However, although most Travellers advocated the legalisation of drugs on the basis on a liberal ethic of individual choice, several with whom I spoke did not take drugs themselves, and indicated that drug use was the basis of a serious split in the New Age Traveller community. For example, a Traveller in Cork City told me that when the Traveller community splintered off from its usual convoy route in the early 1980s, a Bristol-bound group became so renowned for their heavy drug use that the highway to Bristol—the M36—became known in Traveller circles as the M "Dirty fix." In Traveller communities, heavy drug users are known as "jitters," and are regarded with sympathy but suspicion among other Travellers. Similarly, according to the more settled community members on Cool Mountain, several of the more transient Travellers have "serious drug and alcohol problems." In fact, some Travellers claim that ironically it is actually the city Travellers who are more likely to have such problems, because they will gravitate toward the cities where they are more likely to find ways to support their habit.

Another major split in this community occurs between the hippys and the ravers, or what McKay (1996) calls the "crystal versus vinyl" debate. John, for instance, described a conflict between himself and Patty, a "hippie" in her mid-40s who complained that he played his rave music too loud, arguing that his musical choices, like the recent techno trend in general, was politically vacuous. According to John, Patty was constantly trying to turn him and his girlfriend Carre on to folk music and protest songs; to Dylan and Guthrie; and the whole set of 1960s music, which to her still represented the only authentic alternative music. John was becoming increasingly uncomfortable about their difference of opinion, claiming that this conflict had escalated to the form of a "stereo war" where each would play their own music louder to try to drown out that of the other, a fact that others living on the mountain found at times problematic.

However, this folk–techno debate is about much more than just discrepant musical tastes. Rather, it reflects a whole generational and attitudinal difference between the oppositional impulses of youth cultures of those who came of countercultural age during the 1960s hippie movement, and youth culture emerging in the computer-literate, MTV generation of today. Even though 18-year-old John and 45-year-old Patty live side-by-side in a New Age Traveller encampment, and both share an appreciation of the countryside, a critique of consumer culture and an antipathy to the alienation of city life, there are some profound differences in their version of what constituted a counterculture. In John's words "She [Patty] would run around with her Birkenstock sandals and flowers in her hair acting like she had a monopoly on the alternative lifestyle." These differences were based on different opinions both between and within these different groups regarding what constituted an alternative lifestyle.

A diversity of labels are used to refer to this community: English Travellers, Travellers, New Age hippies, crusties, local blow-ins, blow-ins, even settlers. McKay has found an even broader diversity of terms for the New Age Travellers he studied in England: "crusties, drongos, mutants, hedge monkeys, brew crew, soap dodgers, giro gypsies, brigands" as well as even more derogatory names such as "trailer trash" and "vermin" (p. 49). As is frequently the case with the names of subordinate groups, most of labels bestowed on the New Age Travellers were not chosen by them, but rather had been imposed on them by the media, the surrounding locals, or other non-Travellers. Jane from Cool Mountain told me that the label "New Age Traveller" was just another way the media tried to identify, contain, ridicule, and then dismiss them as a community by associating them with both a flaky fringe philosophy (the New Age movement) and with a marginalized social group (the Travellers).

When asked what name they themselves preferred to call themselves, several chose simply "Travellers," a gesture of solidarity to Irish Travellers whose caravan lifestyle they admire and emulate. Others chose to take on the name "Travellers" instead of "New Age Travellers." However, this name thus glosses over important distinctions between Irish Travellers and New Age Travellers, and masks periodic antagonisms, conflicts that emerge when, for instance, the former perceive that the latter are caricaturing their way of life. These antagonisms will perhaps in the future be exacerbated by the potential competition between these two communities for halting sites. However, other New Age Travellers thought attempts to "name" themselves, to impose a unifying label on such a diverse and vibrant community ran counter to the fundamental meaning of the New Age Traveller lifestyle itself. This New Age Traveller refusal of labels represents an attempt to resist the process of naming that would categorize, order, define or contain them. If a part of the project of modernity is to impose an order on disorder, to organize chaos, through the process of naming, organizing, categorizing, as Bauman (1990) claims, then the New Age Traveller refusal to be labeled is indicative of their more general critique of modernity.

However, many New Age Travellers choose to be called just "Travellers" deliberately associating themselves with Irish nomads or gypsies (as distinct from European Romany gypsies), the community that used to be called Itinerants, or Tinkers, and is now considered to be the "Real Irish." As well as emulating their nomadic lifestyle and adopting the traditional Irish Traveller or Gypsy habitat of the caravan, some New Age Travellers expressed sympathy, admiration, and identification with the Irish Traveller/European gypsy community. This admiration extended to all marginalised and dispossessed peoples such as North American and Aboriginal people, but was extended particularly to Irish and Romany Travellers. For example, New Age Travellers on Cool Mountain kept the distinctive piebald horses often kept by Irish Travellers. Although they tend not to live in the same encampments, their paths intertwine at times. For example, one Irish Traveller I picked up hitching who confided that he lived up on Cool Mountain for 2 years while evading the law, claimed that Cool Mountain was one place where New Age Travellers and Irish Traveller communities often merge. McKay identified how these two communities frequently intertwine at horse fairs and carnivals in England where the New Age Traveller lifestyle originated.

However, other subjects I interviewed indicated this admiration only went in one direction. Some Irish Travellers with whom I spoke about their attitude toward New Age Travellers were resentful of the New Age Travellers, who they felt belittled their identity by caricaturing their lifestyle. Others reported feeling that their livelihood was threatened by the exponential increase in New Age Travellers with whom they had to compete for scarce halting sites. Similarly, McKay also discovered that some gypsies in England have strong hostility toward New Age Travellers. For instance, in a conversation with two gypsy men they aired grievance about New Age Travellers "sponging, their laziness, their filthy lifestyles, their provocative flouting of the laws of the land, their drug taking, their music, the way they rip up hedges for firewood, their dangerous vehicles, their begging, their filth again, the length of their dreadlocks" (McKay, 1996, p. 49).

Despite the strong desire that some Irish Travellers/gypsies have to distinguish themselves from New Age Travellers, the law does not actually distinguish between the two communities. Under the British caravan sites act of 1968, gypsies are defined as "persons of nomadic habit of life, whatever their race or origin, other than a group of travelling showmen, travelling together as such" (McKay, 1996, p. 48). Collapsing these two forms of Travellers adequately represents the extent to which both are marginalized from the point of view of the laws, judges, courts, and police. However, it also obscures very important differences in these groups regarding how precisely the distinction between these two communities should be conceived.

What is most interesting about this definition of Travelling communities is that this is a description of identity by lifestyle, not by race or ethnicity. Several non-Travellers with whom I spoke took issue with the New Age Travellers because they were not "authentic," because they "chose" this Travelling identity. This issue brings up the question of the relationship between marginalization, choice, and identity, and the question of whether or not one can assume a marginalized identity by choice. Clearly, some New Age Travellers (the unemployed, the homeless) were already marginalised in the economic sense of the term. However, others claim that they were spiritually marginalized in a strong sense: unfulfilling work, and the conflict and antagonism characteristic of city life had meant that they no longer felt they had a home in Britain.

Thus, Travellers were taking on hybridized identities, identities that are not based on birth, but by choice. New Age Travellers are not a distinctive ethnic group, but rather have an "elective and pastiche ethnicity" (Hetherington, 1996, p. 41) that is in a sense an act of self-creation. This diverse group of people are attempting to reimagine and reconstruct their identities by breaking down conventional categories of identity based on one's place of birth, occupation, level of conspicuous consumption, class position, even gender, and to reimagine them based on an ethos of their own choosing. As I show later, the way in which they do this is by creating cultural spaces that allow for the suspension of boundaries and transgressive performances, for chaos, and for incoherence.

THE NEW AGE TRAVELLER BODY: "AUTHENTIC," "ETHNIC," AND "GROTESQUE"

As well as embracing various subcultures of resistance, New Age Traveller aesthetic also embraces "ethnic" and "New Age" themes. In addition to as the hippie, punk, grunge and rave aesthetic, New Age Travellers at "dress up time" adopt a variety of brightly colored "ethnic" styles such as scarves from Malaysia and Thailand, bright Indian silks, and multi-colored Latin American vests. They also wear a variety of New Age accoutrements such as crystals, Celtic jewelry, and Aboriginal and African talismans said to have healing power, which illustrate their identification to marginalised peoples (Hetherington, 1996). In Hetherington's words, this style involves the adoption of an "authentic body" (p. 43), or the aesthetics of the Other, in order to signify their difference.

However, New Age Travellers also adopt what Hetherington calls a "grotesque body" as a way of radically assuming the position of the Other. For instance, some of the Travellers with whom I spoke seemed extraordinarily dirty, and seemed to revel in their own dirt. Other Travellers who did not share this orientation to dirt were somewhat shocked and disgusted by this, and commented to me that some Travellers went to great lengths to stay "unclean." This dirt did not seem accidental, but rather a deliberate message. For instance, the New Age Traveller production of their own bodies as "grotesque," as filthy, shocking, and "unsanitary" is a furthering of this process of self-marginalization.

This adoption of a "grotesque body" is an instance of a form of embodiment that signifies "resistance through dirt" (Hetherington, 1996, p. 43). As discussed in the last chapter, the body is the site of the swarming of the disciplinary discourses of modernity. However, the body is also the site of the exercise of power. Thus, the New Age Traveller attempts to reproduce his or her own body as a marginalized body is a bizarre but interesting attempt to expose our subjection to the civilizing processes of modernity, and expose our own enslavement in order to imagine an alternative. Our collective repulsion by the New Age Traveller's "grotesque body" reveals to us most clearly the extent to which we are enslaved to modern conventions of the civilized, sanitized body.

McKay (1996), one of the few academics who has written extensively on the New Age Travellers, claims that "dirt is a signifier of difference, of outsiderness, for travellers and other marginal groups" (p. 66). For example, according to ADILKNO (the anarcho-style Foundation for the Advancement of Illegal Knowledge), Travellers in urban Britain deliberately tried to look unkempt as a part of their identity. "The clothing of the movement looked sexless, dirty and ripped. There were hard patches and nasty stains on it. . . . Squat dress resembled the work clothes of miners, chimney sweeps, and tank cleaners. It looked at least as rough and filthy, only it couldn't be traded in after work for a designer sweat suit" (cited in McKay, 1996, p. 66). Similarly, Young, in her book *Femininity in Dissent* illustrates the extent to which media representations of marginalized focus on the grotesque: "It is a preoccupation to which the papers constantly return: dirt, disease, disgust, positioned against cleanliness, health, approval . . . . The grotesque (body) becomes synonymous with the marginal and the deviant, the cast-out" (Young, cited in McKay, 1996, p. 66). As such, "crusty" dirt and filth is proudly and intentionally displayed as a symbol of the rejection of the cosmetic cleanliness of the modern body as a symbol of subjugation to moral regulation of modernity.

Although this particular aspect of the New Age Traveller body is an inversion to the ethic of self-care that animates holistic health, both can be seen as a critique of industrial society, an expression of disillusionment with contemporary politics, and a critique of modern science. First, they can be conceived of as an attempt to inscribe a "green" politics right on to their very own bodies, to "renaturalize" the body they perceived has been violated by perceived evils of industrial society. Second, this assertion of power through the use of their own bodies can be perceived as an acknowledgment of the failure of political representation and a disillusionment with participatory democracy. This politicization of something so intimate, personal as one's own body can be seen as an attempt to reclaim an element of agency or power by embracing a "politics of the local." Third, both the holistic and the grotesque body can be seen as attempts to reclaim bodies perceived to be objectified through Western science and medicine.

This perception of individual bodies as objectified by modern industry, politics, and science is also consistent with what Foucault's (1975) analysis of how modern disciplinary technologies operating in various settings such as workshops, schools, and prisons try to forge a "docile body that may be subjected, used, transformed, and improved" (p. 198). As Rabinow (1983) illustrates, the body is disciplined not only through drills and training, but also through "standardisation of actions over time, and through the control of space" (p. 17). The coordination of individual bodies along particular spatial and temporal grids ensures selves to supervise and discipline individuals. "In a factory, the procedure facilitates productivity; in a school, it assures orderly behaviour; in a town, it reduces the risk of dangerous crowds, wandering vagabonds, or epidemic diseases" (Rabinow, 1984, p. 17).

By Foucauldian standards, the New Age Traveller form of resistance would be a much more profoundly subversive gesture than that of holistic health. In his introduction to *Anti-Oedipus*, Foucault advocates several principles for living a "Non-fascist life" which include his imperative "Prefer what is positive and multiple, difference over uniformity, flows over unities, mobile arrangements over systems." He goes on to say:

> Do not demand of politics that it restore the "rights" of the individual as philosophy has defined them. The individual is a product of power. What is needed is to "de-individualise" by means of multiplication and displacement, diverse combinations. (p. xiv)

From this point of view, the holistic body of the New Age is uniform, orderly, systematic, and unified. In contrast, the "grotesque" Traveller body is different, chaotic, mobile, and diverse. Furthermore, the New Age Traveller advocacy of the "grotesque body" is an attempt to "displace" the body from the spatial and temporal organisation of modernity that would order it, confine it, and contain it.

In this manner, New Age Travellers have attempted to illustrate their agency through the production of their own bodies as sites of resistance not simply to specific forms of authority such as to Thatcher's Britain, and more generally to the civilizing processes of modernity. Although their particular agenda is much more abstract, the use of the body as a site of resistance is, of course, not without precedent. For instance, refusing to keep clean as a form of resistance was one phase in the escalating plan of resistance that predated the hunger strikes of the Irish Republican prisoners in the H-block struggle from 1976 to 1981. These prisoners began their struggle as both a protest against the brutality and harassment of Republican prisoners and as a symbol of resistance against British rule in Northern Ireland by first initiating "Blanket protest," a refusal to wear prison uniforms. This form of protest was intended to illustrate that they were political prisoners, and were only incarcerated in the context of a profoundly unjust system. This protest that then escalated to the "no-wash, no-slop-out" phase, a protest that, according to one of the surviving hunger-strikers with whom I spoke, was experienced as profoundly disturbing to the prison guards. This use of individual bodies as sites of protest in such a heavily regulated and monitored environment is a literal representation of the Foucauldian panoptic society whereby the individual body must be reclaimed as the site of a micropolitical struggle.

This relationship to dirt illustrates the strong strain of asceticism runs through New Age Traveller culture. Despite the public image of city Travellers as hedonists, as "the brew crew," as into cider, hash, and out for a "good time," some of the more rural Travellers I spoke with fairly reveled in self-denial. These people were proud of their capacity to endure achieved life without modern comforts such as running water, conventional heating, appliances, and so on, in abandoned houses, vehicles, tepees, and makeshift homes. In a sense then, this asceticism is one response to the contemporary spiritual crises encountered as a result of the loss of faith in Christianity.

The New Age "grotesque body" perhaps reveals most clearly to us that New Age Travellers spirit of resistance is not opposed simply to Thatcher's Britain, but is aimed more generally to what is perceived as the various ills of modernity. The self-production of the "grotesque body" is a challenge to the modern fear of disorder, of chaos, of the unruly, of the uncategorizable that Foucault argues is so much the anathema to the modern psyche. Insofar as some New Age Travellers assume this "grotesque body," Traveller culture, like punk, adopts a strategy of "visual outrage" of semiotic warfare that Hebdige describes. However, this strategy explicitly opposes the civilizing and moralizing processes of modernity.

This "grotesque body" perhaps reveals the proliferation of classificatory systems and systems of ordering that illustrate modernity's anxiety regarding disorder, chaos, the unruly, and uncategorizable. In *The Order of Things*, Foucault (1973) shows how Borges' description of the bizarre taxonomy of a Chinese encyclopedia shows how the tenuous, unstable boundaries of classificatory systems only exist in the "non-place of language" (p. xvii), and that only the "mere act of enunciation" heaps those "contained" into their "containers." Furthermore, he shows how the very way in which classification systems try to "localise the contagion" of the indeterminate draws attention to that very possibility of indeterminacy, of monstrosity. "It would not even be present at all in this classification had it not insinuated itself into the empty space, the interstitial blanks separating all the entities from one another" (Foucault, 1973, p. xvi).

As Hetherington (1996) illustrates, Francis Bacon uses the term *heteroclite* to refer to anomalies and freaks of nature which defy classification. This image of the heteroclite shows our collective anxiety regarding the "thing" that defies categorization, an anxiety that Foucault (1973) reveals in his own reaction to the possibility of the interstitial space:

> Perhaps there arose in its wake the suspicion that there is a worse kind of disorder than that of the *incongruous*, the linking together of things that are inappropriate; I mean the disorder in which fragments of a large number of possible orders glitter separately in the dimension, without law or geometry, of the heteroclite; and that word should be taken in its most literal etymological sense: in such a state, things are "laid," "placed," "arranged" in sites so very different from one another that it is impossible to find a place of residence for them, to define a *common locus* beneath them all. (p. xvii)

HETEROCLITE, HETEROTOPIA, HETEROCRONIA: THE NEW AGE TRAVELLER SEARCH FOR THE INDETERMINATE IDENTITY/SPACE/TIME

Historically, New Age Travellers adopt a nomadic lifestyle that emulates that of more traditional cultures such as gypsies or Travellers. According to MacKay, this movement emerged out of Britain's travelling fairs when young people from the cities who had mixed with people from traditional Travelling families also "took to the road," and began forming convoys to travel from one site to the next. Many New Age Travellers living in caravans or converted buses in West Cork and West Clare, moved around regularly and returned periodically to the cities, but did not establish a home base anywhere in particular.

However, claiming that their lifestyle is "derivative" overlooks the tremendous significance of this nomadic imaginary to the New Age

Traveller version of space. In choosing a nomadic lifestyle, Travellers are identifying with gypsies, Travelling performers, and other "outlaw" identities, who cannot be defined or explained, because they have an indeterminate point of origin as well. Like their search for the heteroclitic identity, the nomadic lifestyle of the New Age Travellers can also be seen as a way of subverting attempts to find what Foucault (1974) calls "etymological place of residence" (p. xv) for them as well. In other words, from this perspective, nomadicism can be seen as an attempt to shed the constraints of an originary identity.

This reconceptualization of space is even apparent in their organization of domestic life, and is central to understanding their way of life in general. For instance, the New Age Traveller lifestyle and identity is closely associated with a celebration of chaos, of disorder, of the unruly, an ethos that translates into how they eat, think, work, and live. As well as rejecting the process of labeling, New Age Traveller life is an explicit rejection of the organization of space and time underpinning the modern household. First, the New Age Traveller advocacy of (geographical and spiritual) nomadicism is a rejection of the notion of the permanent habitat and of a stable identity that has played a crucial role in processes of modernization. Because the mobility of New Age Traveller life and the practice of living in single "room" shacks, tipis, vehicles, precludes the possibility of modern sanitation, Traveller life opens up the possibility of life without modern conveniences. Although many Travellers with whom I spoke managed to stay scrupulously clean (contrary to the "crusty" image of dirt and dreads), their refusal to acquiesce to the contemporary fetish of the "bathroom" is an implicit rejection of the modern obsession with sanitation. Furthermore, their innovative, multi-functional living spaces are an implicit challenge to the fragmentation of the house into specialised rooms; into bathrooms, bedrooms, and kitchens within which individual bodies are fed, cleaned, regenerated and reproduced to the tempo of the working day. More generally, the multi-functional spaces that comprise New Age Traveller homes, the spatial and temporal (dis)order of New Age Traveller life pose a challenge to the spatial and temporal ordering central to work and home life that is a part of the civilizing and moralizing processes of modernity.

The desire expressed by New Age Travellers to assume bodies that occupy this "interstitial space" in systems of ordering is thus paralleled by their attempt to seek out these "interstitial spaces" in a geographical and cultural sense as well. For instance, New Age Travellers often seek out contested or marginal spaces frequented by other marginal identities, identities that inhabit the margins, the detritus of bourgeois culture located in the brothels, flea markets, gutters, and so on in which Breton, Aragon, and other Surrealists were fond of wandering (Nadeau, 1987). Hetherington (1996) claims:

> Just as outlaws, bandits, revolutionaries, and the dangerous classes have often been associated, in popular representations, with such heterotopic places as forests, deserts, jungles, and slums, so those who elect to construct an alternative lifestyle and new identities, will use the Otherness, difference and liminality of such sites to do so. (p. 39)

As well as outlaw figures, New Age Travellers identify with "outlawed", marginal, or contested space as well. In the New Age Traveller taxonomy of space, the centers become the margins, and the margins become the centers: For instance places like Cool Mountain and the outskirts of the Beara Peninsula are considered to be more desirable or "central" within a New Age hierarchy of authenticity than cities such as Dublin, Galway, or Cork. However, this inversion of margin and center does not mean that countercultures implement a series of countercultural values that bear no resemblance to those other social grouping, or to simplify, that mainstream values bear no resemblance to "fringe" values. Many New Age practices are simply unusual or creative ways of fulfilling everyday needs and desires, desires shared by members of the broader society. For example, New Age Traveller lifestyles are often seen by locals as a threat to "family values." What I discovered is that quite the opposite is the case. Many Travellers have very close relationships with other Travellers, and not with their own families of origin, a characteristic that some non-Travellers see as illustrating their "anti-familialism." However, this does not mean they are anti-family, but rather that Travellers recreate community as family in the context of what for some consider a problematic relationship to their own families—problems that often befall contemporary families and inhibit communication such as divorce, death, and ideological differences. In this way, this subculture has emerged in relation as well to the rise in marital breakdown, the increasing social acceptability of childlessness, and other factors that have challenged the patriarchal, traditional nuclear family. For instance, many Travellers speak of each other as "family," and very often have dogs, ferrets or other "non-human companions" that they consider to be family as well. When I asked several Travellers about why so many of them had pets, they challenged my use of the term pet, which designated ownership, and claimed that "our dogs are our children." The fact that Traveller communities (often called "Tribes") and animals have become a surrogate family doesn't mean that these are indicators that Travellers are a threat to the cherished value of family, but rather that they are attempting to reconstitute this relationship in a unique way. This contemporary tendency for young people to see relationships with friends as a kind of a replacement for more problematic relationships with family, is also strongly apparent in a variety of alternative as well as mainstream communities. For instance, various lesbian communities in Toronto tend to consider or to name their friends their "sisters" or "brothers."

Similarly, the global popularity of the TV sitcom *Friends* demonstrates how one's friendships and relationships are coming to supercede professional, national, familial and other previously significant categories of identity.

Those who embody heteroclitic identities will seek out heterotopic spaces with which they can "play" with boundaries. This New Age Traveller advocacy of nomadism is more than simply about refusing to locate oneself in geographical space, but also illustrates their commitment to "wandering," and to "exploring" conceptual and ideational space as well. However, this exploration is not simply aimless, but seeks out spaces not inhabited by predetermined social scripts and codes of behavior. In short, they wish to challenge what they perceive as the increasingly authoritarian legislation in Britain, the tyranny of a culture of conspicuous consumption, a world inhabited by rules they feel they had no part in making, a world that they feel is not their own. They wish to recreate new identities that defy categorization altogether.

This "Travelling spirit" that the New Age Travellers embrace is encapsulated by the lyrics in the music of prominent Traveller band the Levellers, songs entitled things such as "Exodus," "The Riverflow," "Leave this Town," The Boatman," and others. However, other titles illustrate the Traveller perception of themselves as not moving toward something, but rather fleeing from something, a "something" posed as simultaneously modern life and the various crises characterizing contemporary Britain. For instance, the song "Headlights, White Lines, Black Tar Rivers" documents an attempt to flee the pollution caused by industrial society. "Sell Out" is a critique of commercialism and the suburban way of life. On the other hand, "England my Home and Liberty" documents problems specific to Britain, and symptoms of the decline of the empire such as the fascist element of football hooliganism, race riots, the increasingly authoritarian legislation, the crisis of the welfare state, and unemployment. Such themes illustrate the simultaneous utopian search for a "free space" a "better space," and their critique of the social relations underpinning the "spaces" they left. Despite their diversity, New Age Travellers are unified as a community in terms of their commitment to some sort of utopian imaginary, to some sort of self-determination, despite the living conditions involved in being transient. In the words of one Traveller from Newcastle, "I came out here in search of a better life."

Their nomadic way of life makes New Age Travellers difficult to classify, interview, and research as well. One interesting aspect to studying Travellers for me was that many of my more relaxed interviews and most informative research data were acquired while in transit or on the move as well. For instance, one of the ways I discovered was easiest to interview Travellers was to drive around Travelling encampments and pick up Travellers who were hitching. This way of collecting proved very satisfactory because it allowed an air of leisure and relaxation that only a "journey" affords.

The centrality of travelling fairs to New Age Traveller life is not simply about movement or a refusal to put down roots, but rather it is more directly related to the search for a "free space" within which one can play with the boundaries of their own identity, a free space frequently only found on the margins. This search for free spaces is central to New Age Traveller identity. For instance, Donal, a Traveller, poet, writer, and activist, told me that the search for places to put on festivals in Ireland was an attempt to produce an indeterminate, unregulated (or self-regulated) space where people can talk, share, play music, exchange ideas about mysticism, herbalism, the paranormal, and other beliefs often "outlawed" in "normal society. In his view, Irish society tolerates such beliefs, but frequently does not allow individuals to congregate to practice them.

New Age Travellers in Ireland frequently hold parties and festivals at sites like New Grange, and other places of pagan worship. According to Hetherington (1996), many New Age Traveller festivals in Britain are held in sites of old medieval fairs, or pagan sites like Stonehenge. The centrality of festivals and carnivals to New Age Traveller life can also be explained in terms of this search for indeterminate space. As Bakhtin (1984) points out, the carnival involves the production of identities that are deliberately subversive, grotesque, and threatening, through forms of disorder such as drug-taking, hedonism, anti-authoritarianism, and bizarre costume. As Turner (1982) pointed out, such festivals are liminoid social occasions that release social constraints, overturn the values of society, and establish a new code of behavior.

Free, indeterminate, or marginal spaces will thus hold a strong appeal to those who perceive themselves as marginal to society because these spaces symbolize an uncertainty, an indeterminacy, and ambivalence that mirrors the individual's own experience of identity. From this perspective, the New Age Traveller practice of self-marginalization is not "dropping out" but rather an exploration of an alternate space, a reconceiving of the relations of interiority and exteriority that privileges certain versions of "in" and "out" in the first place. Such metaphors of "space" have been used frequently in feminist literary critics how have argued that we have to open up "the blank page" for women to begin writing their stories, and by feminist geographers arguing feminist scholarship must fight to open up a "free space" within institutions to begin expressing feminist concerns, conceived in both conceptual and logistical terms (see, e.g., Barr, cited in Goodwin & Jones, 1990).

This reconceptualization of interiority and exteriority is first accomplished by inverting the ordering of central and marginal space

(Hetherington, 1996). Although New Age Travellers repudiate "central" spaces such as the city, shopping malls, and the workplace, they seek out "marginal" spaces such as pagan sites, carnivals, and so on, spaces that become central to their identity. In other words, in the New Age Traveller taxonomy of space, the centers become the margins, and the margins become the centers. These marginal spaces themselves become endowed with supernatural powers, become sacred, magical. Hetherington cites Aragon (1987) in saying:

> Man no longer worships the gods on their heights. Solomon's Temple has slid into a world of metaphor in where it harbours swallow's nests and corpse- white lizards. The spirit of religions, coming down to dwell in the dust, has abandoned the sacred places. But there are other places which flourish among mankind, places where men go calmly about their mysterious lives and in which a profound religion is very gradually taking shape. These sites are not yet inhabited by a divinity. It is forming there, a new godhead precipitating in these re-creations of Ephesius like acid- gnawed metal at the bottom of a glass. (p. 28)

Furthermore, this appeal to the order of the "supernatural": to Stonehenge, New Grange, Dolmen, and to other stone circles and pagan sites around England and Ireland, as an indeterminate space because in modern secular society, such places are the sites of highly symbolic but contested meaning.

However, the New Age tendency to seek out such places is not simply about the search for an indeterminate space, but an indeterminate time as well. Some of the Travellers expressed a strong sense that the time of the new millennium is a difficult time for people of the world. Some Travellers, like Jane, articulated their feeling of disconnection from the rest of the world by claiming that she felt like she was "out of time," born in the wrong time, and that she somehow didn't fit with the rest of the world. The feeling of dislocation that Jane describes is a symptom of one of the characteristics Jameson (1992) describes as the condition of postmodernity. Some dealt with this feeling of fragmentation, dislocation, and alienation by frequent participation in pagan pilgrimages, ancient rituals and other so-called premodern practices that give one a sense of continuity with the past, a feeling of oneness which we believe is our heritage or tradition. As Turner (1973) points out, "a pilgrimage centre, from the standpoint of the believing actor, also represents a 'threshold', a place and moment 'in and out of time'" (pp. 213-214). In a sense, then, the New Age isn't solely anti-modern as several authors have noted (e.g., Heelas, 1996), but rather the search for the paramodern, or what Foucault (1989) calls "heterochronia"—a space in time where time is multiple, nonlinear, displaced, and unfixed.

New Age Travellers are not simply refugees from Thatcher's Britain, but are refugees more generally from modernity. This characterization of New Age Travellers as self-proclaimed refugees from Thatcher's Britain, from the dismantling of the welfare state, from the introduction of the Public Order acts, the unemployment crisis, and the clamp down on squatter's rights, however, homogenizes what is in reality a very diverse group. New Age Travellers with whom I spoke living in West Cork and Clare described themselves as self-proclaimed refugees from the city, perceiving themselves as damaged by the fragmentation, the complexity, and the intensity that characterizes the contemporary urban experience. Some conceived of their pilgrimage to rural Ireland as a retreat from urban life, as a quiet place to recover from the excesses of modernity: from personal crisis, assaults, substance abuses, and other traumas associated with modern life. Many of these Travellers are able to articulate the various paradoxes of modernity, and to acknowledge the heavy costs we pay to gain the benefits of processes of urbanization, globalization, and rationalization for both human and non-human actors. Others claimed to be refugees from Thatcher's Britain, from the dismantling of the welfare state. In short, they all saw themselves as refugees from modernity.

NEW AGE TRAVELLERS IN IRELAND: A SUMMARY

To summarize the conclusions of the last two chapters regarding the New Age Travellers, several New Age Travellers with whom I spoke living in West Cork and Clare described themselves as self-proclaimed refugees from Thatcher's Britain, from the dismantling of the welfare state, from the introduction of the Public Order acts, the unemployment crisis, and the clamp down on squatter's rights. Others claimed more generally to be refugees from the city, perceiving themselves as damaged by the fragmentation, the complexity, and the intensity that characterizes the contemporary urban experience. Some conceived of their pilgrimage to rural Ireland as a retreat from urban life, as a quiet place to recover from the excesses of modernity: from personal crisis, assaults, substance abuses, and other traumas associated with modern life. However, one of the implications of this construction of Ireland as the locus of the authentic "Other" and as on the periphery of modernity is to reinforce those very dichotomies between traditional–modern, Ireland–Europe, Ireland, rural–urban that legitimated colonialist domination in the first place.

Although their self-perception as refugees from modernity is the theme that most clearly unifies the New Age Traveller community, this community is extremely diverse. The New Age Traveller community is not a community, but rather an amalgamation of various diverse ethnicities (such as Irish, Spanish, German, Dutch, American, French, Italian, as well as English), and aesthetic or countercultural impulses (1960s hippie, 1970s punk, 1980s grunge, and 1990s rave). When asked what name they themselves preferred, several chose simply "Travellers," a gesture of solidarity to Irish Travellers whose caravan lifestyle they admire and emulate. Others chose to take on the name "Travellers" instead of "New Age Travellers" in order to disassociate themselves from any strong connection with the New Age movement, perceiving it as far too esoteric and ideologically confused. However, this name glosses over important distinctions between Irish Travellers and New Age Travellers, and masks periodic antagonisms, conflicts that emerge when, for instance, the former perceive that the latter are caricaturing their way of life. However, other New Age Travellers thought attempts to "name" themselves, to impose a unifying label on such a diverse and vibrant community ran counter to the fundamental meaning of the New Age Traveller lifestyle itself. This New Age Traveller refusal of labels represents an attempt to resist the process of naming that would categorize, order, define, or contain them. If a part of the project of modernity is to impose an order on disorder, to organize chaos, through the process of naming, organizing, categorizing (as Bauman, 1990, claims), then the New Age Traveller refusal to be labeled is indicative of their more general critique of modernity.

However, what makes the New Age Traveller lifestyle and identity unique and interesting is not simply that it is a celebration of chaos, of disorder, of the unruly, but rather that the New Age Traveller lifestyle is an attempt to turn a critique of modernity into a way of life. As well as rejecting the process of labeling, New Age Traveller life is an explicit rejection of the organization of space and time underpinning the modern household. First, the New Age Traveller advocacy of (geographical and spiritual) nomadicism is a rejection of the notion of the permanent habitat and of a stable identity that has played a crucial role in processes of modernization. Because the mobility of New Age Traveller life and the practice of living in single "room" shacks, tipis, vehicles, precludes the possibility of modern sanitation, Traveller life opens up the possibility of life without modern conveniences. Although many Travellers with whom I spoke managed to stay scrupulously clean (contrary to the "crusty" image of dirt and dreads), their refusal to acquiesce to the contemporary fetish of the "bathroom" is an implicit rejection of the modern obsession with sanitation. Furthermore, their innovative, multi-functional living spaces are an implicit challenge to the fragmentation of the house into specialized rooms; into bathrooms, bedrooms, and kitchens within which individual bodies are fed, cleaned, regenerated and reproduced to the tempo of the working day. More generally, the multi-functional spaces which comprise New Age Traveller homes, the spatial and temporal (dis)order of New Age Traveller life pose a challenge to the spatial and temporal ordering central to work and home life that is a part of the civilizing and moralizing processes of modernity.

Another thing that unifies the diverse New Age Traveller community and sets them apart from the broader community is their attitude and relationship to the formal economy. Although some New Age Travellers work for wages or even own small businesses, work within an informal economy (such as the LETS program in which skills are traded), or operate on an alternative economy (i.e., vending, juggling), many subsist by collecting the dole. For some, "dropping out" was a response to the meaninglessness they experienced in their previous jobs or professions. For instance, some expressed reluctance to participate in reproducing a system they perceived was based on the exploitative division of labor. Others preferred not to participate in what they perceived as an unethical system designed to create false needs. Still others were disillusioned with the alienation, the lack of autonomy they were given in their jobs or professions where they experienced themselves, literally or otherwise as that of an "appendage to the machine." Thus, their reluctance some express toward participation in the formal economy was generally not based on an unreflexive desire to "freeload," but at times a thoughtful, self-reflexive ethical position based on a critique of exploitation, commodity fetishism, and alienation.

Nonetheless, New Age Travellers are often criticized by the broader community for their lack of participation in the formal economy. As was noted earlier, New Age Travellers have been characterized as "parasites" and "freeloaders," as "wasters" and as "knackers." This anxiety expresses a very legitimate concern that the already overstretched welfare state cannot withstand more strain. However, the vehemence with which some of these negative sentiments are expressed would indicate that New Age Travellers are sometimes feared and disliked not because of the potential drain on the welfare state, but because of the possibility that they will further destabilize traditional values already eroded by modernity. In a sense then, some of the critiques of their potential drain on the welfare state are merely give a rational, economic veneer to a more generalized fear of difference, change, and diversity.

These references to New Age Travellers as "spongers" illustrate that the moral economy underpinning one aspect of anti-New Age Traveller sentiments is the notion that participation in gainful employment is a part of one's moral obligation to the community. In contrast, the moral economy underpinning New Age Traveller life is not based on one's relationship to production, but rather is based on its orientation to consumption. Unlike members of the broader community, they do not define "work" exclusively as participation in the formal economy. Rather, what makes New Age Traveller life unique, what unifies this diverse community is their commitment to living off the waste, the leftover, the excess of modernity. For example, several New Age Travellers with whom I spoke diligently scoured dumps for material for clothes, furniture, kitchen appliances, or other household utilities, a practice they called "seagulling." Moreover, some of the more "settled" Travellers used this refuse to create makeshift homes out of tipis, rusty lean-tos, self-made shacks, or abandoned vehicles. Some even routinely searched supermarket rubbish bins for fruit, vegetables, and even bags of thrown-out food from the deli counter, although apparently sometimes supermarket employees had taken up the practice of dying food unpalatable colors such as blue to discourage this practice. Thus, many New Age Travellers do not "work" in the formal sense, or do not engage in paid labor, but rather see their "work" as making the unusable usable, the unproductive productive. In short, they make a vocation, a lifestyle out of living off of the excess of modernity.

Thus, living a lifestyle oriented toward making the unproductive productive, the unusable usable inverts the conventional moral economy that prioritizes one's relationship to production, to the formal economy. Relocating this moral imperative, this ethical responsibility, in the realm of consumption rather than production, reconceptualizing collective responsibility in terms of waste, not wages can be seen as a legitimate and principled value on which to base a lifestyle. The extent to which New Age Traveller life is oriented to finding innovative if laborious ways of reviving various "dead" objects of modernity is particularly apparent on Cool Mountain, a New Age Traveller community near Dunmanway in West Cork. A number of New Age Travellers have "settled" in this community for as long as 12 years, setting up homes in a broad variety of sparse, eclectic, and imaginative habitats out of a broad variety of materials: an old ambulance, a tourist information booth, a makeshift tipi made out of plastic bags. Although their primary orientation to such refuse is functional, some of these habitats ironically signify those very aspects of modernity that many Travellers were trying to escape, such as the "panic" culture symbolized by the ambulance, the commodification of nature symbolized by the tourist information booth, the environmental crisis of industrial society signified by the non-biodegradable plastic bags. As such, the political economy of New Age Traveller life is based on living off the waste of others, and establishing a principled relationship to the global community.

Thus, the New Age Traveller life strongly illustrates the paradox of modernity that on one hand provides the illusion of the possibility of retreat, yet is unable to deliver its utopian promise. On one hand, Travellers on Cool Mountain are utopian, for they conceive of quiet rural life they lead on the mountain as in one sense a refuge from modernity. On the other hand, the Cool mountain people are realists, for their orientation making the unusable usable, the unproductive productive acknowledges the very worst aspects of modernity, and tries to tackle this problem head-on. This experience of being caught between two worlds, the utopian and the real was also apparent in their own feelings of being caught between their old lives and their new lives. For instance, several claimed they felt torn between the lives they had literally carved out on the mountain, and the lives they left behind, and felt ambivalent about staying, and ambivalent about leaving. Thus, mountain life is much more that nostalgic retreat to a rural, mythical, agrarian past. Rather, this life expresses both a longing for the premodern, the traditional, the refuge from modernity, yet at the same time the recognition that there is really no refuge, no utopia, no place outside modernity from which to hide.

CONCLUSION

As I tried to show in the last chapter, one of the things that makes New Age Travellers one of the more interesting, politicized, and radical moments of the New Age movements is their attempt to transform the meaning of the New Age movement from a commodified leisure activity to a total way of life. Through their environmentalist ethic of living off the waste, the garbage, the excess of modernity, New Age Travellers have tried to transform the meaning of environmentalism from an abstract ecological consciousness to a set of principles that involve the everyday material practices of living.

In this chapter, I tried to show how New Age Traveller orientation to time and space transcends the naive nostalgia of other aspects of this movement. The New Age Traveller celebration of order, of chaos, of the unruly, through the adoption of the grotesque body, the carnivalesque space, and their nomadic exploration of marginal or contested space illustrates their rejection of certain aspects of modernity. However, in some ways the search for the time outside modernity or the paramodern, is simply a nostalgic, reactionary retreat to a version of the pre-modern. For instance, New Age Travellers in Ireland like the larger New Age movement of which they are a part, tend toward essentialized and problematic version of what they construct as the rural, and implicitly pose Ireland as premodern in their characterization of this country as a refuge from modernity.

This characterization of Ireland as a refuge from modern life is problematic. However, one of the implications of this construction of Ireland as the locus of the authentic "Other" and as on the periphery of modernity is to reinforce those very dichotomies between traditional–modern, Ireland–Europe, Ireland, rural–urban that legitimated colonialist domination in the first place.

As Memmi (1990), and others noted, whether the colonized is denigrated or idealized, it is still being defined by the colonizer who speaks for her or him. Furthermore, these definitions of the primitive say much more about the tendencies of the Western subject to project onto the past or onto "undeveloped" societies fears and desires we have regarding our own social context. As Torgovnick (1990) illustrates:

> Is the present too materialistic? Primitive life is not—it is a precapitalist utopia in which only use value, never exchange value prevails. Is the present too sexually repressed? Not primitive life—primitives live life whole—without fear of the body. Is the present too promiscuous and undiscriminating sexually? Then primitives teach us the inevitable limits and controls placed on sexuality and the proper subordination of sexuality to the needs of childrearing. Does the present see itself as righteously Christian? Then primitives become heathens, mired in false beliefs. Does the present presume vigorous business expansion? Then primitives cease to be thought of as human and become a resource for industry, able to work mines and supply natural wealth. In each case the needs of the present determine the value and nature of the primitive. The primitive does what we ask it to do. Voiceless, it lets us speak for it. It is our ventriloquist's dummy—or so we like to think. (p. 9)

Thus, New Age Travellers are the geographical representation of the New Age search for another space, another time, another identity. Perhaps represent the best and most exploratory of the New Age. Nonetheless, their idealization of what they construct as premodern is symptomatic of what is most problematic in the New Age movement in general. It is this theme that I explore in the next chapter.

III

The New Age as a Symptom of Postmodernity

Five

Unified Subjects, Unified Communities: The Desire for Reconciliation in the Libidinal Economy of the New Age

The New Age Travellers described in chapter 4 have adopted minimalist, Spartan lifestyles as a critique of consumer culture. As noted in chapter 2, however, other more affluent New Agers practice the New Age purely through leisure-time consumption through purchasing a variety of treatments, seminars, therapies, health care products, and other consumables that comprise the New Age industry. However, what these groups share is that both participate in the New Age in order to find meaning in their lives, to try to establish a more profound connection to others and to nature, and to fill a "spiritual vacuum." In chapter 6 I illustrate how this spiritual vacuum characteristic of modernity can be described as a kind of a psychopathology of modernity, a symptom of what Jameson (1988) calls *postmodernity* (the waning of affect, the play of surfaces, etc.). In this chapter, however, I look at the various psychoanalytic and existentialist perspectives that explain the New Age as a response to the limitlessness on one hand, and guilt on the other that the condition of modernity engenders.

This chapter takes a psychoanalytic perspective on the mechanisms of New Age desire, or more specifically how this desire for for "connection" operates within the libidinal economy of the modern subject. Taking from Freud and Lacan the psychoanalytic model of how fears and desires become projected and transferred, I show how the New Age desire is the desire for reconciliation with various Others: with the divided parts of the self (Zizek, 1989), with Nature (Haraway, 1991), with the "Primitive"/Third World/Aboriginal (Torgovnik, 1990), and other Others, a nostalgic fantasy construction whereby the sites of spirituality, the natural, and the primitive are constructed as the sites of wholeness, fulfillment, and completeness. This desire expresses itself in the essentialized and idealized New Age formulations of the self, spirituality, community, the environment, and the developing world. Thus, this chapter illustrates how the New Age movement is an attempt to reverse the Enlightenment devaluation of nature, the body, and the primitive, through an imagined reconciliation or reintegration with these categories. This desire in the New Age for reconciliation with various "others" through the appropriation of what it perceives as the natural, the third world, the holistic body, is a symptom of the crises of science, rationality, and colonialism. However, the fact that the imagined reintegration of these categories in the New Age is animated by an eradication rather than an acceptance of difference makes the reconciliatory dimension of the New Age politically problematic.

The specific examples I use to illustrate the New Age desire for reconciliation with self and Other are as follows: First, New Age self-help technologies that stress how to achieve an "inner balance," "harmony," and "oneness" represent the New Age fantasy of the unified, accessible, and coherent subject devoid of conflicting desires or a chaotic unconscious. Second, the New Age desire to "protect" nature through its program of "cleansing," "detechnologizing," and "decivilizing" nature constructs nature as the site of some idyllic, preindustrial past that is as much a commentary on the dissatisfaction with the antagonism of the social as it is a fear of environmental destruction. Third, in reaction to the colonialist impetus to consume or annihilate the Other, the New Age has responded by identifying with or in Irigaray's (cited in Moi, 1990) terms "consummating with the Other," a strategy that ironically replicates the same denial of difference found in colonialist narratives of the Other. Thus, what gets coded as the Other in the New Age through the figures of the "aura," the crystal, and the "alien" all reveal how the realms of the spiritual, nature, and the developing world are all sites in which fears and desires, projection, and transference regarding difference and sameness are played out.

THE NEW AGE AND THE SEARCH FOR CONNECTION

The 1994 film *The New Age* depicts clearly how the spiritual quests for higher values, for spiritual regeneration, for some transcendent principles can take place in a limited, compartmentalized, and easily consumable form that is consistent with a consumerist ethos. The film deals with how a wealthy LA couple cope when a series of financial and marital crises force them to radically reassess their lives. Peter Witner is a materialistic, amoral philanderer who is aware of the futility of finding happiness through a series of extramarital affairs (his often-used pick-up line is "How are your morals tonight?"). Katherine Witner is a social-climbing shopoholic. At the beginning of the film, these two characters are living at the height of the "affluent society": they live in a beautiful loft filled with expensive and tasteful paintings, attend fabulous parties, and wear designer clothes, but they experience themselves as superfluous. In a moment of nihilism, Peter claims that "The world doesn't need us. In the old days the laws of nature kept everything thing check . . . now nature is dead and there is no more harmony and we are all pointless." They are right: They are completely unskilled in anything other than consumption, and are simultaneously afraid of "real" work (i.e., of actually creating something—they both have jobs with expense accounts and high salaries that they both realize are not "real" jobs) and of losing the affluent lifestyle they have. Their basically unproductive status is underscored at several points in the film: Peter's piano even plays itself, and as Katherine puts it when both lose their jobs, the only thing they are good at is "shopping and talking." Yet, both are searching for some kind of meaning in their lives: Peter through extramarital affairs, and Katherine through a variety of New Age therapies. Peter's desperate line to a woman in an S and M club—"Isn't it exciting when you make a connection?"—paradoxically illustrates how the Witners are really searching for a feeling of connectedness, of wholeness, of completeness, despite the superficiality of their lives.

However, the Witners search for meaning is characterized by misrecognition: Despite their constant search for spiritual meaning—attending chime rituals, Earth Power seminars, and meditation workshops—they tend to reduce their problems to a need for more money, or for a quick, spiritual fix, to a weekend spiritual retreat or a Shiatsu massage. Faced with financial ruin and socially ostracized from their shallow but trendy social group, they go into more intensive therapy to help them cope, but ultimately are more fearful of the loss of their luxury house, paintings, and status than in changing their lives. Their marriage and self-esteem suffer a temporary boost when they open up an exclusive clothing boutique upon the therapy-induced discovery that their true "hidden talents" are shopping and talking, but the boutique fails, and the two reach the peak of their marital and personal crises. After elaborately planning which candles, music, and designer wear would give the proper effect at their intended double suicide, Katherine extricates herself from her unhealthy marriage and they decide to divorce instead. In the closing sequence, it is clear that they have both, so to speak, survived divorce, and both have found other jobs: Katherine runs a trendy coffee shop and Peter becomes a motivational speaker who trains telemarketers. Yet in the closing shot, Katherine's beautifully made-up eyes are dead as she chats to her clients, and the cynicism in Peter's voice when he tells his trainees, "in Chinese the word for crisis is the same word for opportunity" illustrates he is spiritually dead as well.

This film illustrates how some forms of New Age spirituality are a symptom of the spiritual crisis experienced within the "iron cage" of modernity that Weber (1976) refers to in *The Protestant Ethic and the Spirit of Capitalism*. In particular, this spiritual crisis is a symptom of what Weber calls rationalized acquisition (p. 181). The Witners are desperately afraid of poverty, and when they lose their jobs they try valiantly to come up with solutions so they can keep their house and possessions. However, their desperate attempt to "feel the vibrations and the power of the earth," "to get in touch with your inner child," to "feel the chimes unite you two as the feminine and masculine principles" illustrates the vacuousness of this life, the strength of their desire for re-enchantment with the world in a context where, as Weber claims rationalized acquisition has been stripped of its religious and ethical meaning. When asked incessantly in therapy "what do you want," and "what are you afraid of," the Witners reveal themselves to be the ultimate "specialists without spirit, and sensualists without heart," they are too preoccupied with getting their former lifestyle back to challenge the values on which this lifestyle is based. The nonjudgmental response of their spiritual teachers who encourage them to find what they are good at, even if it is "shopping and talking," illustrates the extent to which New Age therapies encourage some degree of self-reflexivity, but not self-critique or social responsibility.

This film illustrates, in exaggerated form, the extent to which many of the "self-oriented" therapies New Age wherein the search for meaning takes the specific form of an almost obsessive quest for self-knowledge. However, achieving total self-knowledge is an unattainable goal, as Young (1990) illustrates in her summary of Kristeva, "Consciousness, meaning, and intention are only possible because the subject-in-process slips and surpasses its intentions and meanings . . . subjects all have multiple desires that do not cohere: they attach layers of meanings to objects without always being aware of each layer or their connections" (p. 310). Moreover, this incessant search itself can paradoxically inhibit the possibility of self-discovery. A Lacanian formulation of this search would hold that the very process of searching for the chimerical object of our desire, our inner "secret," materializes the void of our desire, and is in a sense posed retroactively in a variety of narratives produced by the analysand with the help of the analyst. Furthermore, Lacan describes how in a way our very subjectivity is defined by our symptoms themselves, and thus to articulate our symptom is to risk losing our consistency. In Zizek's (1989) words:

> if we come to know to much, we may lose our very being . . . The self only exists on the basis of the misrecognition of its own conditions; it is the effect of this misrecognition . . . the subject can pay for such a reflection with the loss of his very ontological consistency . . . in getting too close to it we observe suddenly how our consistency, our positivity, is dissolving itself. (p. 68)

As the example of the Witners illustrates, constantly describing their feelings and their desires does not lead them any closer to self-knowledge. On the contrary, it deflects attention from the fact that in many ways it is the very culture of affluence itself, the very lack of limits that is paralyzing them.

The obsession with the self in the New Age is also countered by an obsession with the Other, and with a connection to nature, the "primitive," the past, with tradition, and with more generally some sort of community. This search for connection that the Witners are seeking must be understood in the context of the affluent society wherein (at least for some) individuals experience themselves as disconnected, fragmented, and alienated. In psychoanalytic terms, the problem is a lack of limits, and is simultaneously one of a lack of recognition and one of supreme omnipotence of the self. In her classic articulation of the dynamic of self and other in the acquisition of personal and gender identity, Benjamin (1988) illustrates how sadism and psychosis can result when individuals do not attain a sufficiently strong version of limits, of the boundaries of his or her will, or a clear enough version of the the Other. As Benjamin puts it "success in the battle for omnipotence is that to win is to win nothing: the result is negation, emptiness, isolation" (p. 35). Psychoanalytically speaking, the popularity of self-oriented New Age therapies particularly amongst the higher-income bracket in North America and Europe is a response to the terror of limitlessness, of boundarylessness that the affluent society produces. Although Benjamin's primary intent is to demonstrate how sadomasochism is a result of a breakdown of the balance of differentiation/recognition and often takes gender-polarized forms, her description of the trauma of omnipotence is also relevant to a description of the ideal subject of the affluent society. In Benjamin's terms, individuals need limits; if the self asserts itself absolutely, there is no recognition or connection.

From this perspective, we can examine the New Age in terms of how it illustrates the fantasy of unity, coherence, nonantagonism whether located in the self (through "self-understanding") or in the other (through an imagined "unified community). For instance, New Age symbolism frequently depicts themes of a unified earth, of the essential commonality of different races, of the unity of "man"and "nature," the timelessness, and therefore connectedness of all living things, and so on. As well, New Age rhetoric consistently is organized around the themes such as wholeness, unity, oneness, harmony, balance, and integration. As well, dominant New Age symbols such as the crystal, are perceived as symbols of connectedness, continuity, oneness, and wholeness. A semiotic reading of this tendency holds that "a sign does not simply exist as a part of reality—it reflects and refracts another reality" (Volosinov, 1973, p. 13). What follows is an attempt to illustrate how these Lacanian themes are a valuable way of reading the dominant themes of the New Age.

THE NEW AGE AND THE DESIRE FOR COMMUNITY

Despite the ethic of individualism inherent in the New Age notion of holistic healing and Harmonic Convergence, the New Age movement is also animated by a very strong desire for a community, a desire that is very much shared by the left. This desire for wholeness is also apparent in the New Age fantasy of community, an appeal, that in a sense can be seen as a response to the increasing social fragmentation and differentiation of modernity. For example, many of the journals I studied (e.g., *The New Age*, *Vitality*) described how the dominant mode of receiving and transmitting alternative techniques and practices (in subversion of the orthodoxy of mainstream medicine and science) was through word of mouth. For example, *Common Ground* magazine discusses how knowledge regarding the effectiveness of a cancer-curing herbal medicine has been very widespread due to this word-of-mouth advertising. As well, most journals I studied made the rhetorical move of asserting clearly "our" common goal that "we" are working toward (couched in terms of global transformation, Harmonic Convergence, environmental awareness, etc.), a flattering and seductive appeal to the reader that implicitly positions him or her as a member. Furthermore, many texts in New Age bookstores (e.g., *Jacob the Baker: Gentle Wisdom in a Complicated World*) appeal to a notion of an agrarian, idyllic, preindustrial past in espousing the wisdom of folk knowledges that have been lost in contemporary life. New Age literature makes many nostalgic references to the "good old days," to shared values, an implicit appeal to a Durkheimian "traditional" collective consciousness.

This formulation of community that expresses the desire for face-to-face, undifferentiated, relations with others can be seen, on one hand as a reactionary reversion to a pre-modern notion of social differentiation, for "mechanical solidarity," a Gemeinschaft community characterized by face-to-face interactions and a notion of "the common good." Thus, the New Age dream of the unitary community, embodied in the notion of Harmonic Convergence, and the unitary holistic subject, is merely a representation, in exaggerated form, of the myth of original unity, apparent in Judeo-Christian mythology in the Garden of Eden. This narrative that poses identity as predicated on an initial unity is a symptom of the totalizing, unifying tendencies of the Cartesian subject, a tendency that is integrally intertwined in the tradition of Western rationalism. As various theorists such as Haraway have pointed out, however, this fantasy of original unity is apparent in the twin myths of Marxism and Psychoanalysis. Haraway argues that these bodies of thought, "in their concepts of labour and of individuation and gender formation, depend upon a plot of original unity out of which difference must be produced and enlisted in a drama of escalating domination of woman/ nature" (p. 151). Thus, leftist or any critique of the New Age for constructing overly utopian notion of the logic of history that appeals to a return to original unity must take account of the fact that such unifying tendencies are apparent in many of the foundational discourses of the left.

This fantasy of the undifferentiated community is one response to the contemporary problem of difference, to increasing heterogeneity, and to the complexity of social differentiation, in a social context where the institutional contradictions of capitalism have violated the utopian promise of the Enlightenment through relations of exploitation based on class, race, gender, and other categories. The recent proliferation of advocacy groups asserting the rights of various interest groups such as feminist, nativist, gay rights, and the differently abled has resulted in an explosion of contemporary debates around the issue of the social, cultural, and political representation. In fact, this problem of how to represent difference is the central focus of debate in such prominent contemporary discourses such as political correctness, affirmative action, aboriginal representation, and multiculturalism. Furthermore, this problem of difference has been the topic of recent debates on the left in the context of concrete political struggles of women, people of color, homosexuals, and others both in North America and the Third World, who have challenged the Marxist designation of the proletariat as the single privileged agent of historical change, and have revealed the new forms of political subjectivity that cross-cut simply defined social and economic categories. As many commentators have noted, the Western sense of identity has been dependent on the construction of a set of binary dualisms whereby the identity and legitimacy of the one has been dependent on the devaluation of various Others, including women, "primitives," Orientals, Blacks, other colonized people, and nature.

However, the New Age attempts to reverse the hierarchies of the Enlightenment through idealizing rather than devaluing various others ultimately results in a denial of difference that is just as totalitarian as the racist, colonialist, antifeminist tendencies it is opposing. The New Age recognizes the tendency of colonialist and other Enlightenment narratives to annihilate the other through consuming it, and seek instead to consummate with, to merge with various others. However, both consuming the other and consummating with it involve a dissolution of the subject–object boundary that advocates, ultimately, a denial of difference. For example, the New Age is motivated by an impetus to find ourselves through identification with the goddess, the shaman, the Celt, the Iron John, the aboriginal, the primitive, animals, crystals, and other essential figures that were once a part of ourselves, constructs a narrative that the other is really ourself in disguise. Similarly, New Age alien contact narratives, virtually always of friendly contact with extraterrestrials, represents another example of the New Age tendency of dealing with difference through eradicating it. Thus, the New Age formulation of community as the reconciliation with various others, is about the denial of the inevitable antagonism that dealing with difference entails.

Furthermore, many dimensions of the New Age share the fantasy of an undifferentiated community, a fantasy that is apparent both in the work of recent feminist and socialist formulations of community. For example, feminist communitarian theorist Dorothy Allison recommends that the ideal feminist community would be based on a "shared feeling of merging and belonging," and would have "an ecstatic sense of oneness" (Young, 1990, p. 309). Similarly socialist communitarian Issac Balbus represents the goal of radical politics and the establishment of community as overcoming the "otherness" of the other in reciprocal recognition (Young, 1990, p. 309). This merging of boundaries, sharing and overcoming subject–object oppositions, themes that recur in socialist, feminist, and other communitarian literature, are not that far removed from the New Age desire for reconciliation with the other. Similarly, Allison's ecstatic sense of oneness sounds very similar to the Harmonic Conversion "explosion into an ecstasy of light and sound" that one of my New Age interviewees claimed she was waiting for. Thus, the left has been plagued with the same desire for unity, the same fantasy of the social, of community, of totality, that characterizes the New Age.

This fantasy of an intersubjective community is being questioned by psychoanalytic and hermeneutic critics of the rational, unified, and coherent Cartesian subject. These critiques challenge the subject's capacity to present its own interests to itself in the first place, and the assumption that it has access to its own desires. In Young's (1990) words, "Subjects all have multiple desires which do not cohere; they attach meanings to objects without always being aware of each layer or their connections" (p. 310). Furthermore, if the subject is unable to represent coherently its own desires, to be present to itself, subjects cannot make themselves wholly transparent, wholly present to each other. As Young puts it:

> If each subject escapes its own comprehension and for that reason cannot fully express to another its needs and desires, then necessarily each subject also escapes sympathetic comprehension by others. I cannot understand another as he or she understands him or herself, because he or she does not completely understand him or herself. (p. 311)

In short, constituting the desires of the "we" is difficult, if not impossible, if those of the "I" cannot even be adequately represented.

In this light, the New Age fantasy of Harmonic Convergence can be read as an attempt to bypass all the complications entailed by the inevitable intersubjectivity of meaning by transposing subjectivity into a prediscursive level, and thus as adhering to the fantasy of communicative consensus in the Habermasian sense. The recent linguistic or discursive turn in the social sciences has rejected the notion of an Archimedean point of objectivity outside the discursive, and focuses instead on how or if we can achieve consensus, or agreement by a linguistic community. The problems entailed by the recognition of decentered subject's unruly unconscious and contradictory desires, however, makes this project fraught with problems. Other dimensions of the New Age movement such as trance channelling, and alien contacteeism gloss over the thorny issue of communication by retaining an essentially modernist fantasy of a unitary language that is amenable to only a singular interpretation. In the New Age, communicative consensus is always presumed, for speaking with, for, and to aliens or spirits is never a problem. This fantasy of a coherent intersubjective community, even among aliens, is also the basis of the Star Trek Universal Translator: With the flick of a switch, any species from any galaxy can be almost perfectly understood.

THE NEW AGE DESIRE FOR RECONCILIATION WITH NATURE

In this type of New Age rhetoric, nature is an original unity that we lost, a state from which we have became separated. As such, the New Age is a clear expression of a desire for reconciliation with nature, a desire to make reparation (Klien, 1986) or atonement, literally "at-one-ment," a desire foiled by our collective guilt at how we (through industrialization, urbanization) perceive we have denatured the world. This desire for reconciliation is expressed in terms of environmentalist programs to "protect" nature through detechnologizing, decivilizing nature, programs that construct nature as the site of some idyllic, preindustrial, essentialized past. Thus, the New Age desire for reconciliation with nature constructs a logic of history that parallels both the Judeo-Christian and the psychoanalytic fantasy of original unity: We were born of Mother Nature/Eden, with which we had an original unity, and were innocent until we were tempted by the serpent of science and the apple of technology, but we can ensure our salvation, and hence reclaim our innocence if we make reparation.

This New Age fantasy of reconciliation with and rediscovery of nature is also animated by the fantasy of reconciliation with our own natures, a fantasy that the essentialist debate in academia tells us has long plagued humanist and feminist formulations of identity. Self-help and personal transformation literature is oriented toward helping us "find ourselves," "rediscovering our inner child," that expresses the desire for reconciliation with our own natures, with the selves we have lost. This type of rhetoric clearly posits some sort of natural, essential human self that has been hidden away, constrained, and suppressed by culture that must be recovered, the search for which (humanism) Foucault reveals to be a source of subjection. Furthermore, the New Age search for our "Wild Woman," or "Iron John" within us, illustrates the desire to recover our own gendered nature, a desire that has been clearly expressed and recently strongly chastised in both cultural feminism (particularly of the 1960s and 1970s) and the more recent "masculinity" movements that are attempting to rediscover the essential male.

The New Age discovery of the healing power of crystals, the revival of herbal folk remedies, the recent explosion of the health food industry, are all symptoms of the New Age tendency to see the natural as the remedy for the ills inflicted on us by civilisation. Clearly, mainstream food, cosmetics, and many other industries have picked up on the tendency of consumers to see the "naturalness" of a product as the final arbiter of whether or not it is good for us. In this type of New Age rhetoric, nature is an original unity that we have lost. Such ideology and rhetoric is not simply espoused by an alternative fringe, but is also apparent in the rhetoric of popular environmental groups such as Greenpeace.

The tendency in the New Age Movement toward the valorization of the natural and toward essentialized identities can be read as a symptom of the crisis of community. These debates conceive of community not simply as geographical or administrative units (i.e., the local, regional, national, or international), but rather in terms of the possibilities for a unified collective identity, and a shared version of the common good. The contemporary recognition of the critique of essential identities, in favor, for instance, of Mouffe's (1988) recognition of the "multiplicity of subject positions" (p. 34) occupied by any social actor has problematized the notion of the pure, singular, or essential identity, and replaced it with the notion of complex, multifaceted, and "hybrid" identities based on the occupation of a multiplicity of subject positions. This recognition of the complexity of identity has called into question the extent to which subjects within a community can share a common identity that forms the basis of common interests, agendas, and subjectivities. New, complex, and multifaceted identities entailing a variety of possible class, race, gender, and ethnic subject locations have emerged out of the increasing heterogeneity and rise in social differentiation that are characteristic of modernity.

This New Age desire for reconciliation with our own natures often gets coded as the desire to find the "primitive" within us, a desire that involves designating a primitive or other who must be emulated. This desire to rediscover the primitive can be seen in the contemporary popularity of Third World fashion, including Latin American clothes, African art, "primitive" statues, figures, and so on. Furthermore, appeals to the "primitive in all of us" are made frequently in New Age literature. However, this cultural appropriation is about more than just a colonialist expansion of market possibilities through ripping off from the periphery what can be sold in the center; it is also about the tenuousness of identity. As many commentators have shown us, the West has constructed nature, the Third World, women, primates, aboriginal, and others as the site of the "primitive" in an attempt to formulate what "civilized" life should look like. However, although modern rationalist and scientific thought is about the attempt to control, contain, and at times enslave what gets coded as primitive, both in our selves and in various others, modern art and literature tells us that this relationship to the primitive has been a profoundly ambivalent one: It has been the repository for both the fears and the desires of the Western subject.

Nonetheless, the problems apparent in the New Age attempts to resurrect the primitive, and to reverse the Enlightenment devaluation of the primitive apparent in the narratives of science and rationalism, tell us that the problems with modernist narratives are not just in their devaluation of the primitive, but in the binary dualisms to begin with. As Memmi (1990) and others have noted, whether the colonized is denigrated or idealized, it is still being defined by the colonizer who speaks for it. Furthermore, these definitions of the primitive say much more about the tendencies of the Western subject to project onto the past or onto "undeveloped" societies fears and desires we have regarding our own social context. Thus, the New Age idealization of the primitive illustrates the problems with a simple reordering of the hierarchies of the Enlightenment. Whether idealized or devalued, nature, women, the Third World, and other Others are still used to prop up the identity of the rational, civilized, usually male Western subject.

THE SEARCH FOR ORIGINS AND THE DESIRE FOR WHOLENESS IN THE NEW AGE MOVEMENT: TRANSCENDENTAL HOMELESSNESS AS A SYMPTOM OF POSTMODERNITY

When theorists of the left discuss the New Age movement, it is usually to dismiss it as individualistic, abstract, and ideologically confused. Although such charges are not untrue, such a dismissal overlooks the extent to which the New Age movement shares similar aspirations, histories, and desires with what we call the left that may be instructive for us. The "New Age manifesto" in a sense, which like other manifestos of the left, expresses the desire for a "break with history," for transformation, for change. However, what distinguishes New Age manifestos (besides their high level of abstraction, their reification of the "spiritual," and their failure to articulate concrete or collective strategies to accomplish their goal of transformation) is the frequency with which they use concepts such as rebirthing, reclaiming, recharging, and other images that imply that we have lost something that must be regained. In the new age imaginary, "we" originally existed in a state of unity with each other, with "nature," with our "selves," a unity that was shattered by the serpent of civilization, the apple of technology. Thus, the New Age positioning of "nature," the "primitive," the "spiritual," and ultimately, the past as sites of wholeness, fulfillment, completeness, can in a sense be seen as one particular response to various "crises" of modernity (i.e., of "science," "reason," and, more generally, the crisis that has accompanied the reevaluation of the project of the Enlightenment). This search for origins, this desire for reconciliation, which appears in exaggerated form in the New Age, is something we need to be wary of in the project of reconstructing the left, and is a symptom of our contemporary "transcendental homelessness," of a condition that some call postmodernity.

The "New Age desire" is the desire to "reconstruct" a community through reconciliation of various "others," with nature, with the third world, with the aboriginal, and with the divided parts of the self, that are posited as once part of the self. Insofar as this New Age fantasy of reconciliation has emerged in reaction to various crises announced by postmodernism, it is in a sense a symptom of postmodernity, and can tell us a great deal about the extent to which we invest in various "origin myths" in order to consolidate our sense of continuity with both the past and the future. We will need to acknowledge the extent to which this fantasy is shared, to some extent by theorists of the left, if any reconstructive project of the left is to be in any way successful. My intention in studying the New Age is not only critical—I also draw out how, despite what some would call the ideological confusion of the New Age, it provides an interesting point of departure for imagining a "postmodern politics," for it is animated by the desire for community, a critique of technological rationality, and a desire for a revival of political agency that underlies the current attempts at reformulating a politics of the left. Furthermore, the New Age fantasy of reconciliation with various "others"; with, for instance, the "third world"/aboriginal, with "nature" and with the divided parts of the self provides a point of entry into the formulation of "difference" and the constitution of the "other" in contemporary social thought. The formulation of difference and the "other" are topics that provide the most pressing challenge to our capacity to formulate a version of postmodern politics.

Part of the appeal of the New Age can be explained because it positions the subject as a traveller who can potentially transcend the epistemological limitations of the body, and social location, through access to another dimension. The figure of the traveller, who can travel both through time and through space, now appears with increasing regularity in contemporary popular culture in movies, television shows, and even advertisements. This positioning of the subject as time traveller reveals our desire to recreate our origins, to rewrite or rediscover our "roots," and, in a sense, to consolidate the fantasy of "autogenesis." The fantasy of time travel is integrally linked then to what Lukacs (1971) calls "transcendental homeless," a condition of the modern Western mind that emerges out of the tenuousness of identity. This condition is characterized by the experience of the self in Lukacs' words as "kaleidoscopic and changeable," as "nefarious and evasive" (p. 189). Thus, the fantasy of time travel is one manifestation for the desire to go home, to recreate our origins. This desire to recreate our origins, this transcendental homelessness is a symptom of the postmodern skepticism toward origin myths, and reveals our ambivalence toward the dissolution of these grand narratives. It reveals the chaotic and contradictory desires of the postmodern, split subject. The New Age desire to be a time traveller, expressed in the phenomena of astral projection, and Harmonic Convergence, is representative of nostalgia without irony, the part of the postmodern subject caught in the abyss that yearns for the sacred, the absolute, the community, and the totality.

Thus, the fantasy of the time traveller as played out in the yearning to recreate our origins is integrally related to the tenuousness of identity in a contemporary context. The West has constructed nature, the third world, women, primates, aboriginals, and others as the site of the "primitive" in an attempt to reconstruct our "past" in order to come to terms with our "present." What gets coded as primitive becomes articulated in a self-sustaining set of binary opposites that become central to consolidating the Western sense of self and other. The primitive becomes a repository for the fears and desires of the Western subject: It is nature to our culture, the field of the unrepressed to our "disciplined" society. Thus, the time traveller represents the fantasy of the Archimidian point, the God's eye view; this traveller is the historian who accurately captures our "essence" through "re-reading" our past.

Furthermore, this phantastic figure, the time traveller, is perhaps the New Age revolutionary subject. The New Age time traveller is an expression of the desire for transformation, for a "break with history" because this time traveller can "re-read" the past and forecast the future. Thus, the New Age manifesto at its most extreme is a call to join in Harmonic Convergence. This transformation, however, has no real vanguard, no concept of species-being, no theory of alienation (beyond the garden of Eden myth that we were corrupted by civilization). The New Age vision of transformation, at least in the phenomenon of Harmonic Convergence thus is both despatialized and detemporalized. We are to "explode in an ecstasy of light and sound" on another dimension when we have reached a sufficient degree of "spiritual elevation." The more moderate, and perhaps, comprehensible, expression of the New Age worldview is encapsulated in the slogans, "think globally, act locally," "one people, one planet," and other phrases that advocate an organicist, holistic philosophy evoking images of harmony, integration, balance. Thus the new age manifesto is in one sense a "final solution" that seeks to impose order, unity, purity, on a chaotic, disorderly, world.

This desire to impose order on the social can be seen our response to the problem of difference. Entrapped in binary logic, we think of the other as something that we can either consume or consummate with, annihilate or merge with, repudiate or identity with, devalue or idealize. The boundary between self and other is experienced as intolerable; we must either forcibly erase all vestiges of the other's existence or construct an ideological fantasy that the other is really us in disguise. In New Right movements such as the neo-Nazism and Heritage Front, the "primitive" is formulated as the other, the object that is devalued; the other must be annihilated in order to consolidate the identity of the subject. In the New Age, however, the other becomes idealized. The New Right is caught at the moment of the dialectic in which the other, for instance what is coded as the "primitive," must be consumed or annihilated to ensure self-certainty, and to consolidate the self–other boundary, whereas the New Age is arrested at the moment of "consummation" with the so-called "primitive," where the self tries to recognize itself in the other through a dissolution of the self/other boundary. Insofar as the New Age movement articulates what some would call an essentialized version of nature, woman, native Celt, oriental, and "others" with which it identifies and seeks to discover in the self, it presents one alternative as to how to deal with the subject object gap that advocates, ultimately, a denial of difference. In effect, such formulations, which are positioned in political rhetoric as vehemently opposed to the New Right, ironically replicate its annihilation of difference, its lack of concern for the other, characteristic of the New Right, through merging with the other. For instance, the New Age is motivated by an impetus to find ourselves through identification with the "goddess," the "shaman," the Celt, the masculine "Iron John," the "aboriginal," the "primitive," animals, crystals, and so on, as ways of reclaiming our own natures, positing these figures as "selves" that we have lost that we can regain. Thus, these figures are formulated only as extensions of the self, to prop up the identity of the Western subject and to patch in the gaps of the exhausted narratives of the Western subject.

The New Age can be seen as a "symptom" of postmodernity: In order to avoid dealing with the messiness of multiplicity, and of polyvocality, the New Age deals with difference by trying to eradicate it. However, the idealization of the primitive in the New Age, in its most generous moments, is symptomatic of an "anthropological nostalgia," a mourning for what we have "lost," and in a sense, an attempt at reconciliation with others that have been hurt by colonialism and industrialization. Furthermore, the fantasy behind the movement, however naive and ideological, is to make reparation with those we have wronged by giving them an exalted, purified status. The figure of the primitive in the New Age is, in one sense, an apology for the past.

Just as the figure of the primitive in the New Age is colored by our desire for redemption from the ravages of colonialism, the New Age figure of the alien is a repository for our hopes for the future, and is an expression of our desire for a postcolonial imaginary. The figure of the alien, both in the New Age and contemporary science fiction, reveals the intense ambivalence we have regarding the unknown, toward the future, as well as toward ethnic, racial, sexual, and other "differences." This figure, however, is more than just an ideological construction, for it represents the fantasy of the nonexploitative relationship between two disparate and even technologically unequal cultures. Thus, New Age narratives of "friendly" contact with extraterrestrial share the same spirit as that which is behind our current theorizations of "postcolonialism," and behind current attempts to formulate representations of and material relations with third world cultures that do not resort to "primitivisms," "orientalisms," or other oppressive tendencies that have characterized first world–third word relationships in the past. A simple critique of the alien as "ideological" overlooks the extent to which the fantasy of alien contact is, in a sense, representative of a new postcolonial imaginary.

Because the alien represents the "most other of the others" that we know nothing about, the characterization of this figure can tell us a great deal about how we view difference. For instance, in popular science fiction, aliens are usually portrayed, at least at moments, as terrifying, hostile, and threatening. In the New Age, however, the alien is benign, friendly, and helpful. Many New Age gurus profess to be able to "trance channel" alien entities who are helpful, beneficent, kind. For instance, New Age literature is littered with references to "transeekers" and other alien entities that offer simple folk wisdom and platitudes such as our favorite uncle or grandmother might do, or as similar to the self-help gurus on late night television. Just as in the case with the colonialist and the New Age characterizations of the primitive, characterizations of the alien reveal how we treat the other as an all-good, fully comprehensible being we must merge with, and as an all-bad, terrifying object that threatens to annihilate us. Alien "difference" in the New Age makes the other appear as merely an extension of the self: The New Age alien's "alienness" is really only a facade that masks its sameness, for it is really one of us. In science fiction, however, the alien is frequently posited as all bad, and as entirely incomprehensible: This alien is an object, it is thinglike, and is waiting to consume us and must annihilate it. In psychoanalytic terms, the figure of the alien is "split" into an all-good or all-bad object; neither of these images, neither the New Age nor science fiction (with the exception of Star Trek) can treat the difference of the alien as something we can tolerate.

One example of how the New Age tendency to transform the strange into the everyday has influenced popular culture and advertising is the "Caramilk" commercial several years ago where the pyramids, Stonehenge, and other unexplained natural wonders are explained as being merely a good-natured but colossal joke on the part of the superior alien entities that created them merely to have "a bit of fun." This theme was also apparent in the Reese's Peanut Butter Cups ad that presents circles left in wheat fields in England as merely alien practice attempts at perfecting this "mysterious" confectionery. Both of these examples reveal the New Age desire to minimize the threatening, unknowable aspects of the alien by denying the alien's "alienness," making this otherness appear in the realm of the explicable, mundane, and in fact, consumable everyday. Furthermore, these examples reveal how the New Age incorporation of the alien into the everyday has been a recent and undeniably popular marketing strategy that has infiltrated mainstream advertising; the other is made to appear as really one of us in disguise, and not really different at all. Like us, they have a sense of humour, and play practical jokes. The appeal of this strategy of anthropomorphizing the alien resides in its capacity to alleviate anxiety regarding difference by domesticating it: If the alien is really human, perhaps different ethnic groups and races, perhaps men and women, are also really the "same."

Furthermore, the fantasy of the alien also tell us about our relationship to difference because it is about the fantasy of community and the struggle with what it means to be human. The significance of the alien for us lies in its gaze: We imagine it imagining us as a singular species, as a "whole" community of "humans," as an object of desire. From the alien's point of view, we are a common species; we have common identifiable characteristics, and we are basically "good." The popularity of this "alien" point of view can be seen in *Star Trek* and *Terminator 2*; to both Lieutenant Commander Data and the "good"

Terminator, we as humans are an object of desire, of perfection, something they would like to understand, and implicitly, to become. Data, for instance, tries to learn to paint, dream, tell jokes, all in an attempt to become more human. The Terminator tries to find out why we cry, why we don't like to kill people (!). Thus, aliens, or in this particular example, android/cyborgs, allow us to imagine ourselves as an idealized imago; in these versions, we are good, compassionate, and ethical.

However, the point I am trying to make is not that these aliens reveal the assurance with which we believe we are "good," or that we are a "global community," but rather, our profound fear that we are not. In the context of global conflict, imagining the alien imagining us enables us to constitute ourselves as a community, for, from the vantage point of the alien, we are a community, a "global village," for the alien does not see our "difference." It is from the point of view of the alien that we can conjure up Earth Day slogans such as "one people, one planet," alongside the satellite/alien view of the planet earth. Ecologism is not, then a human or even an "earthly" imaginary; it is rather an alien imaginary. The figure of the alien reveals the desperation with which we are trying to revive various discredited narratives: the human as essentially "good," and the global community as essentially unified. As such, perhaps it is only from an alien imaginary that we can conceptualize the commonalties that could bind the European economic community together. In a postmodern era, we cannot believe in these narratives ourselves, so we let the alien believe them for us.

The New Age, like several left and feminist theorizations of community, ultimately ascribes to a closure of the gap between subject and object, and articulates difference as something that has to be overcome. For instance, Dorothy Allison (cited in Young, 1990) proposes an ideal feminist community as characterized by a "shared feeling of merging and belonging," with an "ecstatic sense of oneness" (p. 309). Similarly, Issac Balbus (cited in Young, 1990) believes the goal of radical politics and the establishment of community is to overcome the "otherness" of the other in reciprocal recognition (p. 309). This is not to say that all attempts at trying to achieve a recognition of collective interests should be abandoned, but rather, that such formulations must take account of the inevitable antagonism of the social, the impossibility of "fixing" difference, the contingent character of identity, and in particular, of the fragmented, multiple, and conflicting desires of the subject. Any theory of community that denies difference is doomed to failure. Thus, the challenge for radical politics is how to formulate a version of community that stops short of consummating with the other. The problem, in Hegel's terms, is how to cancel the opposition but preserve the difference.

For my second example—the crystal—I show how the New Age posits nature as an other, which, again, becomes a repository for the fears and desires of the New Age subject in response to an antagonistic social, an antagonism that the New Age tries to overcome by annihilating the gulf between the "human" and the "natural." First, insistence on the healing powers of rocks and crystals represents an insistence that both animate and inanimate natural actors are a part of our community, and furthermore, that nature, like the primitive, becomes the source of purity, beauty, happiness, and harmony in response to the corrupting influence of "culture," of technology. Nature, like the primitive, is formulated, in terms of origin myths, as an original unity that we lost, a state from which we became separated. The formulation of "nature" in this manner is a way of coming to terms with the fact that nature is not benevolent, and attends to its own logic rather than that of individual beings who are "in tune" with it. The New Age configures nature as oppositional to culture, to technology, and as a "force" within ourselves struggling against the "alienating," frequently dehumanizing effects of culture. Thus, the New Age buys into the same set of dualisms as scientific rationality, but views nature as an extension of ourselves rather than as an expendable resource. Scientific rationality has been predicated on the construction and systematic domination of nature, on a construction of "nature" that is dependent on a set of mutually sustaining binary dualisms between male–female, nature–culture, civilised–primitive. Whereas the legitimacy of the fundamental premises of Enlightenment rationality rests on the subordination of the latter set of signifiers, the New Age has responded by an elevation of the female–nature–primitive. Nonetheless, the New Age approach still serves to perpetuate the logic of enlightenment rationality through a simple inversion that is still driven by binary logic.

The valorization of nature is, in a sense, one of the "symptoms" in the Zizekian sense, of the postmodern "crisis of the future," a crisis in which the future is virtually unimaginable. In this context, nature comes to symbolize continuity, timelessness, immortality: Through identifying with the inevitable "rhythms" of nature, the ebb and flow of the tides, the inevitability of regeneration after death signified by the seasons, we can imagine a future beyond our apocalyptic visions of tomorrow. Identification with nature as immortal is perhaps most clearly expressed in the symbol of the crystal, because the crystal in popular mythology appears as both a symbol of permanence, and gateway to the future (as in the crystal ball).

The crystal operates as a symbol of continuity, both across time, and across space because it reminds us of our connectedness to others, our community. Ironically, however, these objects serve to act as stand-ins for real relations with other—they come to mediate relations between individuals. For instance, in some versions of the New Age, "attunement" with nature or natural symbols such as the crystal takes precedence over human relations. In this version of the New Age, some crystals are called "healers" and "openers," others are "conditioners" and "cleaners." This association with qualities we commonly ascribe to hair products draws out the New Age emphasis on "cleaning," "clearing away of debris," a theme that is frequently used with reference to the "self-help elements of the New Age" that I call *psychic cleaning*. The antiseptic, sterile metaphors the New Age relies on, are reminiscent of the emphasis on purity and unity in the Nazi final solution.

The fantasy of the coherent, unified essentialized subject is also clearly symbolized by the "aura"; a metaphor for the desire for a protective shield, for clearly identifiable boundaries between self and other, which some New Age practitioners claim to be able to identity visually or photographically. To Baudrillard (1988), this desire for a protective shield is a symptom of "schizophrenic" society, against "a state of terror which is characteristic of the schizophrenic, an over-proximity of all things, a foul promiscuity of all things which beleaguer and penetrate him, meeting with no resistance and no halo, no aura, not even the aura of his own body protects him" (p. 27).

Furthermore, the symbol of the aura reveals more than just a desire for a protective shield, it represents the fantasy of the unity, the opacity of the subject, a subject that recent psychoanalytic literature has called into question. In effect, the image of the aura is an example of the desire to annihilate the other in the self. The New Age subject's desire, then is to become fully comprehensible to itself, for once the subject is "read" through aura readings, astrological readings, and so on, unconscious and conflicting desires, multilayered meanings, ambiguities, all conveniently dissolve into one description, one reading that reorders them. The split subject is superimposed with a "reading" that "organises her actions, behaviours and gestures in to a unifying framework which 'explains' them." Thus, the chaotic unconscious, contradictory conflicting desires, aspects of the subject that are inaccessible, incomprehensible, ambiguous, or in other words, the parts of the self that we designate as other, are annihilated.

Thus, the phenomenon of the aura on one hand reveals the fantasy of the transparency of the social, the desire for unmediated intersubjectivity, unobscured by language, social location, or cultural specificity. Aura readings on one hand engage us in the fantasy that, like the universal translator in *Star Trek*, we can all read each other once we know the code, once we have the appropriate technology. On the other hand, aura readings stress individual interpretation, and the active participation of the subject in inserting him or herself into the "reading." In a sense, aura, horoscope, palmistry, tarot cards and other such "readings" can be seen as merely an enactment of the analytic situation in which the subject can be seen as exhibiting an openness to the social, since he or she is opening him or herself up to the influence of "other." This other in the New Age is some times a "radical" other since aura readings are frequently "channelled" through "spirits" or "aliens." Other aspects in the New Age such as past life regression, hypnosis, lessons on trance channelling, and automatic writing, encourage the subject to develop an openness to the other in the self; in these technologies, aspects of the self that are conflicting, desires that are contradictory and ambivalent, are acknowledged by actually attributing them to a "past life," a "spirit," a doppelganger. In a convoluted way, then, the New Age perhaps can be read as more acutely aware of the conflicting desires of the divided subject than conventional analysis, because it actually literalizes the notion of the other in the self. For instance, trance channelling "other entities" or "past lives" as well as the New Age therapeutic move of "speaking to the inner child" can be read as literalizing the postmodern notion of the multiple subject.

In conclusion, these examples bring up the question that, perhaps I started with: How do we construct a principled relationship to difference that keeps the other alive in her otherness, and resists closing the subject–object gap in favor of either annihilation of the other on one hand, or total identification and merging with the other on the other hand? In Hegel's terms, the question is how to cancel the opposition but preserve the difference. Irigaray (1987) alludes to this when formulating sexual difference when she suggests, following Descartes, that we retain that sense of wonder we first experience when encountering difference. "Wonder might allow (the subject and object) to retain an autonomy based on their difference, and give them a space of freedom or attraction, a possibility of separation or alliance" (p. 124). This autonomy is based on the recognition that the interval between subject and object should not be crossed; rather the gap should remain open so that one is never consummated or consumed by another. This gap, this space marks the inevitability of difference, of discontinuity, of the antagonism of the social. It is only in the preservation of this space that a tolerance of difference can be formulated.

Thus, the New Age incapacity to deal with difference, to tolerate "openness," antagonism, ambivalence, and so on is a part of Enlightenment tradition from which we have emerged. This intolerance, this anxiety toward openness, this desire for a suturing of the social, that appears in exaggerated form in the new age is perhaps the "return of the repressed" of modernism. The primal father, the fully self-conscious subject, who emerged from a sutured and self-defined society, has been slain, but returns to haunt his homeland as the spectre of the New Age imaginary, because he does not know he is dead. Insofar as the left is the progeny of Marxism, psychoanalysis, and other discourses that originally posited an undifferentiated unity out of which difference has emerged, this spectre could haunt the political left as well, unless we become more honest about our own investment in "origin myths." We are, in a sense, caught between the modern and the postmodern: perhaps postmodern theory posits an openness that real humans cannot (yet) accept. Thus, any reconstructive project of the left, any version of postmodern politics must become more self-conscious of how its subjects simultaneously fear and desire the dissolution of grand narratives. Lukacs (1971) captures this ambivalence is his claim that we are both "secular, but yearning for the sacred, ironic but yearning for the absolute, individualistic, but yearning for the wholeness of community, asking questions but receiving no answers, fragmented but yearning for imminent totality" (p. 189).

Alongside the New Age desire for closure, however, resides another moment that may in fact be particularly instructive for the left. The New Age openness to influence, and sustained desire to engage with the other exhibit a playfulness and creativity not apparent in the increasingly rigid, prohibitive, and bureaucratically oriented tendencies of "political correctness." Furthermore, the figure of the alien represents an attempt to imagine how "making contact" with other cultures, other species could be accomplished in a non-exploitative fashion, and as such, could be integral to developing a version of postcolonialism. Thus, the New Age imaginary, which expresses desire for reconciliation with various "others"; with nature, the third world, the aboriginal, and the divided parts of the self, can tell us a great deal about our own desires, and in this way perhaps can contribute to the formation of a postmodern political imaginary.

BEYOND THE NEW AGE: THE REPRESSION OF ANTAGONISM IN MARXISM AND FORMULATIONS OF COMMUNITY

Although the New Age clearly ascribed to this fantasy of unity, coherence, and non-antagonism at both an intra- and an inter-subjective level, Zizek (1989) critiques Marxism for repressing social antagonism as well. On one hand, Zizek claims that Marxism poses a fundamental social antagonism that possesses an ontological priority that mediates all other antagonisms, that of class or economic exploitation. One the other hand, he shows how within the logic of Marxism, those very conditions that brought about this fundamental antagonism produce the historical possibility of overcoming this antagonism. The problem with this formulation, according to Zizek, is that "it is not possible to solve any particular question without solving them all—that is, without solving the fundamental character of the social totality" (p. 3). The Marxist fantasy, then is that the abolition of this basic or primary social antagonism will abolish all social antagonisms, "enabling the formation of a transparent, rationally governed society" (p. 3).

To Zizek, however, Marxism is not alone in advocating a fundamental antagonism, which if solved will resolve all others. For him, feminism has its own fundamentalist belief that the liberation of women will enable a global liberation. Democratic fundamentalism is apparent in the way democratic theory sees the application of democratic principles as solving all other problems. Similarly, ecologism views the ecological deadlock as the problem of all humankind. To Zizek (1989), psychoanalysis also expresses this utopian desire, as illustrated by Marcuse's claim that "the key to liberation lies in changing the repressive libidinal structure" (p. 4). From this perspective, the ecologist's dream of a "return to nature", the feminist's vision of non-antagonistic relations between the sexes, the psychoanalytic fantasy of the unified self, and the Marxist's fantasy of the classless system are all fantasy constructs in order to mask the inevitability of social antagonism.

This difficulty in coming to terms with the inevitable antagonism of the social is not in itself inherently "negative". Rather, it is this very process of trying to come to terms with the radical impossibility of non-antagonism, this Lack, that animates us, that drives us, and which forms the basis on which all culture is based. Within this paradigm, it is this very Lack which structures the human psychic apparatus in the sense that it is the catalyst for what Freud would call "blind automatism of repetition beyond pleasure-seeking, self-preservation" (Zizek, 1989, p. 4). According to Zizek, all culture is a "reaction formation, an attempt to limit, canalise—to *cultivate* this imbalance, this traumatic kernel, this radical antagonism through which man cuts his umbilical cord with nature, with animal homeostasis" (Zizek, 1989, p. 5).

However, the problem is that at times coming to terms with the impossibility of non-antagonism involves invoking utopian solutions that claim to have the capacity of abolishing all antagonism, solutions that tend strongly toward totalitarianism. He says, "the greatest mass murders and holocausts have always been perpetrated in the name of man as harmonious being, of a New Man without antagonistic tension" (p. 5). He even claims that Hegel was the first post-Marxist for recognising that "the antagonism of civil society cannot be suppressed without a fall into totalitarian terrorism" (p. 5). Thus, solutions that impose a unity and harmony by radical measures are internally destined toward totalitarianism.

He says, "the only thing man can do is accept fully this cleft, this fissure, this structural rooting-out, and to try as far as possible to patch things up afterwards; all other solutions . . . are a direct path to totalitarianism" (Zizek, 1989, p. 5). However, he argues that psychoanalysis, at least in its Lacanian application, is the only paradigm that breaks with this essentialist logic that claims that after the (Marxist, feminist, ecological) revolution, we will all be reconciled. His claim is that Lacanian psychoanalysis, unlike these other fundamentalisms, is predicated on the notion of a fundamental split, a radical negativity, that cannot be overcome or abolished, but rather is a part of the human condition. To Zizek, this is the only perspective that forces us to recognize that we have no alternative but to come to terms with the inevitability of this fundamental antagonism, the impossibility of this reconciliation. For instance, he commends Laclau and Mouffe for acknowledging this position in their reconceptualisation of Marxism through their theory of "radical democracy":

> Ernesto Laclau and Chantal Mouffe have developed a theory of the social field founded on such a notion of antagonism—on an acknowledgement of an original "trauma", an impossible kernel which resists symbolisation, totalization, symbolic integration. Every attempt at symbolisation— totalization comes afterwards: it is an attempt to suture an original cleft—an attempt which is, in the last resort, by definition doomed to failure. They emphasise that we must not be "radical" in the sense of aiming at a radical solution: we always live in an interspace and in borrowed time; every solution is provisional and temporary, a kind of postponing of a fundamental impossibility. Their term "radical democracy" is thus to be taken somehow paradoxically; it is precisely not radical in the sense of pure, true, democracy; its radical character implies, on the contrary, that we can save democracy only by *taking into account its own impossibility*. (p. 6)

This failure to acknowledge the impossibility of non-antagonism is not to him simply a theoretical error, but rather an ethical and political necessity. From this point of view, we must be aware that all attempts to "suture" this lack, to patch over this original trauma are doomed to failure, since that very search for non-antagonism has historically resulted in the imposition of totalising hegemonizing, and often totalitarian versions of so-called non-antagonism onto various Others. We may desire oneness, integration, unity, and harmony, but our very efforts to achieve these states may make them even less attainable. This is not to say that Zizek is advocating that we desist from trying to achieve something better, but rather that we acknowledge the extent to which any solution to this original trauma are provisional, temporary, and subject to renegotiation. Lacan does in fact claim that one must "not give way on one's desire" (Zizek, 1989, p. 3) but in doing so, "we must not obliterate the distance separating the Real from its symbolisation" (p. 3).

Six

The New Age and the Crises of Modern Narratives of Progress: The New Age as a Symptom of (Post) Modernity

In the last chapter, I illustrated how the New Age desire is one for reconciliation with antagonistic Others of the self, Nature, the colonized, and with community. What I show here is that this New Age desire for reconciliation is a "symptom" of more general, more profound crises of modernity. It also expresses an anxiety about the limits of modern narratives of progress. This impulse can be read, in a sense, as an expression of a disillusionment with dominant political, social, economic, and academic institutions, a disillusionment that is the focal point for discourses around modernity. As such, this impulse can be read as a response to the crisis of modernity; to the increasing social fragmentation and heterogeneity of modernity; to the disarticulation of the scientific project of the Enlightenment; to the progressive liberatory project; to the tendency of advanced capitalism to fragment and exploit people along the lines of class, sex, and race; to the increasing academic and popular awareness of the crises of scientific rationality; and to the popular disillusionment with modern liberal democratic institutions and their capacity to ensure political representation, tendencies that are currently being discussed in contemporary debates in the social sciences.

In short, what I hope to demonstrate here is that the New Age movement is a symptom of the crisis of Western Reason, a crisis discussed under the rubric of debates around the limits of modernity–postmodernity. Insofar as the New Age formulates, albeit problematically, alternative (although, as Ross, 1991, points out, not necessarily oppositional) ways of thinking about science, technology, and human emancipation to those subsumed under enlightenment discourses of rationality, positivism, or liberalism, the New Age is a symptom of our anxiety regarding the limits of reason, of science, of the environment, of authority, and of democracy: categories that postmodern theorists have identified as being in crisis.

The "crisis of rationality" has been the focal point of what are frequently called postmodern, but include various psychoanalytic, hermeneutic, linguistic, and poststructuralist critiques of science and philosophy. Such critiques have illustrated the extent to which one of the central projects of Enlightenment rationality, the cultivation of an emancipatory reason, is deeply problematic. The most significant challenges this critique of reason presents to contemporary versions of science and politics, specifically with regard to the possibilities of scientific objectivity and of a coherent political identity or subjectivity, illustrate ways in which various critiques of reason have challenged assumptions underpinning the Western traditions of positivism and humanism. These issues are thus integrally related on one hand to the New Age relationship to science and to the tendency for certain aspects of the New Age apparent in the Toronto community to retreat to essentialist identities and to utopian and homogeneous versions of community.

THE NEW AGE AND THE DREAM OF THE ENLIGHTENMENT

In the foregoing discussion, I have looked at the New Age as ideological, as a form of micropolitical resistance to consumer society, and to scientific and medical authority, as the expression of desire for reconciliation with various Others, with Nature, and with the divided parts of the self. When examined at a higher level of abstraction, however, the New Age can be seen as a response to Enlightenment philosophy: as both a symptom of the failure of the Enlightenment's utopian aspirations, and as an attempt to recreate a utopia through other means.

Enlightenment philosophy expresses a profound faith in the capacity of reason to emancipate humanity. To Enlightenment philosophers, the goal of the Enlightenment was to free humans from the corrupt influence of traditional authority, and from the tyranny of unreason, of superstition, prejudice, and illusion through the pursuit of knowledge. Francis Bacon, for instance, believed purging the human mind of these "idols" of unreason involved establishing universal truths based on experience, precepts that are now considered an integral part of positivist scientific methodology (p. 5). To Bacon, "Truth is not to be sought in the good fortune of any particular conjuncture of time, which is uncertain, but in the light of nature and experience, which is eternal" (p. 4). Thus, to Bacon, as to other Enlightenment philosophers, establishing these truths involved freeing the mind of its ties to a particular time and place, variables which he indicates are always unstable. The Enlightenment concept of reason, then, is of a transcendental, universal reason that, when freed from cultural and historical particularities can assume an Archimedean point or God's eye view from which universal "truths" can be clearly apprehended. This concept of reason is based on the fantasy that reason constitutes an axis of power external to discourse.

Twentieth-century critiques of modernity have documented the inability of science, positivism, democracy, liberalism, humanism, and other modern narratives of progress to deliver their promise of unlimited social and technological growth through the pursuit of reason. These critiques have revealed how the modernist scientific project's promise to liberate humanity from toil, on one hand, and the modernist political project's promise of the gradual extension of human rights and freedoms (enshrined in concepts of democracy and liberalism) on the other, have failed to fulfill their utopian aspirations. The proliferation of debates about the "crisis" of reason, technology, science, and positivism on one hand, and of reason, the political, community, and identity on the other are a testament to the limits of these narratives of technological and social growth. It is these debates around the crises and limits of modernity that have both reflected and facilitated what some theorists are calling the loss of utopia in contemporary society.

This loss of utopia, this skepticism toward metanarratives, is one of the elements Hebdige (1988) defines as characterising the contemporary era. To him, one of the markers of postmodernism is a "strongly marked vein of skepticism concerning any collective destination, global framework of prediction, any claims to envisage, for instance, the 'ultimate mastery of nature', the 'rational control of social forms', a 'perfect state of being', the 'end of all (oppressive powers)'"(p. 196). This skepticism regarding utopias entails the recognition that efforts toward engineering the "perfect society" have frequently been justifications for the eradication of, and in some cases, the literal annihilation of difference, and that totalitarian projects such as social engineering and eugenics can and have been legitimated as progress. In his words, "All Holy Wars require casualties and infidels, all utopias come wrapped in barbed wire" (p. 196). At the level of culture, this antiutopianism is expressed both in the exhaustion of innovation and of the possibility of the avant garde in art and architecture (Foster, 1983; Jameson, 1992), and in the rise of forms of apocalyptic culture. For instance, Kingwell (1996) claims that the current popularity of conspiracy theories, distrust of government, renewed religiosity, sex and gender flux, . . . body piercing all express a "millennial anxiety" that is consistent with the postmodern skepticism towards utopias.

One of the symptoms of this crisis of reason that characterizes the contemporary era is the "crisis of science" indicated by the proliferation of critiques of positivism, technology, the scientific method, and objectivity advanced by environmentalists, feminists, social scientists, philosophers, and even positivist scientists themselves. Many 20th-century critiques of science have challenged scientific rationality on various grounds. For instance, the Frankfurt School, feminists, environmentalists, and post-colonialists have critiqued modern science on the grounds that it is predicated on the domination of nature, women, the third world, and other "Others." Kuhn's (1970) *The Structure of Scientific Revolutions* revealed science to be a socially constructed paradigm rather than an eternally true, objective model; and hermeneutic, and poststructuralist critiques have critiqued scientific rationality because it is based on a dualistic epistemology predicated on the omniscience of an abstract, Cartesian knowing subject (Hekman, 1986, 1990). The most startling contributors to the dissolution of the old model of scientific certainty have been propagated from within the field itself. For instance, scientists have now told us that conventional assumptions about time, space, matter, and objectivity have been displaced by discoveries made this century in quantum physics, the Heisenberg principle, and so on. As the paradigmatic science of the positivistic hierarchy of the sciences, such developments in physics have had the effect of profoundly challenging established notions about the nature of science, and its presumed autonomy from metaphysical issues. Thus, these critiques have had the effect of profoundly destabilising scientific claims to authority.

Y2K ANXIETY AND THE LIMITS OF TECHNOLOGY

One interesting and recent example of anxiety about the limits of science and technology was the profound anxiety regarding the Millennium bug (named the Y2K bug) in the last half of 1999. The Y2K bug has interesting resonances with the New Age because in the public imaginary, the Y2K bug, like the New Age, was a metaphorical repository for the fears and desires we hold regarding our collective future. Although at the surface the Y2K bug is the diametrical opposite of the New Age because it is a condensed, dystopian metaphorical representation of the approaching limits of science (and the New Age in contrast is utopian, "natural" and "spiritual"), the libidinal economy underpinning each is the same, for each is a symptom of the anxiety about the limits of modernity. The concern around the Y2K bug was an expression of the fear of our interface with technology, that the information society will force us to live in the eternal present, and will divest us of collective memory, history and identity because the constant flow of information in the words of a character from the film *Johnny Pneumonic* reduces our attention span to a sound-byte. (The central character in this film, Johnny, lives in the perpetual present—he is an information courier with no last name who had to purge childhood memories that would give him a sense of identity in order to improve the storage capacity of his computer implant-enhanced brain). Moreover, the Y2K problem captured the public imagination because it encapsulates in exaggerated form some of the paradoxes of the information age: the Y2K bug as a figure named after an insect with with no material consistency, and occupies cyberspace but not real space. As well, this bug existed outside of time and is thus frozen in infinity, for it only came to life at the verge of the year 2000, where we were caught between the 20th and 21st centuries. It was a liminal, indeterminate cyborgian figure that existed at the boundary of the informatic and the material, temporal and spatial. It is a symbol of disorder, for like the chimeras in Foucault's Chinese puzzle cannot be ordered, categorized, contained.

As well as signifying potential loss of memory and history, the Y2K bug also confronted us with the our fears regarding our own vulnerability to technological breakdown, and thus was a symbol of risk society that reveals our vulnerability to the unintended consequences or side effects of modernity, for the response to the Millennium bug can be seen as a classic example of what Beck (1994) would call the management or normalisation of risk. He claims the predominant response to issues of risk are legal (i.e., calculating and assigning blame), and current organizational forms (i.e., assigning spheres of responsibility) are responses that provide the illusion of rational control but have little power to predict what potential risks are. The predominant reaction by the Canadian and U.S. governments to the Y2K problem was to craft responses that, on one hand, were intended to alleviate potential panic and to provide the illusion that everything was under control, and, on the other hand, disavow responsibility and clarify that an apocalypse was a possible "risk scenario," and even the experts were not certain what the effects of Y2K would be. This is what Beck (1994) would call the "normalisation of risk" response whereby calculations of probabilities are drawn up, but which in effect mean nothing, for they "rule nothing out" (p. 9). In Beck's words, "it is possible to chase away critics with a risk approaching zero today, only to bemoan the stupidity of the public tomorrow, after the catastrophe has happened, for misunderstanding probability statements" (p. 9).

This simultaneous discourse of control and potential apocalypse was apparent in the response of the U.S. and Canadian federal governments, responses that in ways showed how the discourse around Y2K represents the convergence of anxiety around both the unanticipated effects of risk society and quasi-religious rhetoric around the apocalypse. In the months and even years preceding the year 2000, both governments published regular progress reports on their respective "Y2K Readiness Projects" containing very reassuring graphs illustrating the continuous growth in "readiness of mission critical functions" toward "Y2K compliance" invoking simultaneously militaristic and positivist scientific metaphors of mastery and control. On one hand, the claim was made that everything possible was done to contain the risk: that through centralized planning and calculations of probability, Y2K was under control. On the other hand, both governments made statements to the effect that 100% Y2K readiness would not be enough to avert all potential problems, since criterion establishing what 100% readiness (computer testing, complex organizational structures designating areas of responsibility) can't nullify. The co-existence of these two contradictory discourses illustrates Beck's central point regarding the limits of our institutional, and imaginative resources rooted in instrumental rationality to prevent risk. In this context, the rhetoric of concern around the capacity of instrumental rationality to contain risk converges with the rhetoric of the doomsayers and apocalypse nuts, in interesting and strange ways: It was often hard to tell expert and popular advice apart, or to asses what constituted a "reasonable" response. Insofar as the Y2K problem illustrated the convergence between expert predictions of possible "risk scenarios" and apocalyptic predictions of radical millenarianists, it is an example of the contemporary crisis of expert knowledge.

The Y2K bug represents our deepest fears regarding the ecological crisis and other potential crises that threaten our future, as well as our fear of our "cyborgisation," or the effacement of the boundaries between human and machine. However, the belief in the destructive capacity of the Y2K bug was utopian as well, and in some ways similar to the New Age desire for Harmonic Convergence for it reflects the desire for transcendence, for a radical break with history. Although much of the millennium bug hype has provided an opportunity for marketing of a huge array of "Bug Zapper" scams. the thought of disaster was in actual fact eagerly embraced by survivalists, journalists, and experts alike who gleefully predicted a variety of disasters from nuclear meltdown to air traffic chaos. As well, it reflects the dream of a new Information society wherein we are all equal within a new uncolonized utopian space outside of time and in cyberspace, a vision increasingly revealed to be too optimistic in the context of the encroaching commercialization and colonization of the Internet. Y2K anxiety thus illustrates our collective desire simultaneously for re-enchantment with the world, and for radical change and hardship, for in Millenarianist fantasies we are rightfully punished for our wrongs this millennium and specifically this century: the Holocaust, Hiroshima, Chernoble.

In a sense, the Y2K bug was a sublime object which was a collective representation of the fears and desires at the end of the 20th century, as a symbolically overdetermined, condensed, metaphorical representation of the limits of risk society and of technology. In a similar vein to the claim I am making, Zizek (1989) claimed the Titanic operated as a symbol of the fears and desires of the 19th century, an argument that is interesting in the context of the recent popularity of the movie *Titanic*, and the public fascination with the near catastrophe of the luxury liner "The Norwegian Dream" in the summer of 1999. The destruction of the Titanic operated as a symbol of the end of an era of peaceful progress, of stable class distinctions, the end of which was already part of the Zeitgeist of the 19th century even before this disaster occurred. Thus, Zizek claims that although "the sinking of the 'unsinkable ship' was a shock, 'the time was waiting for it' even before it actually happened, there was already a place opened, reserved for it in fantasy- space. It had such a terrific impact on social imaginary by virtue of the fact that it was expected" (p. 69). Whereas the Titanic was a symbolically overdetermined condensed, metaphorical representation of the approaching catastrophe of European civilization, a sublime object that symbolizes the fears and desires of the 19th century, the millennium bug operates in a similar way in the collective libidinal economy.

However, this sense of impending punishment or retribution, I argue, is not limited to a fringe group of doomsayers (although if the net is anything to go on, this fringe is pretty big), but rather is clearly apparent in the discourse of both expert and popular opinion around Y2K or the millennium bug. However, the most interesting fear regarding the millennium bug was not the way in which it illustrated our fear of disaster, but rather the extent to which we desired such a disaster. Radical fringe survivalists and experts alike were gleefully predicting that markets would crash, telecommunications would break down, airplanes would fall out of the sky, nuclear missiles would launch, and electricity and heat would fail. For the radical survivalist in North America, Y2K was an opportunity for the reemergence of the individualist, frontier mentality that would test our self-reliance and reharmonize the disintegrating nuclear family. For Y2K experts, it was the chance for different nations to bond together regarding compliance strategies in the face of an alien, technological other in a way which could destroy our social fabric. Clearly, Y2K anxiety is a symptom of a latent millenarianism is a part of depressive unconscious of modernity, a symptom of our increasing guilt in the eyes of the big Other of History. The real fear is not that the world will be destroyed, but that it will persist;that there is in fact no accountancy done, no deeds and misdeeds noted, and no rewards and punishments meted out. Our real fear is not that millennial prophesies are true but rather that they are absolutely meaningless, that there is no God, no Other, or no Nature seeking her revenge. It is not that we are afraid to know that We are Not Alone, but rather we are terrified at the thought that we are. The idea that we are, in fact, all alone, that God, Extraterrestrials, and Nature will not punish us, and that we are left with only our decisions and our conscience to guide us is the most terrifying of all. As such, Y2K anxiety is a symptom of our desire for "reenchantment of the world" in the context of the "disenchantment" of technological society.

THE NEW AGE AND THE CRISIS OF SCIENCE

The New Age movement can be seen as a response to the crisis of science, as a powerful utopian voice originating from the anti-science side of the spectrum of our ambivalent positions on science. Environmentalist, holistic health, and self-help dimensions of this movement have all tried, in various ways, to displace conventional scientific, medical, and psychiatric authority. However, the New Age relationship to orthodox science is more complex than merely being a derogation of scientific authority. Like many other discourses critical of science and rationality, including those of social critics, environmentalists, and feminists, the New Age relationship to orthodox science is a complex and often simultaneously a combination of a disavowal and a piracy of the legitimacy claims of established scientists. As Ross (1991) noted, this movement rejects the authority claims of positivist scientists while simultaneously citing these "legitimate" authorities, particularly the names of Nobel prize winners (p. 64). Some New Age practitioners paradoxically enthusiastically embrace the help of sophisticated technologies such as biofeedback and "brain machines" (p. 64), as a means to achieving "balance," "harmony," and other characteristics they ascribe to "nature." The paradoxical coexistence of anti-technologist and technophilic attitudes apparent in some aspects of the New Age movement is perhaps a testament to the complexity of this movement, as well as a reflection of our collective ambivalence toward technology shared by the broader society.

These contradictions involved in the New Age's appropriation of the legitimacy of scientific orthodoxy is indicative of the more general paradoxes confronting critics of rationality. If, as Lyotard (cited in

Nicholson & Fraser, 1990) asks, dominant cultural authorities are being displaced, as epistemic and political metanarratives can no longer reside in philosophical metanarratives, "where . . . does legitimation reside?" (p. 87). These contradictions are currently facing those who are trying to challenge dominant paradigms of Western rationality and science: problems that are facing feminists and other critics of rationalism who are anxious to challenge certain dualistic assumptions on which Western rationality is based, yet are unable to speak in a language that does not replicate these binary dualisms.

Such contradictions entailed by the paradox of rationality which underpins this New Age love–hate affair with science remind us of the extent to which, in Ross's (1991) words, "assuming a rationalist style is an indispensable discourse for those whose business it is to contest orthodox claims about the natural world" (p. 17). Similarly, Aronowitz (1988) claims that the privileging of science in our knowledge hierarchy is echoed and emulated, to some extent, by all cultures subordinate to it, even when their identity is marked as alternative. Derrida (1979) makes a similar point when discussing the possibilities of escaping phallogocentrism of language; to paraphrase, it appears that the only choices available to us are to enter the master's house or stay outside. Even when we are critiquing rationality, we must rely on the traditions derived from the more general paradigm of western rationality in which our dominant modes of communication and legitimation are inscribed, since the tradition of Western rationalism is the only one that is collectively meaningful or intelligible to us.

The New Age celebration of the feminine, the non-White, the natural and primitive identities can be located in the context of these critiques of rationality. Critiques of rationality illustrate how rational authority has been historically predicated on the construction of mutually sustaining binary dualisms such as rational-irrational (or emotional), culture–nature, mind–body, civilized–primitive, white–black, and male–female, where the hegemony of the former set of signifiers is sustained at the expense of the latter, dichotomies that have sustained Western thought in general. For example, these critiques argue that the western sense of identity has been dependent upon the devaluation of various Others, including women (De Beauvoir, 1953), so-called primitives (Torgovnick, 1990), Orientals (Said, 1978), Blacks (Fanon, 1952), other colonized people (Memmi, 1990), and nature (Haraway, 1991). These critiques claim that such dualisms inscribed in rationalism have been used to justify the superiority of the rational, culture, the mind, the civilized, the White, and the male over the irrational, nature, the body, the primitive, the Black, and the female, and thus have legitimated the colonialist, imperialist, and patriarchal imperatives of instrumental rationality.

The New Age movement has also responded to the crisis of science and reason by advocating a repudiation of the "civilized" and an identification with nature. In this way, the New Age response to this crisis of rationality is to challenge not the Enlightenment dualisms on which Western rationality is based, but rather their hierarchical ordering. The New Age system of values inverts the natural–civilized dichotomy of Enlightenment rationality and poses the natural as the positive side of the binary dualism that is defined in opposition to the corrupting influence of civilization, technology, science, and industry. The New Age belief in the healing power of crystals, the revival of herbal folk remedies, the recent explosion of the health food industry, are all symptoms of the New Age tendency to see the natural as the remedy for the ills inflicted on us by civilization.

Furthermore, the holistic health version of the unified body is a response to the repression of materiality (Butler, 1994), and the body (Bordo, 1990) characteristic of Western philosophy. For Cartesian epistemology, the body is the site of epistemological limitation because it fixes the knower in time and space, and relativizes perception and thought. Thus, the knower must transcend or, as recent psychoanalytic theorists has pointed out, repress the body in order to achieve the Archimedean view (Butler, 1993). As feminists have also pointed out, this repression of the body also entails a repression of the feminine, since the etymology of the word matter is linked in both Latin and Greek to mater and matrix (the womb), an association perhaps most clearly revealed in Aristotle's assumption that women contribute matter in reproduction, and men, the form. As many theorists such as Derrida have pointed out, Western philosophical thought is fundamentally grounded in a mutually sustaining set of gendered dualisms whereby the former signifiers in the reason–emotion, mind–body, form–matter, culture–nature, and so on are valorized and seem to be associated with the masculine, whereas the latter are devalued and seen as feminine. As such, the modernist epistemic subject, the abstract knower is only achieved at the expense of repressing its materiality, its body, and hence its particularity.

In denying itself a body that would situate it, this modern epistemic subject, in Bordo's (1990) words, "claims to descend from the heavens of pure rationality or reflect the inevitable and progressive logic of intellectual or scientific discovery" (p. 137), and hence represses the particularity of its point of view. Hence, this subject presumes to see from nowhere, and presumes access to reason without race, class, gender, or history; yet it claims to have access to the Archimedean point or God's eye view. Recent moves in attempting to situate or embody knowledge claims, show us that, in Haraway's (1991) words, these knowledge claims are in actuality "situated knowledges" (p. 183). Haraway for instance uses the metaphor of vision to emphasize the inevitably perspectival nature of knowledge claims, reminding us of the importance of the subject position from where the knowing subject "sees." This metaphor is enlightening, because vision is limited and situated; its journey from electrochemical impulses in the retina to stimuli in the brain involves interpretation; objects appear differently to people in different places, and to different species, which reminds us that the knowing subject sees from somewhere, which cannot be abstracted from what it sees. Thus postmodern attempts to embody the knowing subject seek to both situate the knowing subject and reveal the modern episteme's homocentrism, the human-centeredness of modernist claims to authority.

The tendency in the New Age Movement toward the valorization of the natural and toward essentialized identities can be read as a symptom of the crisis of community. The contemporary recognition of the critique of essential identities, in favor, for instance, of Mouffe's (1988) recognition of the "multiplicity of subject positions" (p. 34) occupied by any social actor, has problematized the notion of the pure, singular, or essential identity, and replaced it with the notion of complex, multifaceted, and hybrid identities based on the occupation of a multiplicity of subject positions. This recognition of the complexity of identity has called into question the extent to which subjects within a community can share a common identity that forms the basis of common interests, agendas, and subjectivities.

The difficulty that difference presents to the possibility of a unified notion of a shared version of the common good in any community is also exacerbated by the recognition that individuals themselves are divided by contradictory and incoherent desires. For instance, the assumption that collective identity can provide a point of departure for the political organization, mobilization, and representation of a variety of subjects with common interests have themselves been critiqued by early 20th-century psychoanalytic, linguistic, and hermeneutic critiques of the rational subject. As mentioned earlier, Freud and Lacan have shown that the notion of a unified ego and coherent desire is a fantasy that does not take account of the chaotic unconscious or the conflicting and contradictory desires of the subject. It also glosses over the difficulties confronting subjects when trying to make themselves transparent or wholly present to each other. This critique of identity challenges the assumption that the community is a coherent and unified totality that determines the identities of the elements within it. In other words, constituting the desires of the "we" is difficult if those of the "I" cannot be adequately represented. The critique of the unified, fully self-conscious, fully self present subject that make it more difficult to conceive of community as retaining a shared version of "the common good."

The New Age tendency to organize community around identification with and internalization of essentialized identities is one response to this problem of how to deal with the complexity and level of social differentiation that characterize modern communities. For example, New Age communities are often organized around identification with the goddess, the Shaman, the aboriginal, the masculine Iron John, the Wild Woman, the "Celt," the primitive, and "nature," all posited as once a part of ourselves that we have lost. As well, New Age literature frequently appeals to the fantasy of an undifferentiated, unified community characterised by face-to-face interaction and a unified notion of the "common good" that is a reaction to the heterogeneity and social differentiation that theorists such as Simmel, Durkheim, and Tonnies claim sets apart modern from premodern societies. New Age journals such as *Common Ground* magazine, *Vitality*, *The New Age*, and *Shaman's Drum* all rhetorically position the reader as a member of a large, mythical community which they pretend frequently interact face to face and transmit these alternative knowledges word of mouth by frequently and inclusively using the term *we*. This is because, since these journals themselves would not be necessary if this community was as undifferentiated, tightly knit, and based on face-to-face interaction as the journals suggest. These journals resort to the fantasy of the agrarian, idyllic, preindustrial past by frequently referring to the superiority of "folk wisdom" over science, to the "good old days," appealing to a traditional version of shared common values. In this way, the New Age fantasy of an undifferentiated community is a reactionary reversion to a Gemeinschaft community, based on mechanical solidarity, a fantasy that valorizes the traditional, itself a modern invention.

If the New Age identification around essentialised identities is a reaction to the crisis of community, the New Age reversion to abstract spirituality and individual self-empowerment can also be seen as a response to the "crisis of (political) representation." This crisis refers to the contemporary recognition of the limits of the capacity of participatory democracies to ensure the rights and freedoms of its citizens because of the limited and purely formal notion of rights embodied in their concepts of citizenship and public participation. For instance, many 20th-century critiques have emerged, which have tried to show the disparity between the ideal of democracy and the lived experience of those historically excluded from such "human" rights. For example, Pateman (1986) showed that classical theories of democracy were based on the exclusion of women. Many of these critiques have argued that concepts of citizenship central to the liberal democratic notion of human rights problematically presume that all are born equal. These critiques claim that the assumption of equality of opportunity in the face of historically documented inequalities on the basis of race, gender, ethnicity, nationality, or sexual orientation, is itself discriminatory. This is the logic behind policies of affirmative action, or positive "reverse discrimination" that give preferential treatment to women and ethnic minorities in the workforce in an attempt to equalize gender and ethnic ratios.

In this way, the New Age focus on individual empowerment and on the individual–mind–body spirit can be located in the context of the contemporary skepticism toward utopias. The limits of concepts of citizenship and justice are an indication of the failure of our modern narratives of progress, democracy, liberalism, and humanism, to fulfill their utopian promise. As such, the limits of these categories are a testament to the failure of the more general promise of the Enlightenment—the assumption that modernity, through the discourses of liberalism, democracy, and humanism would involve the gradual extensions of human rights and freedoms. Adorno and Horkheimer's (1972) *Dialectic of Enlightenment* shows how the utopian assumption that Reason is harnessed to the project of human emancipation was shown to be false after fascism, when it became apparent that despite its utopian aspirations, the liberatory component of Enlightenment reason descends all too easily into its negative counterpart, instrumental reason, or reason as domination. In the words of Benjamin (1973), "there is no document of civilisation which is not at the same time a document of barbarism" (p. 248).

This crisis of the political has also been associated with the failure of socialism on a global scale and the current disarray of the "left" in Western industrialized countries. In this context, the New Age formulation of community and of identity are instructive for social scientists who are interested in the contemporary debates on collective identity and politics. The inability of modern narratives of progress such as democracy and liberalism to fulfill the Enlightenment promise of the gradual extension of human rights and freedoms has been attributed not only to the limited and purely formal notion of rights embodied in their concepts of citizenship and public participation, but also to the ideology of individualism, the fantasy of an autonomous, self-constituting subject. Furthermore, left and communitarian attempts to formulate versions, advanced, for example, by Marxists, socialists, and feminists have been guilty of formulating totalizing, exclusionary, and ethnocentric versions of community based on essentialized identities. For example, this problem of difference has been the topic of recent debates on the left in the context of concrete political struggles of women, people of color, homosexuals, and others both in developed and developing countries, who have challenged the Marxist designation of the proletariat as the single privileged agent of historical change, and have revealed the new forms of political subjectivity that cross-cut simply defined social and economic categories. Similar debates have occurred in feminism which have argued that feminism to date has represents only the interests of White, bourgeois-educated women at the expense of those of non-White, working-class, non-Western women. The inability of either liberalism or democracy on one hand, or left/Marxist/socialist/feminist versions of community on the other to formulate versions of community that are sufficiently nuanced to accommodate the proliferation of differences in terms of race, gender, sexual orientation, ethnicity, nationality, or identity has produced what some theorists are calling the crisis of (political) representation, the crisis of community, the crisis of identity, that are all symptoms of the more general crises of modernity. However, representing difference and the complexity of identity in formulations of community are crucial issues in terms of how to ensure the representation of diverse interest groups in North America, apparent in prominent contemporary discourses such as political correctness, affirmative action, representation of indigenous peoples, and multiculturalism, as well as how to ensure the representation of various national interests and cultural identities in Europe in the context of European integration.

One response to this crisis of community, to the contemporary problem of difference, to increasing heterogeneity, and to the complexity of social differentiation has been a nostalgic retreat into the fantasy of an undifferentiated community. Such a fantasy is clearly apparent in the New Age version of community. This formulation of community that expresses the desire for face-to face, undifferentiated, relations with others can be seen, on one hand as a reactionary reversion to a premodern notion of social differentiation, for a "mechanical solidarity," a Gemeinschaft community characterized by face-to-face interactions and a unified notion of "the common good." This fantasy of the undifferentiated community is to a notion of an agrarian, idyllic, preindustrial past in espousing the wisdom of folk knowledges that has been lost in contemporary life. New Age literature makes many nostalgic references to the "good old days," to shared values, to authenticity.

The New Age's attempt to deal with difference expresses a version of a community that is animated by the fantasy of totality, of all-inclusiveness, that denies both the impossibility of representing totality, and the open and incomplete character of every social identity. In Mouffe's words, we are "multiple and contradictory . . . subjects, inhabitants of a diversity of communities constructed by a variety of discourses, and precariously and temporarily sutured at the intersection of those subject- positions" (p. 372). In other words, as the complexity of contemporary identity shows us, we inhabit many communities simultaneously. Furthermore, Mouffe's point challenges the legitimacy of the claim we "belong" to a community to begin with, for it shows that our relationship to any community is precarious and contingent. The same holds true with recent attempts to reconstruct coherent versions of oppressed communities apparent in doctrines of affirmative action, political correctness, and the feminist standpoint position. Thus, the standpoint position version of subjugated communities overlooks the complexity of identity and the multiplicity of communities to which we belong. As Haraway (1991) points out, "there is no way to 'be' simultaneously in all, or wholly in one of the privileged (i.e., subjugated) positions structured by gender, race, nation, and class" (p. 193).

In many ways, the New Age attempt at reviving these "subjugated knowledges" such as those of First Nations people, witchcraft, herb lore, and others is integrally related to contemporary issues of affirmative action. Postmodern critics have illustrated many ways in which the modern epistemic subject's claims to authority, emphasising how knowledge claims are always made from a particular social and discursive location. However, recent critiques of this transcendental knowing subject have emerged in contemporary theory and out of political movements which have attempted to situate the precise location from which such a subject "knows," and have discovered that although this subject denies its own locatedness, the knowing subject of modern philosophical discourse has been predominantly White, Western, and male. This transcendental subject has been challenged on the basis that subjects can only know from the vantage point of particular social locations, and as such have certain vested interests in legitimating particular accounts of the world. As leftist and feminist critiques of the 1960s and 1970s have shown us, legitimacy claims of official accounts are the products of historically situated individuals with very particular class, race, and gender issues. Thus, claims to epistemological objectivity, foundations, and neutral judgment are not only false, but are authorised at the expense of marginalized cultures, unheard voices, and suppressed narratives.

Furthermore, New Age models of communication embodied by their persistent belief in mind-reading, in trance channelling, and in communication with aliens illustrates the fantasy of the intersubjective community who can unproblematically communicate one-to-one. Such a fantasy is what Zizek (1989) would call a reaction formation to the recent hermeneutic, linguistic, and psychoanalytic problematization of this fantasy of intersubjective communication. This fantasy emerges out of a failure to acknowledge the inevitable antagonism of the social, the refusal to face this hard kernel of the Real, a refusal that can only be dealt with by "going through the fantasy." In contrast Zizek would point out how the very tenacity of the belief in this fantasy of the intersubjective community, the great pains that this community goes to illustrate that "we are all the same" is itself evidence of the truth of Lacan's dictum "There is no Metalanguage" (p. 153). Although Zizek does not speak of the New Age, he argues that this fantasy of the intersubjective community is held by Habermas, who adheres to in Zizek's words, "the ethics of the unbroken communication, the Ideal of the universal, transparent intersubjective community" (p. 2).

However, I contend that this critique of the potentially totalitarian tendency to deny difference and to search for an essentialized, authentic identity is not just relevant to naive communitarians, New Agers, or North American tourists, but is relevant to issues around multiculturalism and identity facing North America and Europe. By keeping in mind how essential identities are frequently constructed against an "other," a "them," against which an "us" can be formulated, this critique of essentialism can also warn us about the dangers of essentialist or dualistic constructions of identity. Capturing the cultural and historical particularity of any identity without resorting to essentialized, potentially totalitarian notions of "purity" or authenticity is a challenge that faces citizens, social theorists, and politicians in the future.

CONCLUSION

In conclusion, the New Age Movement is a complex and multifaceted movement that exhibits a variety of sometimes contradictory tendencies and agendas. As such, I have used a different analytic framework for examining different aspects of this movement depending on what seemed most applicable. When looking at the proliferation of New Age commodities such as natural foods and cosmetics and spirituality books and seminars, the New Age can be seen as exploiting the spiritual vacuum in modern life, and as consistent with the ideology of consumer society illustrated in chapter 2. When looking at self-help therapy and holistic health in chapter 3, the New Age is expressing a desire to democratize scientific, medical, and psychiatric authority. When looking at New Age Travellers who live off the waste of modernity the New Age illustrates an environmentalist ethos and a micropolitics of resistance to consumer society. New Age Travellers' merging of the New Age with identities of other "subcultures of resistance" allows the expression of hybridized identities, a theme illustrated in chapter 4. Despite the sophistication of some New Age Travellers' version of ethics, resistance, and identity, by trying to build an alternative rural community in which they can find themselves, these Travellers can be seen as expressing the desire for reconciliation with the self, Nature, and various Others, a desire underpinning many strains of the New Age, and outlined in chapter 5. Finally, chapter 6 shows how the search for alternative paradigms of science in the face of twentieth century challenges to notions of objectivity, the Comptean hierarchy of the sciences, and the doctrine of naturalism is perhaps mirrored in the search for alternative cultural authorities in the face of the dissolution of notions of community, identity, and meaning. Both these crises are symptomatic of deeper and more generalized crises of modernity, of science, and reason on one hand and of community and identity on the other.

References

Abercrombie, N., Hill, S. and Turner, B. "Determinacy and Indeterminacy in the Theory of Ideology" in *Mapping Ideology*, S. Zizek (ed). London: Verso, 1994.

Adorno, T. *The Stars Down to Earth and Other Essays on the Irrational in Culture*. London: Routledge, 1994.

Aragon, L. *Paris Peasant*. London: Picador, 1987.

Alcoff, L. "Cultural Feminism versus Post-Structuralism: The Identity Crisis in Feminist Theory" *Signs*, Spring 1988.

Aronowitz, S. *Science as Power: Discourse and Ideology in Modern Society*. Minneapolis: University of Minnesota Press, 1988.

Bakhtin, M. M. *Rabelais and His World*. Bloomington: Indiana University Press, 1984.

Basil, R. *Not Necessarily the New Age*. New York: Prometheus Books, 1987.

Baudrillard, J. (Mark Poster, ed). *Jean Baudrillard: Selected Writings*. Stanford, CA: Stanford University Press, 1988.

Baudrillard, J. *In the Shadow of the Silent Majorities*. New York: Semitext(e), 1983.

Bauman, Z. *Thinking Sociologically*. Oxford: Blackwell Publishers, 1990.

Beck, U. "The Reinvention of Politics: Towards a Theory of Reflexive Modernisation" in *Reflexive Modernisation: Politics, Tradition, and Aesthetics in the Modern Social Order*, U. Beck, A. Giddons, and S. Lasch (eds.). Cambridge: Polity Press, 1994.

Benhabib, S. "The Critique of Instrumental Reason" in *Mapping Ideology*, S. Zizek (ed). London: Verso, 1994.

Benjamin, J. *The Bonds of Love*. New York: Pantheon, 1988.
Benjamin, W. *Illuminations*. London: Fontana, 1973.
Berman, M. *All that is Solid Melts into Air*. New York: Penguin, 1985.
Bernstein, R. "Introduction" in J. Habermas *The Philosophical Discourse of Modernity*. Cambridge: Polity Press, 1985.
Bordo, S. "Feminism, Postmodernism and Gender-Skepticism" *in Feminism/Postmodernism*, L. Nicholson (ed). New York: Routledge, 1990.
Butler, J. *Bodies that Matter*. New York: Routledge, 1993.
Capra, F. and Spretnak, C. *Green Politics*. London: Hutcheson, 1984.
Clifford, J. *The Predicament of Culture*. Cambridge: Harvard University Press, 1988.
Coser, L. and Rosenburg, B. eds. *Sociological Theory: A Book of Readings*. New York: Macmillan, 1965.
Coupland, D. *Generation X*. New York: St. Martin's Press, 1991.
Coward, R. *The Whole Truth*. London: Faber and Faber, 1989.
Daly, M. *Gyn/Ecology: The MetaEthics of Radical Feminism*. London: The Woman's Press, 1979.
Davies, N. "Inquest on a Rural Riot", *Observer* 9 June 1985.
De Beauvoir, S. *The Second Sex*. New York: Knopf, 1953.
Derrida, J. *Spurs*, B. Harlow trans. Chicago: University of Chicago Press, 1979.
Diamond, I. and Quinby, L. eds. *Feminism and Foucault: Reflections on Resistance*. Boston: Northeastern University Press, 1988.
Dreyfus, H. and Rainbow, P. *Michael Foucault: Beyond Structuralism and Hermeneutics*. Los Angeles: Harvester Press, 1982.
Dreyfus, H. *What Computers Can't Do: A Critique of Artificial Intelligence*. 2nd ed. New York: Harper and Row, 1979.
Eagleton, T. *Ideology*. London, Verso, 1991.
Earle, F. et al. *A Time to Travel? An Introduction to Britain's Newer Travellers*. Lyme Regis: Dorset, 1994.
Eichler, M. *Families in Canada Today: Recent Changes and their Policy Implications*. Toronto: Gage, 1988.
Fanon, F. *Black Skin, White Masks*. New York: Grove Press, 1952.
Ferguson, M. *The Brain Revolution: Frontiers of Mind Research*. Los Angeles: Toplinger Press, 1973.
Ferguson, M. *The Aquarian Conspiracy: Personal and Social Transformation in Our Time*. Los Angeles: J.P. Tarcher, 1980.
Flax, J. "Postmodernism and Gender Relations in Feminist Theory" in *Feminism/Postmodernism*, L. Nicholson (ed). London: Routledge, 1990.
Foster, H. "Introduction" in *The Anti-Aesthetic: Essays in Postmodern Culture*, H. Foster (ed). Seattle: Bay Press, 1983.
Foucault, M. *The Order of Things*. London: Tavistock, 1989.
______. *Discipline and Punish*. London: Penguin, 1991.

______. *The History of Sexuality*. New York: Vintage, 1980.

______. "Introduction" in *Anti-Oedepus: Capitalism and Schizophrenia*, G. Deleuse and F. Guattari (eds). Minneapolis: University of Minnesota Press, 1983.

______. *Technologies of the Self: A Seminar with Michael Foucault*. London: Tavistock, 1988.

______. *The History of Sexuality: Volume 1*. New York: Vintage Books, 1980.

______. *Discipline and Punish*. New York: Pantheon, 1975.

Fraser, N. and Nicholson, L. "Social Criticism Without Philosophy: An Encounter Between Feminism and Postmodernism" in *Feminism/Postmodernism*, L. Nicholson (ed). New York: Routledge, 1990.

Gardner, M. *The New Age: Notes from a Fringe Watcher*. New York: Prometheus Books, 1991.

Geertz, C. *The Interpretation of Culture*. New York: Basic Books, 1973.

Giddens, A. *Capitalism and Modern Social Theory: An Analysis of the Writings of Marx, Durkheim and Max Weber*. Cambridge: Cambridge University Press, 1971.

______. *Central Problems in Social Theory*. Berkeley: University of California Press, 1979.

Goodwin, S.W. and Libby, F.J. (eds) *Feminism, Utopia, and Narrative*. Knoxville: University of Tennessee Press, 1990.

Groothuis, D. *Confronting the New Age*. Downer's Grove, IL: Intervarsity Press, 1988.

______. *Unmasking the New Age*. Downer's Grove, IL: Intervarsity Press, 1986.

Grossberg, L., Nelson, C., and Treichler, P. (eds) *Cultural Studies*. New York: Routledge, 1992.

Habermas, J. *Legitimation Crisis*. Boston: Beacon Press, 1975.

______. *The Theory of Communicative Action Vol II*. Boston: Beacon Press, 1987.

Hall, S. "Introduction" in *Resistance through Ritual: Youth Subcultures in Postwar Britain*, S. Hall and T. Jefferson (eds). London: Unwin Hyman, 1989.

Haraway, D. *Simians, Cyborgs, and Women*. New York: Routledge, 1991.

Harding, S. "Feminism, Science, and Anti- Enlightenment Critiques" in *Feminism/Postmodernism*, L. Nicholson (ed). Routledge: London, 1990.

Hartstock, N. "Foucault on Power: A Theory for Women" in *Feminism/Postmodernism*, L. Nicholson (ed). Routledge: London, 1990.

_____. *Money, Sex, and Power: Towards Feminist Historical Materialism*. New York: Longman, 1983.

Hebdige, D. *Subculture: The Meaning of Style*. London: Routledge, 1979.

______. *Hiding in the Light*. New York: Routledge, 1988.

Heelas, P. *The New Age Movement*. Oxford, Blackwell, 1996.

Hegel, G.W.F. *The Phenomenology of Spirit*. Oxford: Oxford University Press, 1977.

Hekman, S. *Hermeneutics and the Sociology of Knowledge*. Notre Dame: University of Notre Dame Press, 1986.

Held, D. *Introduction to Critical Theory*. London, Hutchinson, 1980.

______. *Gender and Knowledge*. Cambridge: Polity Press, 1990.

Hetherington, K. "Identity Formation, Space and Social Centrality" *Theory Culture and Society*, vol. 13 no. 4, pp. 33-52, 1996.

Horkheimer, M. and Adorno, T. *The Dialectic of Enlightenment*. New York: Herder and Herder, 1972.

Hunt, D. and McMahon, T.A. *America: The Sorcerer's New Apprentice and the Rise of the New Age Shamanism*. Concord, CA: Harvest House, 1988.

Irigaray, L. "Sexual Difference" in T. Moi *French Feminist Thought*. Oxford: Basil Blackwell, 1988.

Jameson, F. *Postmodernism, the Cultural Logic of Late Capitalism*. Durham: Duke University Press, 1991.

Jay, M. *The Dialectical Imagination*, Boston: Little, Brown & Co., 1973.

Jeffers, S. *Feel the Fear and Do it Anyways*. New York: Vermillian, 1991.

Kingwell, M. *Dreams of the Millennium*. Toronto: Viking Press, 1996.

Klein, M. 1986. *Love, Guilt and Reparation and Other Works; 1921-1925*. London: Hogarth Press, 1986.

Kristeva, J. *Powers of Horror: An Essay on Abjection*. New York: Columbia University Press, 1982.

Kuhn, T. *The Structure of Scientific Revolutions*. Chicago: University of Chicago Press, 1970.

Laclau, E. "God Only Knows" *Marxism Today*. December, 56-59, 1991.

Laclau, E. and Mouffe, C. *Hegemony and Socialist Strategy*. London: Verso, 1985.

Learner, H. *The Dance of Intimacy*. London: New York, 1989.

Lowenthal, L. *Ten Years on Morningside Heights: A Report on the Institute's History, 1934-1944* (Unpublished, 1944) (Lowenthal Collection). Cited in Martin Jay, *The Dialectical Imagination*. Boston: Little, Brown and Co., 1973.

Lukacs, G. *History and Class Consciousness*. London: Merlin, 1971.

Lyotard, J. *The Postmodern Condition*. Manchester, Manchester University Press, 1994.

McKay, G. *Senseless Acts of Beauty*. London: Verso, 1996.

Mahon, E. "Ireland: A Private Patriarchy?" in *Environment and Planning*, A 1994, vol. 26, pp. 1277-1296.

Malesevic, S. *Ideology*. Unpublished manuscript, 1997.

Marcuse, H. *One Dimensional Man*. Boston: Beacon Press, 1964.

Marx, K. *Early Writings of Karl Marx*. Ed. by Tom Bottimore. New York: McGraw Hill, 1964.

Marx, K. *The German Ideology*. London: Lawrence and Wishart, 1965.

______. *The Communist Manifesto*. London: Penguin, 1985.

Martin, B. "Feminism, Criticism and Foucault" in *Feminism and Foucault: Reflections on Resistance,* C. Diamond and L. Quinby, (eds). Boston: Northeastern University Press, 1988.

McIntyre, A. *After Virtue*. London: Duckworth, 1981.

Memmi, A. *The Coloniser and the Colonised*. London: Earthscan Publications, 1990.

Mills, C. *The Sociological Imagination*. New York: Oxford University Press, 1959.

Mouffe, C. "Radical Democracy: Modern or Postmodern?" in *Universal Abandon?,* A. Ross (ed). Minneapolis: University of Minnesota Press, 1988.

____. "Feminism and Radical Politics" in *Feminists Theorise the Political,* J. Butler and J. Scott (eds). New York: Routledge, 1992.

_____."Feminism, Citizenship, and Radical Democratic Politics" in J. Butler and J. Scott (eds) *Feminists Theorise the Political.*. New York: Routledge, 1992.

Nadeau, M. *The History of Surrealism*. London: Plantin Publishers, 1987.

Nicholson, L. (ed.) *Feminism/Postmodernism*. New York: Routledge, 1990.

Nietsche, F. *Thus Spoke Zarathustra*. Baltimore: Penguin, 1967.

O'Neill, J. *The Millenial Madonna*. Unpublished inaugural lecture given as visiting distinguished research fellow at Goldsmith's College, University of London, 1999.

Pateman, C. *Feminism and Participatory Democracy.* Unpublished paper presented to the Meeting of American Philosophical Association, St. Louis, MO.

Rabinow, Paul (ed) *The Foucault Reader*. New York: Random House, 1984.

Rabinow, P. and Sullivan, W.M. "The Interpretive Turn" in *Interpretive Social Science: A Second Look*, P. Rabinow and W.M. Sullivan (eds). Berkeley: University of California Press, 1987.

Riley, D. *War in the Nursery: Theories of Child and Mother*. London: Virago, 1983.

Ross, A. (ed) *Universal Abandon? The Politics of Postmodernism.* Minneapolis: University of Minnesota Press, 1988.

Ross, A. *Strange Weather: Culture, Science, and Technology in the Age of Limits*. London: Verso, 1991.

Said, E. *Orientalism.* New York: Pantheon, 1978.

Schumacher, E.F. *Small is Beautiful*. London: Abacus, 1974.

Smith, D. *The Everyday World as Problematic*. Toronto: University of Toronto Press, 1987.

Steedmen, M. "Who's on Top" in *Who's on Top: The Politics of Heterosexuality*, H. Buchbinder, V. Burstyn, D. Forbes and M. Steedman (eds). Toronto: Garamond Press, 1987.

Therborn, G. "The New Question of Subjectivity" in *Mapping Ideology*, S. Zizek (ed). London: Verso, 1994.

Torgovnick, M. *Gone Primitive: Savage Intellects, Modern Lives*. Chicago: University of Chicago Press, 1990.

Turner, V. "The Centre Out There: the Pilgrim's Goal". *History of Religions*, vol. 12, number 3, 1982.

Volosinov, V.N. *Marxism and the Philosophy of Language*. Cambridge: Harvard University Press, 1973.

Wallis, R. *The Elementary Forms of the New Religious Life*. London: Routledge and Kegan Paul, 1984.

Weber, M. *From Max Weber: Essays in Sociology,* H.H. Gerth and C. W. Mills (eds and trans). New York: Oxford University Press, 1958.

______. "Some Consequences of Bureaucratisation" in *Sociological Theory: A Book of Readings*, L.A. Coser and B. Rosenberg (eds). New York: MacMillan, 1965.

______. *The Protestant Ethic and the Spirit of Capitalism.* New York: Charles Scribner's Sons, 1976.

Weed, S. *Healing Wise.* Woodstock, NY: Ashtree Publishing, 1989.

Weedon, C. *Feminist Practice and Poststructuralist Theory*. London: Basil Blackwell, 1987.

Wittgenstein, L. *Philosophical Investigations*. London: Blackwell, 1994.

Young, I. M. "The Ideal of Community and the Politics of Difference " in *Feminism/Postmodernism,* L. Nicholson (ed). New York: Routledge, 1990.

Zizek, S. *The Sublime Object of Ideology*. London: Verso, 1989.

______."The Spectre of Ideology" in *Mapping Ideology,* S. Zizek (ed). London, Verso, 1994.

______. *The Matrix, or, the Two Sides of Perversion*, 2000, taken from http//: www.mail.britannica. com <nettime list>

Author Index

Subject Index

Printed in the United States
16089LVS00001B/157-210

9 781572 735200